OXFORD WORLD'S CLASSICS

PLATO

Timaeus and *Critias*

Translated by
ROBIN WATERFIELD

With an Introduction and Notes by
ANDREW GREGORY

T0130604

OXFORD
UNIVERSITY PRESS

OXFORD

UNIVERSITY PRESS

Great Clarendon Street, Oxford OX2 6DP

Oxford University Press is a department of the University of Oxford.
It furthers the University's objective of excellence in research, scholarship,
and education by publishing worldwide in

Oxford New York

Auckland Cape Town Dar es Salaam Hong Kong Karachi
Kuala Lumpur Madrid Melbourne Mexico City Nairobi
New Delhi Shanghai Taipei Toronto

With offices in

Argentina Austria Brazil Chile Czech Republic France Greece
Guatemala Hungary Italy Japan Poland Portugal Singapore
South Korea Switzerland Thailand Turkey Ukraine Vietnam

Oxford is a registered trade mark of Oxford University Press
in the UK and in certain other countries

Published in the United States
by Oxford University Press Inc., New York

Translation © Robin Waterfield 2008
Editorial material © Andrew Gregory 2008

British Library Cataloguing in Publication Data

Data available

Library of Congress Cataloging-in-Publication Data

Plato.
[Timaeus. English]
Timaeus and Critias / Plato; translated by Robin Waterfield;
with an introduction and notes by Andrew Gregory.
p.cm.—(Oxford world's classics)
Includes bibliographical references.
ISBN 978–0–19–280735–9
1. Cosmology—Early works to 1800. 2. Atlantis. I. Waterfield, Robin.
II. Gregory, Andrew. III. Plato. Critias. English. IV. Title.
B387.A5W37 2008
113—dc22
2008027751

Typeset by Cepha Imaging Private Ltd., Bangalore, India
Printed in Great Britain
on acid-free paper by
Clays Ltd, Elcograf S.p.A.

ISBN 978–0–19–280735–9

17

For Keith Critchlow, contemporary Platonist,
and in memory of W.G.D.

TIMAEUS AND CRITIAS

PLATO (c.427–347 BCE), Athenian philosopher-dramatist, has had a profound and lasting influence upon Western intellectual tradition. Born into a wealthy and prominent family, he grew up during the conflict between Athens and the Peloponnesian states which engulfed the Greek world from 431 to 404 BCE. Following its turbulent aftermath, he was deeply affected by the condemnation and execution of his revered master Socrates (469–399) on charges of irreligion and corrupting the young. In revulsion from political activity, Plato devoted his life to the pursuit of philosophy and to composing memoirs of Socratic enquiry cast in dialogue form. He was strongly influenced by the Pythagorean thinkers of southern Italy and Sicily, which he is said to have visited when he was about 40. Some time after returning to Athens, he founded the Academy, an early ancestor of the modern university, devoted to philosophical and mathematical enquiry, and to the education of future rulers or 'philosopher-kings'. The Academy's most celebrated member was the young Aristotle (384–322), who studied there for the last twenty years of Plato's life. Their works mark the highest peak of philosophical achievement in antiquity, and both continue to rank among the greatest philosophers of all time.

Plato is the earliest Western philosopher from whose output complete works have been preserved. At least twenty-five of his dialogues are extant, ranging from fewer than twenty to more than three hundred pages in length. For their combination of dramatic realism, poetic beauty, intellectual vitality, and emotional power they are unique in Western literature.

ROBIN WATERFIELD is a writer, living in Greece. He has previously translated, for Oxford World's Classics, Plato's *Republic*, *Symposium*, *Gorgias*, and *Phaedrus*, and *Meno and Other Dialogues*, Aristotle's *Physics*, Herodotus' *Histories*, Plutarch's *Greek Lives* and *Roman Lives*, Euripides' *Orestes and Other Plays* and *Heracles and Other Plays*, Xenophon's *The Expedition of Cyrus*, and *The First Philosophers: The Presocratics and the Sophists*.

ANDREW GREGORY is Reader in History of Science in the Department of Science and Technology Studies, University College London. His books include *Plato's Philosophy of Science*, *Eureka! The Birth of Science*, and *Ancient Greek Cosmogony*.

OXFORD WORLD'S CLASSICS

*For over 100 years Oxford World's Classics have brought
readers closer to the world's great literature. Now with over 700
titles — from the 4,000-year-old myths of Mesopotamia to the
twentieth century's greatest novels — the series makes available
lesser-known as well as celebrated writing.*

*The pocket-sized hardbacks of the early years contained
introductions by Virginia Woolf, T. S. Eliot, Graham Greene,
and other literary figures which enriched the experience of reading.
Today the series is recognized for its fine scholarship and
reliability in texts that span world literature, drama and poetry,
religion, philosophy, and politics. Each edition includes perceptive
commentary and essential background information to meet the
changing needs of readers.*

CONTENTS

INTRODUCTION

Plato's *Timaeus* and *Critias* are works of perennial philosophical and historical interest. *Timaeus* gives us an account of how the cosmos and everything in it — stars, earth, and living creatures — came into existence. It also gives an account of the origin of human beings, their place in the cosmos, and what they should aspire to. It is a complex and multifaceted work, offering important ideas in philosophy, theology, and the study of the natural world. The unfinished *Critias* gives us the beginnings of a fascinating account of the supposed ancient city of Atlantis.

Timaeus offers a pattern of explanation for all natural phenomena: they are to be explained teleologically, in terms of why it is best that they occur in the way that they do. Teleological explanation itself was not original to *Timaeus*, nor indeed to Plato. Anaxagoras (*c*.500–*c*.428 BC) had previously proposed that a cosmic intelligence brought order to the universe. In his earlier work, *Phaedo*, Plato had criticized Anaxagoras for not employing this type of explanation fully enough. What *Timaeus* offers, then, is the first thoroughgoing, exhaustive teleological analysis of all natural phenomena. If we take the account literally, a craftsman god, the demiurge (the word literally means 'craftsman'), imposes order on a pre-existing chaos because order is in all ways better than chaos. So the elements, the cosmos, and all living things are given a teleological ordering by a single god who acts only for the best. This makes *Timaeus* the first manifesto of teleology, and ever since, whenever explanations of natural phenomena based on matter, mechanism, and chance have been perceived to be implausible, the idea of a designer god has been an alternative. Another aspect of this design is that the craftsman god employs mathematics and geometry in the construction of the cosmos. Stars, sun, moon, and planets move with regular circular motions, the elements earth, water, air, and fire are conceived of as having specific, ideal shapes, and the ultimate building-blocks for the elements are two types of triangle.

The ideas of *Timaeus* were much discussed by Plato's followers in the Academy, and by those who developed Plato's thought into ancient neoplatonism. They influenced the Stoic philosophers, and had an important effect on the early Christian theologians, which is still felt in modern Christianity. Those who opposed the ideas of design and teleology felt the need to address and criticize *Timaeus*. Aristotle was both deeply influenced by *Timaeus*, in producing his own teleological account of the natural world, and highly critical of it. There were several Greek and Latin commentaries on *Timaeus*, seeking to interpret and explain its theories. The Renaissance also found *Timaeus* a fascinating and influential work, and Renaissance neoplatonism, an important movement in early modern philosophy and science, took it as its main text. *Critias* has been less influential, though some have seen in it evidence of an ancient tradition concerning a lost city of Atlantis, and so find support for the idea that there was a historical Atlantis of some form.

Dramatis Personae

There are four characters in *Timaeus* and *Critias*. Socrates needs little introduction: a philosopher who lived in Athens, and the main character in many of Plato's works, he lived from 469 to 399 BC, when he was prosecuted and executed by the people of Athens. Socrates, at least as Plato's dialogues represent him, had no specific philosophical views of his own, but was very good at exposing the deficiencies in the views of others, and was particularly concerned with issues of ethics and knowledge. Socrates' life, his manner of doing philosophy, and the manner of his death all seem to have had a significant effect on Plato. It must be said, though, that Socrates in *Timaeus* is very much more subdued than he is in Plato's earlier works. After a brief and very friendly introduction, he drops out of the conversation entirely, leaving Timaeus to make a long, uninterrupted speech describing the origins of all natural phenomena. One odd aspect of this, relative to the Socrates of the early dialogues, is that Timaeus is introduced as an expert in astronomy. Elsewhere, this would be a cue for Socrates to interrogate the expert and show the shortcomings of his supposed expertise. Why does Socrates not play a greater role here? One common suggestion is that Plato has portrayed Socrates as being uninterested in natural phenomena in earlier works, so it would look odd to have him knowledgeable about them here. At *Apology* 19b Socrates denies ever having had any interest in natural philosophy, while in *Phaedo* he says he became disenchanted with it. Aristotle reports that Socrates investigated ethics rather than nature (*Metaphysics* 987b).

Critias in *Timaeus* and *Critias* is very old, so old he finds it easier to recollect the events of long ago rather than those of yesterday (26b). This means that he cannot be the Critias who was one of the Thirty Tyrants in 404.[1] If he is a representation of a real person, most likely he is Plato's great-grandfather, who was grandfather of the Critias of Thirty Tyrants fame.

The Hermocrates of *Timaeus* and *Critias* may be the Hermocrates mentioned by Thucydides (IV. 58 and VI. 72). He lived in Syracuse in Sicily, and was a military leader, taking part in the defeat of the Athenian attack against Sicily in 415–413 BC. He was also a prominent oligarch in Syracuse.

It is unlikely that Timaeus himself was a real person. We are told quite a lot about him, that he was rich and well-born, that he was an excellent philosopher, that he was the best astronomer and had made a special study of the nature of the cosmos, and that he had held the highest political offices in Locri. There is no trace of any such person, which, given these attributes, would be surprising if he were real. Later in antiquity a work called *Timaeus Locrus* was produced. This was taken to be a genuine work of Plato's Timaeus, but was in fact a forgery.

Setting and Outline

The dramatic setting for *Timaeus* is a meeting between Socrates and three of the four people he has been talking to the day before,

---

[1] Athens was briefly ruled by the Thirty Tyrants after its defeat by Sparta.

Timaeus, Hermocrates, and Critias. The fourth person, who apparently has fallen ill, is not mentioned by name, and nothing is known of him. The occasion is a Panathenaea, a yearly festival in Athens celebrating the goddess Athena. Grand Panathenaeas were held every four years, but there is no indication whether this is an ordinary or grand Panathenaea. The speech which Socrates made on the previous day, and which he gives a summary of in *Timaeus*, has clear affinities to parts of *Republic*. Does Socrates summarize the actual speeches of *Republic*? If so, then the dramatic dates of *Republic* and *Timaeus* are only two days apart, as *Republic* gives an account of a conversation that happened the day before. This seems unlikely, however, as the action of *Republic* takes place on the festival of Bendis, and it is improbable that the Panathenaea would follow two days after this festival. Nor does Socrates give a summary of the whole of *Republic*, or even the whole of the political parts of *Republic*. It is probable, then, that the meeting of the day before *Timaeus* is some other day, real or imagined, when Socrates discussed his ideal city. After giving his summary, Socrates compares his description of the ideal state in yesterday's speech with a painting depicting animals. In both cases, he says, one wants to see the subject in action. Critias then gives a brief summary of a tale he heard long ago, of a city with similarities to Socrates' ideal city, a tale which he is to take up again in *Critias*.

Timaeus divides naturally into an introduction and three main sections. In the introduction, Timaeus is given the task of describing the birth of the world and the nature of mankind. Critias is then to give an account of how the ancient Athenians fought a war against the people of Atlantis. Before proceeding to the main part of his account, Timaeus gives us a philosophical preamble, making distinctions between being and becoming, and between knowledge and opinion. The main discourse of *Timaeus* then falls into three main parts, all well signposted. After the introductory niceties, Timaeus begins to give his account of the origins of the cosmos and its contents. These are the works of intelligence, and Timaeus tells us of the nature of the cosmos and the world-soul, of the nature of the stars, sun, moon, and planets and their orbits, and of the nature of human beings and their relation to the cosmos. Timaeus then shifts (47e) to what comes about of necessity. Here we are introduced to the receptacle, something in which every-thing occurs, though the exact nature of the receptacle is unclear. Timaeus also describes the nature of earth, water, air, and fire, and how they interact with one another. He then gives an account of the nature and function of the human senses. The final section of *Timaeus*, from 69a to the close, concerns the cooperation of reason and necessity. Essentially, this is an account of the anatomy and physiology of the human body, underpinned by the principles of intelligent design from the first section of *Timaeus* and given in terms of the theory of the elements developed in the second section. *Critias* begins to give an account of the lost city of Atlantis and its part in an ancient war with other city-states led by Athens. It does not get beyond a description of the city and island of Atlantis before it comes to an abrupt, unexpected, and inexplicable end.

Timaeus is the closest of Plato's major works to being a mono-logue. There are other works where there are long individual speeches, but nothing on the same scale as Timaeus' main speech here. There are passages in other works where the interlocutor has very little to contribute (for example, the latter part of *Parmenides*) but none where there is no interlocutor at all for such a long period. It is not known why this should be so. One might speculate that this has something to do with the subject-matter, but there are other works where Plato discusses the natural world and how we might explain it (*Phaedo*, *Republic*, and so on) where he uses dialogue rather then monologue. Similarly, *Critias*, after some opening niceties, settles down into a monologue from Critias.

The characters of *Timaeus* advertise it as part of a trilogy: *Timaeus*, *Critias*, and *Hermocrates*. *Timaeus* is complete, *Critias* abruptly ends after a few pages, and there is no record of *Hermocrates* hav-ing been written. We have no indication that *Critias* was actually finished but that the ending has subsequently been lost; what we have appears to be all there ever was of the work. It is a matter of speculation why *Critias* is unfinished, and why *Hermocrates* was never begun.

Plato's works are usually divided into three groups: early, middle, and late. *Timaeus* and *Critias* are generally taken to be among Plato's later works, along with *Theaetetus*, *Statesman*, *Sophist*, *Philebus*, and *Laws*. The actual date of composition of *Timaeus* and *Critias* is probably around 360 BC, but there is nothing to fix that with any great precision. Some of Plato's works can be dated fairly accurately if they refer to datable historical events, but *Timaeus* and *Critias* have no such references. Depending on the order and manner in which Plato wrote his later works, the date of composition could even be later.[2]

The dramatic date of *Timaeus* partly depends on whether or not we believe that Socrates is summarizing *Republic* in the introduction. If he is, then the action takes place on the second day after the festival of Bendis, though we do not know which year, and there is the problem mentioned above of the relation of the festival of Bendis and the Panathenaea.

Timaeus *and Teleology*

Timaeus offers the first thoroughgoing teleological account of the world, with order being imposed on chaos by an external deity. *Timaeus* is infamous for its teleological approach to the explanation of nature. A standard view from the history of science would have it that only with the revival of the views of the ancient atomists by seventeenth-century thinkers such as Descartes and Gassendi did science free itself from the restrictive tentacles of the teleology of Plato and Aristotle. Since then science has progressed rapidly, relying on a mechanistic conception of the world in which there is no place for teleology.

[2] G. E. L. Owen, 'The Place of the *Timaeus* in Plato's Dialogues', *Classical Quarterly*, NS 3 (1953), 79–95, argued for a much earlier date for *Timaeus*, giving philosophical reasons why it should be dated before the middle-period work *Parmenides*. H. F. Cherniss, 'The Relation of the *Timaeus* to Plato's Later Dialogues', *American Journal of Philology*, 78 (1957), 225–66, replied to this, reasserting the orthodox view. While the issue is not entirely closed, the orthodox dating is generally accepted nowadays.

Why does Plato feel that he requires this teleology? There can be no doubt that Plato wants to link his account of the natural world to ethics and politics. In particular, the heavens stand as an exemplar of well-ordered motion. Just as the cosmos is well ordered, we, individually and collectively, should order our lives well. There is a good, that good exists independently of us, and we should aspire to that good. *Timaeus* 47a is a clear example of this, where we hear that we should try to bring the wanderings of our mind into order to match the unwandering motions of the heavens. *Timaeus* 90a ff., close to the end of the dialogue, ties up the preceding theme of ordering our minds along the same lines as the universe is organized, and exhorts us to be as much like god as possible. What else, though, does Plato get from his use of teleology in explaining natural phenomena?

First, he gains an important decision-making criterion. Where there is a multiplicity of possibilities, the demiurge selects what is best. The demiurge is faced with the problem of which triangles he should choose to be the basic elements of the geometrical atomism. There is a multitude to choose from. The demiurge is able to make a rational choice, on the grounds of selecting the two best types of triangles. We are able to develop an account of what the demiurge must have chosen if we assume that at all times he makes the best choice. Arguably, this begins an important tradition within the philosophy of science. In modern philosophy of science there is a problem known as underdetermination, describing a situation where the data (however good) are insufficient to allow us to determine which theory to adopt to explain them, and non-empirical criteria must be employed. It is always possible to generate a multiplicity of theories for a single set of data, all of which will account for that data. How can we have a rational choice between these theories, which are all empirically adequate? Plato develops a solution involving teleology, but one which nevertheless contains certain important affinities with modern realist attempts to solve the underdetermination problem by applying criteria such as beauty, simplicity, and unity. If the demiurge constructs the cosmos on the principles of beauty, simplicity, and unity, and does so employing mathematics and geometry, then we can understand that cosmos by applying the same principles. This is important for understanding how Plato goes about solving certain problems in astronomy and cosmology in *Timaeus*, especially those problems where he argues for a single solution from an indefinite field of possibilities.

The second advantage Plato is able to gain from his adoption of teleology is that he is able to oppose an important new explanatory trend in ancient natural philosophy, developed by Empedocles and by the atomists Leucippus and Democritus. Complex entities, such as the cosmos and living creatures, can be thought of as the result of a multiplicity of chance occurrences. So, for Leucippus and Democritus there is an unlimited void, in which there are an unlimited number of atoms of all shapes and sizes. When, by chance, some atoms form a vortex, the processes of cosmos formation begin.[3] There is a sorting of 'like to like' which generates the earth and the heavens.[4] Many of these worlds are generated, all different from one another, and our cosmos is just one of them. It is not in any way designed. It has its characteristics entirely by chance, but that is made plausible by its being one of an infinite array of accidental worlds.

For Empedocles, the types of living creatures we are now familiar with are the result of the chance meeting of their parts.[5] He envisions, in a somewhat nightmarish fashion, parts of the human body wandering about and joining up by chance, the two most gruesome passages being:

Here many heads sprang up without necks,
Mere arms were wandering around without shoulders,
And single eyes, lacking foreheads, roamed around.[6]

Many grew with faces and breasts on both sides,
And man-headed bull-natured creatures, and again there arose

---

[3] See Diogenes Laertius IX. 31.
[4] See Sextus Empiricus, *Against the Mathematicians* VII. 116–18.
[5] See Aetius V. 19, 5.
[6] Empedocles, Fr. 57.

Bull-headed man-natured creatures, and mixtures of male
And female, equipped with shade-giving limbs.[7]

Many chance meetings of parts produced creatures which were
not able to survive, or were not able to reproduce and quickly died
out. Ultimately, though, creatures which were able to reproduce
came about purely by chance. So living things too can be seen as
the result of a multiplicity of accidents.

Plato's alternative is clear. There is one and only one cosmos,
which has been designed. We can explain the complex features of
that cosmos by the use of teleology. There are single, fixed species
which have been designed and, again, we can explain their complex features in teleological terms. It is also significant that instead
of having an unlimited multiplicity of atoms of all shapes and
sizes as the basic constituents of the physical world, as Leucippus
and Democritus believed, Plato opts for a small number (two) of
geometrically well-defined basic entities, which are chosen specifically by the demiurge as being best for their purpose.

One might object to the multiplicity-of-accidents view either
on philosophical grounds or on the grounds of plausibility. Is it
possible for the cosmos to come together accidentally? According
to Plato, it is not. As we have seen, Leucippus and Democritus
make use of a like-to-like principle; according to Plato at *Laws*
889b, though, a cosmos is a 'fitting and harmonious' blend of
opposites, such as hot and cold, dry and moist, soft and hard.
How do these come together by chance when the sorting is like to
like? In the absence of any ordering by the demiurge, but in the
presence of a like-to-like principle, wouldn't there simply be a
sorting out of the elements into areas of earth, water, air, and fire,
rather than the coming together of a cosmos? It is significant in
this context that *Timaeus* tells us that:

It's like when things are shaken and sifted by sieves or other devices
for cleaning grain: the heavy, dense material goes one way, while the
light, flimsy material goes and settles elsewhere. Likewise, when these
four were shaken at that time by the receptacle (which was itself in

[7] Empedocles, Fr. 61.

motion, like an implement for shaking stuff), the least similar among them ended up the furthest apart, and those that were most similar were pushed the closest together. (53a)

So a like-to-like principle will produce a sorting, but not interesting order and not a cosmos. Plato never mentions Leucippus or Democritus by name, but one can take this passage to be directly critical of anyone who supposes that a like-to-like principle is sufficient in cosmogony, the account of how the cosmos comes into being. Plato similarly refers tacitly to Empedocles, when he says: 'Not wanting the head to roll around on the ground without the ability to climb over the various rises and out of the various dips, they gave it the body to be its vehicle and means of transport' (44c). Empedocles needs the parts of the body to move around and associate with each other accidentally for his account of zoogony to work. But, Plato implies, if heads, and possibly many other body parts as well, are going to get stuck in every rut, the account is not going to work, or at the very least is going to become much less plausible. There are philosophical objections to the multiplicity-of-accidents view as well. *Timaeus* 30a presents an argument for there being a single cosmos. In *Philebus* Plato says: 'The indefinite plurality of things and in things makes you in each case indefinite of thought and someone of neither status nor account, since you have never yet examined the number in anything.'[8]

A third possible advantage of teleology is this. In the Socrates' dream passage of *Theaetetus* 201e ff., Socrates argues that composite entities can be analysed into their parts, and so we can have accounts of them. However, that which is incomposite cannot be given the same sort of analysis or account, and on this conception of knowledge the incomposite is unknowable. Employing one of his favourite analogies, Plato argues that we might have an account of syllables (in terms of the letters which constitute them) but not of letters. One problem for natural philosophy here is what sort of account we can have of the ultimate parts of the physical world.

---

[8] Plato, *Philebus* 17e; cf. *Philebus* 64e and *Theaetetus* 183b.

We cannot account for them or analyse them in terms of further physical parts. Plato in *Theaetetus* is happy just to present the problems. In *Timaeus*, however, we are given a theory of geometrical atomism, couched in the same terminology of letters and syllables; and after the elements of earth, water, air, and fire have been analysed into planes and then into the basic triangles, we have further teleological accounts of the nature of the basic triangles. This is not to say that a switch to teleology is a general answer to all the philosophical problems raised by the Socrates' dream passage in *Theaetetus*. It is significant, though, that *Timaeus* does give a teleological account of incomposite entities in his natural philosophy.

The Context of Timaeus' Teleology

Plato has reasons, then, for wanting teleology in his natural philosophy, independent of the demands of his ethical programme. We ought also to place Plato's teleology in context. In Greece of the fourth century BC, how plausible were the accounts of Empedocles, Leucippus, and Democritus? That their accounts have affinities with modern material and mechanical explanation ought not to lead us into overestimating the plausibility of their theories. They lacked many of the tools and discoveries that have made modern theories acceptable, and to many ancients the notion that a cosmos or living beings could come about solely by chance would have seemed radically implausible. Add in Plato's criticisms, that a like-to-like principle on its own cannot produce the requisite order, and that body parts on their own are going to be immobile, and these theories look even more unlikely.

It is also easy to look back and be critical of Plato's teleological programme; but it should be remembered that here is an idea that had yet to be put to any sort of test. With it, Plato is able to give a comprehensive account of physical phenomena, one that is at least as plausible as its rivals. The theory of combinations of regular circular motions produces a better model of the motions of the sun, moon, and planets than anything previously, and arguably produces one of the most important and progressive research programmes in antiquity. In the context of fourth-century Greece, Plato's teleological approach was a plausible and viable project.

Subsequently, the debate between the multiplicity-of-accidents view and the unique-entities view took an interesting course. In zoogony, the multiplicity-of-accidents view has won out in the form of the theory of evolution. It is significant, though, that this did not happen until the nineteenth and twentieth centuries, with the development of Darwin's theory and the discovery of DNA, and until then design theories of various types flourished whenever new phenomena were discovered which the mechanical approach had difficulty explaining.

More controversially, in modern atomism we think in terms of a relatively small number of mathematically well-defined ultimate particles rather than an indefinite multiplicity of shapes and sizes. So too, we believe that these particles form well-defined structures in specific manners, rather than that they come together in an accidental fashion. It is not necessary to think of the ultimate particles as being designed, but there are ways in which they have more in common with Plato's atomism than that of Leucippus and Democritus.

It would be wrong to see the seventeenth century as solely reviving atomism to the exclusion of Plato's geometrical atomism. This is historically important, as one of the great claims for the atomism of Democritus, Leucippus, Epicurus, and Lucretius is that it inspired this revival, and that this was important in the fight against scholasticism, the combination of Christian and Aristotelian thought which dominated the Middle Ages. But in fact seventeenth-century thinkers also felt the need to cure atomism of atheism, and this was not merely a religious predilection, but a borrowing from Plato. The philosophical problems with presocratic atomism, of why atoms should have certain shapes and combine in certain ways, which Plato addressed with teleology and the demiurge, were now addressed with a Christian deity. So we can find Robert Boyle saying that: 'The provident demiourgos wisely suited the fabric of the parts to the uses that were to be made of them.'[9]

So too, there was a considerable debate between those who advocated a universe consisting of a plenum of particles and those who favoured atoms and void. It is notable that those who favoured the plenum and rejected the idea of action at a distance, such as Descartes, adopted a similar solution to Plato for the awkward cases of gravity and magnetism. *Timaeus* 80c argues that the attractive powers of static electricity and magnetism are not due to any action at a distance, but can be explained by the fact that there is no void and the atoms jostle each other and move to their own region. Descartes, while using vortices to explain gravitational effects, did without a void, and used screw-shaped particles moving among smaller particles to explain magnetism.[10]

In cosmogony, there is still very much a live debate about whether or not we should consider our universe to be one of a multiplicity of accidental universes. The modern question is slightly different from the ancient one, in that it asks why the values of certain fundamental constants (such as the speed of light, or the value of the gravitational constant) have values set within the extremely tight limits which allow for the generation of planets and life. One type of answer to this is the descendant of the view of the ancient atomists. It is that there is an infinite number of universes and that the fundamental constants have different values in other universes. Our universe is one of an infinite array, and that is all we need to explain the (apparently fortuitous) values of the fundamental constants in our universe. Another type of answer descends from Plato: there is one universe, and the values of the fundamental constants are part of the design of that universe.

Finally, it is worth drawing some comparisons between Plato's and Aristotle's teleology. For Plato, order is imposed on

---

[9] Robert Boyle, *A Disquisition about the Final Causes of Natural Things*. Similarly, we can find Newton saying that: 'It seems probable to me that God in the beginning formed matter into solid, massy, hard, impenetrable movable particles, of such sizes and figures and with such other properties and in such proportion in space, as most conduced to the end for which he formed them' (*Optics* IV 260).

[10] René Descartes, *Principia Philosophiae*, IV 133 ff.

the cosmos rather than being inherent in it. For Aristotle, the cosmos has always existed (it has no beginning) and it has always had its order inherently. Plato requires something to impose order upon the cosmos, the demiurge. Aristotle's god may be important as an object of love, and has an important explanatory function in his scheme, but this god does not order anything. For Plato, it is the demiurge who acts purposively, not nature.

Cosmology

The cosmology of *Timaeus* marks both an important development in Greek thinking about the nature of the cosmos and some important developments in Plato's own thinking. *Timaeus* attempts to integrate mathematics into thinking about cosmology in a new way; it contains an essentially animate conception of cosmology, where the cosmos and the heavenly bodies are alive, but have regular behaviour; it offers a more stable conception of the cosmos than in Plato's earlier works; finally, it gives us the first argument that there is one, and only one, cosmos, possibly in reply to those presocratic thinkers who believed there to be more than one.

At *Phaedo* 108e ff. Plato had conceived of the earth as free-floating and immobile. The Myth of Er in *Republic* 616c ff. then made a significant conceptual leap, and began to talk of the integrity of the cosmos and how the cosmos might be supported. Here the cosmos needs bonds or braces (which may be internal or external to the cosmos; Plato uses a technical term from shipping, which we do not now fully understand) to hold it together. It is notable that here the cosmos is not referred to as a living entity and requires bracing, while in *Statesman*, *Timaeus*, and later works the cosmos is a living entity (mortal in *Statesman*, immortal in *Timaeus*) and needs no such bracing.[11]

Further important contrasts are that, while in previous works the cosmos turns on a pivot (*Republic* 616b ff., *Statesman* 270a), the *Timaeus* cosmos is entirely free-floating (33d and 34a), and

---

[11] See e.g. *Timaeus* 36e.

that while in previous works the cosmos does not have an immortal soul (no soul in *Republic*, a mortal soul in *Statesman*), in *Timaeus* it does. In *Timaeus* the cosmos is all there is, so it can have no external bracing nor can it rest on a pivot. This move to an unsupported cosmos is the culmination of a strand of presocratic thought. According to Aristotle, Thales proposed that the earth did not fall because it floated on water.[12] Then came theories of the earth not falling by being supported by air, or being in equilibrium. Plato, then, asked similar questions of the cosmos itself.

The integrity of the cosmos (and indeed of all the celestial bodies) is explained by their having souls, so no bracing is required, and as these souls are immortal, there is no degeneration. So too, the motions of the cosmos and the celestial bodies are generated by their souls. While there is a sense in which we can easily think of the cosmos in the Myth of Er as having a top and bottom (as it is supported by a sitting goddess), *Timaeus* 62c ff. makes it very clear that terms such as 'above' and 'below' are not suitable. One must make due allowance for the highly metaphorical language of the Myth of Er and the fact that cosmology is not Plato's primary concern there, but still there are important differences in the structure of the cosmos between *Republic* and *Timaeus*.

There are further contrasts to be made, concerning the regularity of circular motion and the stability of the cosmos. In *Republic* and *Statesman*, where there is a pivot for the cosmos to turn on, celestial motion is not entirely regular and degenerates, while with the free-floating *Timaeus* cosmos it is regular and stable. In *Timaeus* the cosmos is unageing and free from any disease, and indissoluble unless the demiurge wills otherwise, which he will not. There is an indication of a degenerating cosmos at *Phaedo* 110a, where the world is said to have been 'corrupted and eaten away'. At *Republic* 530b Socrates, talking about the motions of the heavens, says that it would be 'ludicrous to suppose that these things

---

[12] Aristotle, *On the Heavens* 294a.

are constant and unvarying, and never change in the slightest'. In the *Statesman* we have something more forthright:

At first, it carried out the commands of its father-maker quite exactly, but later—due to the fact that at least some of its components were material—some precision was lost, because before attaining its current ordered form as the cosmos, materiality (which is a primordial and inherent aspect of the universe) was steeped in a great deal of disorder . . . While the universe was under the helmsman's guidance, then, it used to engender little bad and plenty of good in the creatures it maintained within its boundaries. But then the helmsman departs. In the period immediately following this release, the universe continues to keep everything going excellently, but as time goes by it forgets his injunctions more and more. Then that primeval disharmony gains the upper hand and, towards the end of this period, the universe runs riot and implants a blend of little good and plenty of the opposite, until it comes close to destroying itself and everything in it. (*Statesman* 273b ff.)

That this change affects the heavenly bodies is confirmed at *Statesman* 269a. We might also infer this from Plato's general conviction that the stars have physical bodies and the myth's statement that all physical bodies degenerate. If the cosmos is continually degenerating towards chaos—and as *Statesman* 273b makes clear, this will be a radical and fundamental chaos (unless god intervenes, the cosmos will be 'storm-driven by confusion and broken up into an endless sea of unlikeness', *Statesman* 273de)—then clearly the periods of the planets will be subject to deviation. In the *Statesman*, though, either god must perpetually guide the cosmos or it degenerates of its own inherent nature, and is saved from sinking into 'an endless sea of unlikeness' only by the active intervention of god (*Statesman* 273b ff.). The cosmos of *Timaeus*, then, is more stable in its nature and more sophisticated in its conception.

One of the criticisms of Plato's natural philosophy is that he had an essentially animate conception of the cosmos. Plato indeed considers the heavenly bodies to be gods, to be animate, to be intelligent, and to have souls, and so too for the cosmos as a whole.

Coming after the materialism of the atomists, is this not a regressive move in Greek cosmology? After all, Plato is well aware of the views of the atomists and Anaxagoras' theory that the celestial bodies are hot stones.[13] For Plato, regular and orderly behaviour requires further explanation. Matter, on its own, will not, by chance and necessity alone, exhibit the sort of regularity we see in the heavens. *Laws* 967b says in relation to astronomy: 'Those who studied these matters accurately would not have been able to make such wonderfully accurate calculations if these entities did not have souls.'[14]

Timaeus states that the cosmos does not have many of the things we would usually associate with an animal (or even, within either a pagan or a Christian tradition, with a god). From *Timaeus* 33b onwards we are told that this 'animal' is perfectly spherical; has neither eyes nor ears, as there is nothing external to see or hear; nor does it have any need of organs to receive food or to excrete the remains, as it is entirely self-sufficient and nothing comes in or goes out. As it needs neither hands to defend itself nor feet to stand on, and has no need of legs or feet to propel itself, it has no limbs, and at 34b we are told it is a god. To say the least, this is a somewhat strange animal, and certainly could not be considered anthropomorphic, even if it does have intelligence and soul. Plato's claim in *Timaeus* that the cosmos is like an animal is a claim for the integrity and the internal organization of the cosmos, and the ongoing order of the cosmos, even though there are properties that animals have but inanimate matter does not.

What does this god do, though? All it does is revolve uniformly in one place (34a). The stars are spherical and intelligent like the cosmos (40a), and are divine and living creatures (40b). As with the cosmos, they have motions befitting their intelligence, and so we are told that:

He endowed each of the gods with two kinds of motion: even rotation in the same place, to enable them always to think the same thoughts

---

[13] *Apology* 26cd, *Laws* 886e; cf. Hippolytus, *Refutatio* 1. 8. 3–10.
[14] Cf. *Laws* 897b and *Epinomis* 982b on intelligence and regularity.

about the same things; and forward motion, under the sovereignty of the revolution of identity and sameness. But with respect to the other five kinds of motion, they were to be stable and unmoving, so that each of them might be, to the fullest extent, as perfect as possible. And so all the fixed stars were created as divine, ever-living beings, spinning evenly and unerringly for ever. (40a)

The essential point here, then, is that the celestial bodies have no freedom of action (or no desire to deviate from regular circular motion). They have the intelligence to carry out their assigned duties, and not to do anything else. It is their intelligence which explains their regular and orderly behaviour. That they move, and do so without any external compulsion, is explained by their having souls. For Plato, the soul is a principle of motion.[15]

Although the cosmos and the heavenly bodies have life, soul, divinity, and intelligence, they have these in a highly circumscribed and attenuated manner, from a modern point of view. If this is describable as vitalism, it is a highly depersonalized version, where the attributes of animate beings that are required for the description of the cosmos have been carefully sorted from those that are not. This allows us to distinguish quite sharply between Plato and the mythological and magical traditions. The key issue here is that these souls/gods are not capricious. They always act for the best, and so will always act in the same manner. There is nothing unpredictable or irregular about their behaviour.

As we now express physical laws in terms of equations, we slip very easily into a mathematical model of physical law. That is, we consider physical laws to be unbreakable in a manner analogous to mathematical or geometrical laws. It is very easy to assume that physical law has always been modelled on mathematical law, but this is not so, the scientific revolution of the seventeenth century being the watershed. Prior to the seventeenth century, in the Western tradition and in other cultures, it is common to find physical law modelled on civil law instead. So while physical law ought to be upheld, it is conceivable that it will not be, and then

---

[15] On soul and motion see *Laws* 895c, *Phaedrus* 245c, and *Timaeus* 37b.

there may even be a punishment for a breach of the law. So we find Heraclitus saying that: 'The sun will not overstep its measures, or else the Furies, the allies of Justice, will find it out.'[16]

Plato's conception of physical law in *Timaeus* is based on a civil rather than a mathematical model. The heavenly bodies have intelligence, understand what they ought to do for the best, and, being good souls, carry that out. While it is conceivable that the heavenly bodies will deviate from the intelligent course, due to their nature they will not in fact do so. We might compare here the fate of the cosmos in *Timaeus*. As the cosmos was generated, it is dissoluble, but as the demiurge is good, this will not in fact happen, and the cosmos will continue indefinitely.

There is also a question of resources here. The Greeks had no conception of gravity, so that what we take to be gravitational phenomena had to be explained in different terms. Hence we get like-to-like theories of why heavy objects fall to the ground, or Aristotle's theories of natural place and natural motion. What ancient physical explanation could be given of the heavens? The atomist notion of a vortex sweeping the heavens around may account for the simple motion of the stars, but as becomes evident in the astronomy of *Timaeus*, it cannot account for the more complex motions of sun, moon, and planets. Once one employs more than one circular motion to explain the motion of a celestial body, it becomes difficult to see how the motion of that body can be explained in terms of a single force. As the Greeks held that the earth is central and stable, they had to treat all the movements of the heavens as real motions. We understand many of these to be apparent, due to the motion of the earth. We think in terms of a force emanating from the sun controlling geometrically relatively simple, elliptical orbits, but this was not an option for the Greeks, as they had to explain the highly complex motions of the heavens (as seen from the earth) as if they were real. No force emanating from the earth could explain these, which meant they had to seek different types of explanation.

---

[16] Heraclitus, Fr. 94.

Plato was not alone, then, in the history of scientific thought in using divine entities to explain regular behaviour—there has been a long tradition within Christian thought, right down to the current day, of asserting that God ensures the regularity of the universe. The key question is whether these entities are law-abiding or not, and for Plato they most certainly are. In the sense that teleology is imposed on the world by the demiurge and so is not an original feature of the world, Plato's teleology is unnatural. It is also important to recognize, however, that Plato's demiurge is a god subject to natural law and regular behaviour, as are his demigods, and so there is a sharp contrast with the caprice of the gods of Greek myth. Nor is Plato alone in the ancient world in using biological analogues for physical processes. Aristotle is perhaps a good example of how biological analogues can intrude into physics in a more subtle manner, and this is something which is continued by the Stoics. With modern science having moved away from the use of biological analogues, the essential question is: is it evident, in the context of fourth-century Greece, that one should be using mechanical rather than biological analogues? The answer to that is quite clearly no. There are several reasons for this. If one wishes to explain order and regularity, mechanisms are not a good option for the Greeks. While mechanisms, and particularly clockwork, are paradigms of regularity and predictability to us, the mechanisms available to the Greeks, such as the cart and the winch, cannot serve as such models. It is not surprising, then, that even where the Greeks might be described as materialists, they are not mechanists.

Mathematics, Geometry, and Harmony

Timaeus is one of the first attempts to bring together mathematics and cosmology. Indeed, the demiurge can reasonably be described as a geometer god. One of the odd aspects of this from a modern point of view is that Plato employs a theory of harmony in cosmology: the spacing of the orbits of the planets is related to the musical scale. Musical notes can be expressed as the ratio between two numbers, as can the size of the planetary orbits. Why does Plato do this? First, when we express physical laws now, we often write them as equations, but has it always been evident that we should express physical laws in this manner? The answer to that is a definite no, and in fact physical laws have only been systematically written in this form since around the seventeenth century. Prior to that, many possibilities of how mathematics in general might relate to the world were open. The relationship might be arithmetical, the world itself consisting of numbers, as the Pythagoreans suggested; or it might be based on harmony, as there is clearly some relation between harmony and number (string-lengths for musical instruments, and so on); or the relation might be geometrical, the world being constituted from shapes, or shapes playing an important role in the ordering of the world. The idea that physical laws should be expressed in equations was not intuitively obvious, and had to be hard fought for; indeed, even over the last century science has refined its use of mathematics, with the introduction of the theory of probability. One reason why Plato does not express the motions of the heavens as equations, then, is that this is not really a resource that is open to him. Another is an extension of the idea of civil law being applied to the intelligences that guide the celestial bodies. There is no question here, for instance, of there being a force impressed and there being a resulting action in proportion to the size of that force, nor any question of an expenditure of energy or fuel. The heavenly bodies simply manage their own motions.

In order to illustrate what Plato may be doing here, let us take a short digression via Johannes Kepler (1571–1630), the great astronomer famous for his three laws of planetary motion. Kepler was an ardent Platonist, and an avid reader of *Timaeus*. Two millennia after Plato, was the modern relationship between mathematics and cosmology clear to one of the most important figures in the history of astronomy? Or did he struggle with problems similar to Plato's, and if he did, how did he propose to resolve them? Kepler attempted to derive the size and number of the planetary orbits from the Platonic solids[17]—the cube, tetrahedron, octahedron, icosahedron, and dodecahedron. The precise details need not concern us here, but in outline Kepler's thinking is this: for each of these solids, we can imagine a sphere touching each of the surfaces on the inside, and another touching each of the vertices on the outside. It is then possible to calculate a ratio, $r:R$, of the radius of the inner sphere and the radius of the outer sphere. This is most easily illustrated in two dimensions for a square face of a cube of earth and a triangular face of a tetrahedron:

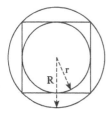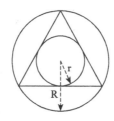

It is then possible, given some assumptions about how planetary orbits nest together, to generate ratios for the relative spacings of the orbits of the planets visible to the naked eye. In one of the most remarkable phenomena of the history of science, this process can be made to give very good results, certainly by the standards of seventeenth-century observation.

Once he had discovered that planetary orbits were elliptical, Kepler needed a reason why they have their specific eccentricities and why the planets had their specific velocities.[18] It is possible to express many of the properties of a planetary orbit as ratios, such as the ratio of the lengths of the axes of the ellipse or the ratio of the speeds of a planet as it crosses the axes. With some mathematical processing, Kepler could then produce the harmonies expressed by the planets. The more pronounced the ellipse (as with Mercury), the more notes a planet produces; the more nearly circular (as with Venus), the more monotonous it is.

[17] The Platonic solids are constructed from similar faces—so the cube from six similar squares, the tetrahedron from four similar triangles, etc.

[18] Kepler does not abandon his spacing for the orbits based on spheres inside and outside Platonic solids, but uses the mean radii of the ellipses.

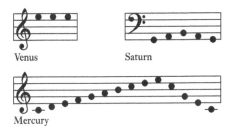

Venus   Saturn

Mercury

Why do Plato and Kepler approach cosmology in this manner? If we ask modern science why there are eight planets in the solar system, with specific spacings of the orbits and specific orbital speeds, the answer is likely to be that this is largely a matter of chance. Kepler, though, has an explanation of why there are only a specific number of planets (there are only a determinate number of Platonic solids to space their orbits with), and why the planets have specific eccentricities and velocities (to produce a celestial harmony). In a cosmos generated by a benevolent demiurge there is nothing which is produced arbitrarily, and the demiurge has a reason for all that he does. Or, to put this another way: what sufficient reason is there for the demiurge to use one set of orbit sizes for the planets rather than any other? Plato and Kepler recognize the need for criteria here. Possibilities open to them, but closed by the developments of the seventeenth century, are forms of geometrical or harmonic ordering.

Kepler's work illustrates that the Renaissance was still struggling with the relation of mathematics and cosmology. Kepler asked a slightly different question from modern science, but a perfectly rational and reasonable one within his historical context, and one that many others of his time were asking. Kepler himself is adamant that there is nothing mystical in his work, and I would agree with him. At no stage does he say that anything is inexplicable; rather, he is always seeking some form of mathematical explanation. So if a major figure in the history of science was still struggling with the relation between mathematics and cosmology nearly 2,000 years later than Plato, we can perhaps be a little more sympathetic to Plato's plight. He too wished to know why the demiurge had formed the cosmos in this specific manner, and pursued what to him would have been open possibilities for the mathematical structure of the cosmos without any recourse to numerology or mysticism.

The Demiurge

The demiurge, the primary god, plays an important role in *Timaeus*, though we are told frustratingly little about him. He is a craftsman god, which is not how one would describe the gods of Greek myth. Since manual labour was looked down upon in cultured circles in Plato's time, this conception of the demiurge is very radical.[19] Plato's god needs to be skilled, as the production of the cosmos and everything in it is something which requires skill, but Plato does not tell us exactly how the demiurge is supposed to exercise that skill.

It is significant, relative to previous Greek mythology, that Plato's demiurge wishes everything to be in the best possible state of order and has no jealousy. In previous mythology the gods often begrudge any gift to mankind, and disagree among themselves about such gifts, and sometimes the gifts turn out to be double-edged; but the demiurge freely gives his gifts, and they are of undoubted benefit to mankind. The relation between humans and god is also significant. Where previously humans had sought to become gods, or sought to be physically like gods, and had suffered for their hubris, Plato attempts to channel human aspirations towards being intellectually like god. There is no sense in *Timaeus* that it is an act of hubris to try to become intellectually as like god as possible.

Relative to earlier Greek cosmogony, this is the first time that we have an independent god imposing order on a pre-existing chaos. In other cosmogonies there is often a principle of 'steering' by which the cosmos is formed, but that which does the steering does not seem to be separate from that which is steered.

---

[19] Xenophon, *Oeconomicus* 4. 2, tells us that: 'What are called the mechanical arts carry a social stigma, and are rightly dishonoured in our cities. For these arts damage the bodies of those who work at them or supervise them, by compelling the workers to a sedentary life.'

Alternatively, there were the chance-dominated cosmogonies of the early atomists and Empedocles, or the rejection of cosmogony in Heraclitus or Parmenides' 'Way of Truth'. Plato's demiurge is the first god to impose order explicitly by using mathematics, geometry, and harmony.

That Plato's demiurge is entirely good and free from jealousy, and is unlike humankind, can be seen as a development away from Greek mythological conceptions of god, a trend that was begun in the sixth century by Xenophanes, who tells us that:

> Homer and Hesiod have attributed to the gods
> Everything that men find shameful and reprehensible—
> Stealing, adultery, and deceiving one another.

> But mortals think that the gods are born,
> Wear their own clothes, have voices and bodies.

> If cows and horses or lions had hands,
> Or could draw with their hands and make things as men can,
> Horses would have drawn horse-like gods, cows cow-like gods,
> And each species would have made their gods' bodies just like
>   their own.

> Ethiopians say that the gods are flat-nosed and black,
> And Thracians that theirs have blue eyes and red hair.[20]

That god is entirely good and behaves in a predictable and invariant manner, and imposes that sort of order on the cosmos, is of considerable importance for the philosophical and scientific ideas of believers from Plato onwards. In *Timaeus* the demiurge is not one god among many, or even the first among equals as we find in myth. He is the only god of his type, and prior to his ordering of the cosmos he is the only god at all, although then he produces demigods to aid him in ordering the cosmos and, in particular, in forming mankind.

There is still some distance, though, between Plato and a Christian conception of God, and we must be careful not to attribute later theological ideas to Plato. While Plato's god is

---

[20] Xenophanes, Fr. 11, 14, 15, 16.

omni-benevolent, he is not omnipotent, in that he cannot do the physically or the logically impossible. It is an important theme in *Timaeus* that the demiurge does as well as he can with the materials available to him, but that reason can only persuade necessity so far and no further. In early Christianity there was considerable debate about whether god created the universe from nothing, or from some pre-existing matter, the former view eventually winning.

Timaeus is not really a religious work, at least in the sense that it does not say that we should worship god, nor does it lay down how god should be worshipped, nor give any structure for the organization of a religion. Rather, it tells us how we can embark on a programme of intellectual improvement, based on an analysis of the relation between the cosmos and god. We should strive to become like god.

Timaeus was much discussed in antiquity in relation to two related theological issues, both stemming from the idea of the creation of the universe by a benevolent deity. First, there is the question of divine providence. If god has created a good world, as far as possible, and continues to care for that world, how exactly does that work? How do we understand the nature of the world as the product of providence? How do we understand our own actions, goals, and fate in relation to god's providence?[21] Secondly, there is the question of evil. Why is it, if god is entirely good, that human beings do bad things and there is evil in the world?

Timaeus' Account and Natural Philosophy

The narrative which Timaeus gives is described as an *eikos logos*, a 'likely account' (29d, 30b), but it would be misleading to consider it a myth in the orthodox sense. Timaeus does not just assert the existence of a god, a world-soul, and so on, but assigns important function to each of these things. In other words, he can justify the existence of everything he supposes to exist, whereas myths are more profligate in what they suppose to exist (many gods,

---

[21] Cf. *Timaeus* 42d ff., where the demiurge is said to be blameless for anything that may happen after the initial ordering; cf. *Republic* 380c ff.

monsters, titans, and so on). Plato's god also behaves in an entirely rational manner, unlike the gods of myth. Plato does use the Greek word *muthos* in *Timaeus* (29d, 68d), but this need not be translated as 'myth'. It can mean any oral account, or any tale, story, or narrative. As Timaeus' account is also referred to as a *logos* (30b), which in philosophical contexts has strong connotations of explanation, it is probably best to think of Timaeus' narrative as a likely account.

The 'likely' part of this description stems from a word-play in the Greek, between *eikones* 'likenesses' and *eikos* 'likely'. One of the important metaphysical themes of *Timaeus* is that the cosmos is in some sense a copy or a likeness. The demiurge looks to an unchanging original, and makes our changeable cosmos as much like that original as possible. Timaeus offers us the principle that explanations have to be of the same order as what they explain. So an account of the forms,[22] which are stable, secure, and manifest to the intellect, should itself be stable and reliable. An account of what is a likeness, on the other hand, can only be likely. But it is difficult to determine the degree of likelihood the account can aspire to. Certainly this is not just one story among many, as several times we are told that this account is second to none in its likelihood. While there are passages where Timaeus is quite tentative in his claims, there are others where he is considerably more confident. We can, for instance, make entirely correct calculations about the motions of the heavenly bodies. Or again, Timaeus seems quite confident about his choice of the two basic sorts of triangle for geometrical atomism, but goes on to say if anyone can think of better triangles than these he will be welcomed as a friend (54a). That the account is currently second to none does not preclude its being improved, though whether it could ever be a definitive account would be open to question. What the 'likely account' cannot do and could never do is produce knowledge, in the sense that Plato believes we can have knowledge of the forms.

[22] The exact nature of Plato's forms has been a matter of debate since antiquity. It is reasonable to say, though, that there is a distinction between a form and what participates in a form (e.g. the form of the good versus a good action). A form is non-physical, non-spatial, and atemporal, and can only be thought of, not perceived with the senses. A form can be known and is entirely unchanging.

What does this mean for Plato's attitude towards natural philosophy and the investigation of nature? In Plato's sense of the word, we cannot have knowledge of the physical world. Plato's use of the word 'knowledge' is very strong, however, and there are differing degrees of opinion we can have concerning the physical world; we may even hold true opinions about it. Plato was highly critical of the *physiologoi*, the presocratic natural philosophers, particularly in his earlier work *Phaedo*. This should not be taken to indicate that he was hostile to natural philosophy, but rather that he had his own conception of how natural philosophy should be done. That, of course, involves the sort of teleology that *Timaeus* supplies. *Phaedo* does not argue that the shape and position of the earth or the constitution of the body are matters of no interest, but rather that purely material explanations of these phenomena are inadequate. *Timaeus* delivers, it can be argued, Plato's more fully worked-out riposte to the *physiologoi*, offering teleological explanations for all phenomena. In *Phaedo*, Socrates says this about causes:

It would be quite true to say that without possessing such things as bones and sinews, and whatever else I possess, I shouldn't be able to do what I judged best; but to call these things the reasons for my actions, rather than my choice of what is best, and that too though I act with intelligence, would be a thoroughly loose way of talking. Fancy being unable to distinguish two different things: the reason proper, and that without which the reason could never be a reason! (*Phaedo* 99a)

Timaeus has a slightly different view: 'we should discuss both kinds of causes, but keep those which fashion good and beautiful products with the help of intelligent craftsmanship separate from those which produce random and disorderly results, with no part played by intelligence' (46e). Plato still talks of two sorts of causes, but no longer is one a real cause and the other not. Plato has the reputation of being rather anti-empirical. In part this is deserved, as he often emphasizes that forms are intelligible entities and not the subject of sense-perception. This attitude is easy to exaggerate, though, and the best antidote is perhaps to quote

Timaeus on the benefits of eyesight:

sight is enormously beneficial for us, in the sense that, if we couldn't see the stars and the sun and the sky, an account such as I've been giving of the universe would be completely impossible. As things are, however, the visibility of day and night, of months and the circling years, of equinoxes and solstices, resulted in the invention of number, gave us the concept of time, and made it possible for us to enquire into the nature of the universe. These in their turn have enabled us to equip ourselves with philosophy in general, and humankind never has been nor ever will be granted by the gods a greater good than philosophy. (47a)

Astronomy

Timaeus gives us a model for the motions of the heavenly bodies: the earth is central and unmoving, and there are the fixed stars, which rotate around the earth once every day. Typically for the ancient world, these stars are all presumed to be equidistant from the earth and to undergo no change of position relative to one another. Unlike Aristotle, where the stars are fixed in a sphere, Plato's stars are freemoving and hold their pattern due to the intelligences that guide them. Each of the other seven heavenly bodies visible to the naked eye (the sun, the moon, Mercury, Venus, Mars, Jupiter, and Saturn) has a second circular motion, in addition to the first, with a different axis. So each time the fixed stars complete a revolution, the sun, moon and five planets will be in slightly different positions (see figure).

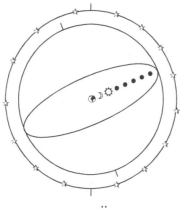

We do not know what angle Plato supposed there to be between the axis of revolution for the fixed stars and that of the sun, moon, and planets, though he does describe the relation between the two as like the Greek letter *chi*, X (36bc). The angle required is around 23.5 degrees, which is the difference between the plane of the earth's motion around the sun and the axis of earth's rotation (see figure).

If one plots where the sun sets through the year, it sets due west at equinox (when day and night are of equal length) and at 23.5 degrees north or south at the solstices (when either the day is longest and the night shortest, or vice versa):

Winter solstice	Equinoxes	Summer solstice
☼	☼	☼
23.5°	due west	23.5°

If you observe which stars rise at the point where the sun sets, you get a line called the ecliptic. The sun changes position relative to the stars by about 1 degree a day (the earth completes an orbit of 360 degrees in around 365 days). In Plato's model, it is the sun which moves, and completes its second circular motion in one year, so it will move by around 1 degree a day relative to the fixed stars and will move along the ecliptic, assuming the correct angle has been chosen. The planets also appear close to the ecliptic. The reason for this is that, if we draw a line from the sun through the earth, the orbits of the other planets are relatively close to this line. So, in the following diagram, the figures indicate the angle between the planets' orbit around the sun and that of the earth:

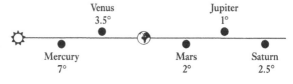

The planets deviate slightly from the ecliptic, and the band of sky they move in is known as the zodiac. Plato also has Timaeus tell us that the moon completes its second revolution in a month, the sun in a year, but that few have taken note of the other celestial bodies (39c). The second circular motion will produce motion along the ecliptic, moving the planets relative to the fixed stars, but it will not produce any deviation from the ecliptic.

In *Timaeus*, all the celestial bodies move in a perfectly regular manner. At 34a Timaeus tells us that the universe itself revolves uniformly and has no trace of any other motion. If the universe as a whole and the fixed stars have regular motion, there cannot be any metaphysical reason why the rest of the heavenly bodies cannot move in a regular manner as well. Timaeus tells us that the motions of the planets constitute time (39c). If so, their motion must be regular or time will be irregular. But Plato mentions no irregularity in relation to time, nor is there any need for time to be irregular in *Timaeus*. All that is needed for a distinction between time and eternity is that time flows while eternity stands still. At 39d Timaeus tells us of the 'great year', the time taken for all the heavenly bodies to repeat their positions relative to each other and to the fixed stars. This is a calculable amount of time, so the motions of the planets must be regular. The general idea that the visible heavens are amenable to calculation proliferates throughout the *Timaeus* (e.g. 40d and 47c). The motions of the heavens are also the visible manifestations of the movements of the world-soul, and these motions are entirely regular (47c).

That the heavens move in a perfectly regular fashion is very important. It marks a significant change from *Republic*, where Socrates asks:

Don't you think that a genuine astronomer feels the same when he looks at the movements of the heavenly bodies? He'll certainly think that the artist of the heavens has constructed them and all they contain to be as beautiful as such works could ever possibly be, but what about the ratio between night and day, between them and a month, between a month and a year? And what about the relations of the heavenly bodies in general to these phenomena or to one another? Don't you think he'd regard it as ludicrous to suppose that these things are constant and unvarying, and never change in the slightest, when they're material and visible, and to devote all one's energy to discovering the truth about these things? (*Republic* 530a–b)

At *Laws* 822a, however, Plato adopts a similar position to that of *Timaeus*: 'The usual opinion concerning the sun, moon, and other planets, that they occasionally wander, is not the case; precisely the opposite is true. For each of these bodies always travels on one path, and not many, although this may not seem so.' This is important for the history of astronomy; previously, the Babylonians had called the planets *bibbu*, 'sheep', and our own word planet derives from the Greek *planetes*, meaning something that wanders, or a vagabond. There is a tradition that Plato set problems in astronomy for others to solve. Simplicius reports that: 'Plato assigned circular, regular, and ordered motions to the heavens, and offered this problem to the mathematicians: which hypotheses of regular, circular, and ordered motion are capable of saving the phenomena of the planets? And first Eudoxus of Cnidus produced the hypothesis of the so-called unrolling spheres.'[23] Plato recognized that there are no irregular motions in the heavens and, in supposing that all the motions of the heavenly bodies are either simple regular circular motions or combinations of regular circular motions, he set the parameters for one of the longest and most fruitful research programmes in the history of science. The concentric-sphere astronomies of Eudoxus, Callippus, and Aristotle all developed from this, as did the epicyclic astronomies of Ptolemy and his followers. Even as late as 1543, Copernicus, supposing the earth to be in motion around the sun, stayed with combinations of regular circular motion. It was not until 1609 that Kepler suggested that planetary orbits are simple ellipses about the sun.

There are, of course, problems with the astronomy of *Timaeus*. As it is one of the earliest models of the cosmos that makes a serious attempt at accommodating the phenomena, it would be very surprising if there were not. Plato was aware of at least some of these.

---

[23] Simplicius, *Commentary on Aristotle's On the Heavens* 492. 31 ff.; cf. 488. 18 ff.

We are told that Venus and Mercury are placed in circles with speeds equal to that of the sun, but that due to having a tendency that opposes the sun (38d), these two planets overtake and are overtaken by each other. This overtaking and being overtaken cannot be generated by a combination of two regular circular motions, so the tendency opposing the sun must involve some other motion. That may be some further regular motion that Plato leaves out of the account for simplicity, or it may be that he has no answer for this problem as yet. Two further major difficulties are that Plato cannot account for the retrograde motion of the planets, and his account of eclipses is seriously astray.

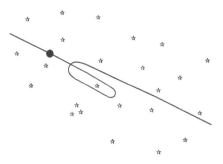

The planets appear to do a little dance (see figure).[24] They move relative to the fixed stars, stop, move backwards, stop again, and then move forwards again. The backward movement is known as retrograde motion, and though Plato is aware of it, he cannot account for it, as on his model the planets move with a uniform speed along the ecliptic. If the sun, moon, and planets were all permanently in the same plane, along with the earth, there would be a lunar eclipse every full moon, and a solar eclipse every new moon. These eclipses would always be of the same type, both in the sense of the linear alignment of the sun, moon, and earth giving identical total/partial eclipses and in the sense of the relative

[24] This is an apparent effect, due to the relative motion of the earth and the planet producing this effect against the background of the fixed stars. One problem with thinking that the earth does not move is that then all the motions of the heavenly bodies must be real and not apparent motions.

distances of sun and moon giving either a complete or an annular eclipse each time (see figure). [25]

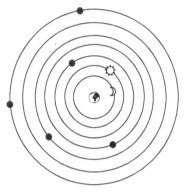

It is wrong to assume that ancient thinkers believed that their models could solve all the problems of astronomy. Simplicius tells us that: 'The unrolling spheres of Eudoxus' school do not save the phenomena, not only those that were found later, but also those known before and recognized by them.'[26] The three phenomena Simplicius cites are that (1) Venus and Mars appear at times much brighter than at others; (2) there is variation in the apparent size of the moon; (3) there are variations in the type of solar eclipses relating to the apparent size of the moon.

Plato's model is best viewed as a prototype. It is strong on philosophical and cosmological principle (all the motions of the heavenly bodies are either simple regular circular motions or combinations of regular circular motions), but weaker in its application to specific problems in astronomy. It is an advance on previous theories, including the model put forward in the Myth of Er in *Republic*, but it is not as good as later theories. We might

---

[25] Depending on its distance from the earth, the moon sometimes covers the entire sun, while sometimes a small rim of the sun is visible around the moon. The latter is an annular eclipse. The reason why there are not eclipses every month is that the orbit of the moon is inclined at around 5 degrees to the plane of the earth's orbit. The moon has to be in the same plane as the earth and sun as it passes in front of or behind the earth for an eclipse to occur.

[26] Simplicius, *Commentary on Aristotle's On the Heavens* 504. 17 ff.

reasonably suppose, given Plato's philosophical predilections, that he was more concerned with generating a teleological cosmology than with astronomy. Clearly, for such a cosmology to be plausible it has to be able to give a reasonable account of the phenomena, but Plato's priorities are surely with cosmological principles.

Cosmogony

Timaeus gives us an account of the origins of the cosmos. Prior to the intervention of the demiurge, there is a chaos. There is no order to the constituents of the cosmos, in two senses: what there is in this chaos is not distributed through space in any orderly fashion, and it is not properly formed into orderly elements. Plato subscribes to the usual Greek view that there are four elements: earth, water, air, and fire. Prior to the ordering of the cosmos, there are only accidental traces of these. So Plato's vision of chaos is quite radical. Matter itself has no order, as well as being randomly distributed. There is also, in an important sense, no time prior to the ordering of the cosmos. There is no measurable time because time is bound up with the movements of the sun, moon, and planets. It is their regular motions which constitute measurable time, and this sort of time comes into existence with the establishment of the heavens.

The pre-cosmic chaos is non-progressive, a dead end. This is different from modern cosmogony, and is critical to Plato's view. In modern cosmogony there is the chaos of the Big Bang, then gravity does the work. Small areas of greater density (the 'wrinkles in space-time') act as attractors and pull matter towards them, eventually forming stars and so on. We can then give an account of the formation of stars, the sun, earth, and the solar system without recourse to a designer. For Plato, though, the pre-cosmic chaos is non-progressive and will remain a chaos unless there is an intervention to generate order, and that is the task of the demiurge. That order will not come about by chance. *Timaeus* does give us a like-to-like principle, but it would be wrong to think of it as a principle of attraction, as with gravity. Rather, when many things are agitated, like things aggregate together. This like-to-like principle will not produce a cosmos from a chaos, however. It will merely sort like things together, and that is not sufficient. There is an important passage in *Laws* where Plato says:

Let me put it more clearly. Fire, water, earth, and air all exist due to nature and chance, they say, and none to skill, and the bodies which come after these, earth, sun, moon, and stars, came into being because of these entirely soulless entities. Each being moved by chance, according to the power it has, they somehow fell together in a fitting and harmonious manner, hot with cold or dry with moist or hard with soft, all of the forced blendings happening by the mixing of opposites according to chance. In this way and by these means the heavens and all that pertains to them have come into being and all of the animals and plants, all of the seasons having been created from these things, not by intelligence, they say, nor by some god nor some skill, but as we say, through nature and chance.[27]

A cosmos, then, has a 'fitting and harmonious' blending of opposites, something that will not be generated by a like-to-like principle. There is a need for the demiurge to intervene in order to establish a cosmos, and the demiurge has considerable work to do. Not only must he create an orderly distribution of the elements; he must form those elements themselves.

There is another aspect to Plato's cosmogony, which is that the cosmos has to have a soul as well as a body. The creation of the soul takes place on a more metaphysical level. The soul is compounded from sameness, being, and difference. This is in order that the world-soul will be able to make judgements of existence, sameness, or difference (the primary characteristics of the world), and so will be able to live an intelligent life. This mix is then split up according to harmonic principles and bound together to form the cosmos and the paths of the sun, moon, and planets. This is not something that can come about by chance either, as there must be precise proportion in the mixing, precise division to form the world-soul, and the different is described as 'difficult to mix'.

[27] Plato, *Laws* 889b.

The key to Plato's cosmogony is that the cosmos cannot have come about by chance. The demiurge must act on a non-progressive chaos. He has to generate the elements, the cosmos, and the soul of the cosmos, as well as humans and animals.

Soul, Macrocosm, and Microcosm

Timaeus develops an analogy between the nature of the world-soul and the nature of our own soul. Our own souls, the microcosms, have very strong similarities to the world-soul, the macrocosm. The world-soul is constituted from sameness, being, and difference. It consists of two revolutions, the same and the different, which move with perfect regularity. The world-soul is intelligent, and all the judgements it makes about sameness (or identity), being, and difference in relation to the objects it encounters are correct. The human soul is constituted in a similar manner, though the mix of sameness, being, and difference is not as good as it was for the world-soul. We too have a pair of mental revolutions. Ours, though, do not move in a perfectly regular manner. When our souls are bound into our bodies, the revolutions of our minds are disrupted by the sudden influx of sensations. Because of this, our judgements of sameness, being, and difference in the objects we encounter is flawed, especially in our early years before the revolutions have had a chance to settle down again (43d).

Plato may not mean all of this quite literally, but it is of great importance for what we should be doing with our lives. Our goal should be to correct our mental revolutions and try to bring them as far as possible to resemble those of the world-soul. If we are able to control our sensations and to bring our mental revolutions under control, we will live justly; if we do not, we will live unjustly. While we should not neglect the health of the body, it is the health of our minds that is really important. Our goal should be to become as much like god as possible, in having perfect mental revolutions. The study of astronomy has a key part in this: 'the gods wanted us to make a close study of the circular motions of the heavens, gain the ability to calculate them correctly in accordance with their nature, assimilate ours to the perfect evenness of the god's, and so stabilize the wandering revolutions within us' (47c). What happens if we do not lead a good life? A good life is an end in itself for Plato, but there are consequences in subsequent incarnations for wrongdoers. The highest part of the soul is immortal and undergoes incarnations, first in the body of a man. If a man should lead a poor life, on the next incarnation he will have the body of a woman. Men who are light-witted and make only a superficial study of astronomy come back as birds. Men who take no part in either philosophy or astronomy become land animals, and the most stupid of these become snakes, or even sea creatures (90e–92c). If this seems harsh, remember that in *Timaeus* humans are responsible for their own mental condition. Everyone is capable of improving his or her condition by study, or of allowing his or her mind to deteriorate through laziness or folly. It is an important principle of *Timaeus* that god is blameless and man generates his own evil.

It is up to us, then, to correct the revolutions in our heads that are so badly disrupted when we are given bodies. These revolutions do settle down of their own accord, to a certain extent, but we must do all we can to encourage this. The housing of the soul in the body has its own problems. The higher part of the soul is placed in the head, in order to keep it as far away as possible from the baser passions of other parts of the body. There is a skull to protect it, but this skull cannot be so thick that it seriously hinders perception. The demiurge favours a short, intelligent, well-lived life over a longer life lived at a lower level, and this informs the disposition of the body around the soul when the demiurge generates humans.

The macrocosm/microcosm analogy also features in the strictures on the health of the body (88d). The receptacle shakes what is in it, and this shaking helps to keep the elements in their order. Similarly, we should keep our bodies in motion, that is, we should take some exercise, in order that the movement of our bodies keeps the elements in their proper places.

The macrocosm/microcosm analogy inspired at least one important scientific breakthrough. Giordano Bruno, in the latter part of the sixteenth century, associated soul with the blood, and speculated that as the soul of the macrocosm had a circular motion, so the blood of the microcosm (that is, humans) must circulate around the body. William Harvey, who discovered the circulation of the blood around 1619, supported his view largely with argument and experiment, though a macrocosm/microcosm relation was an important part of his thinking too.

Intelligence and Necessity

After he has described what he calls the works of intelligent crafts-manship, at 47e Timaeus switches to discussing what comes about by necessity. Timaeus tells us that intelligence persuaded neces-sity for the most part to produce good results. What does Plato mean by necessity, and how is it that necessity can be 'persuaded' by anything? As reason scores only a partial victory over necessity, there is some residual chance and disorder. Now, it seems strange that necessity should be associated with these things. However, one might take both chance and disorder in two separate senses, depending on what they are contrasted with:

(1) An event might be said to occur by chance because there is no causal chain that leads to its occurrence, contrasting chance with causal determinism.

(2) An event might be said to occur by chance in the absence of design. If we were to blindly throw paint at a canvas, in an attempt to generate a portrait, it would be mere chance if anything good were the result, though no causal chain need be broken if such an event were to occur.

We can take the same sort of approach with disorder. The order that it is contrasted with might be that of physical law, or that of a teleological arrangement of phenomena. The ordinary emission of light, for instance, might be law-like but disorderly (with no order to wavelength or direction), relative to a stimulated emis-sion of light and its ordering into a laser beam (ordered in wave-length and direction). An ancient analogue here might be that the principles of military strategy apply to all groups of men, but some groups are well-ordered formations while others are disordered rabbles. Plato often uses the word *taxis* and its cognates for 'order' (e.g. 30a), and it is also the regular word for good military formations.

There are, then, a number of possibilities for how intelligence persuades necessity:

(1) There is only a partial imposition of causal determinism. So there will be 'turbulence', in the sense that there will be unpredictable behaviour by matter.

(2) There is causal determinism, but there is an ordering of the elements by the demiurge such that they produce good results.

(3) The demiurge generates the best bodies for earth, water, air, and fire. Although these are the best possible bodies, they still have limitations for instantiating the best possible world.

(4) It may be that the attempt to completely instantiate the good produces a set of conflicting demands which cannot all be jointly met. A good example of this might be the question of the human skull, discussed at *Timaeus* 75bc. In order for us to have acute perception, the skull ought to be as thin as possible; in order for it to protect our brains and ensure a long life, it should be as thick as possible. Similarly, at 75e there must be some flesh around the skull for the purpose of temperature control, but as little as possible so as not to obstruct perception. If we think of necessity in this manner, then reason can only persuade it as far as logical possibility will allow.

(5) According to Timaeus, it is necessary that the human soul is housed in a body. As the mortal appetites will have bad effects on the soul, these are housed as far away from the head, the seat of the immortal soul, as possible. So while mortal appetite and immortal soul cannot be completely separated, the action of intelligence is to separate them as far as is possible, given that they are to be housed in one body.

Of these possibilities, we can rule out only the first one, as there is no need in Timaeus' account for unpredictable behaviour in this sense, and there is no evidence that he recognizes any such unpredictable behaviour, at least after the demiurge has ordered the cosmos. There are examples of the other four possibilities for intelligence persuading necessity.

How is necessity persuaded by intelligence? Primarily this must be down to the actions of the demiurge, who is able to order the pre-cosmic chaos into the elements and sort those elements into a good order. The demigods and the world-soul must also play a part, though, as their souls direct the motions of the heavens and it is the demigods who produce human beings.

The Receptacle

The receptacle is probably the hardest and most philosophically challenging concept in *Timaeus*. Plato introduces a third thing, apart from the forms and whatever participates in forms. The receptacle is that in which phenomena occur, and out of which they are formed. So the receptacle seems to be space and also to be matter: it provides the space in which perceptible phenomena can occur, and also is the substrate from which phenomena are generated.

The problem which introduces the receptacle is how we refer to changing phenomena. It appears that all four elements can change into one another. If we identify something as water, and it changes into air, should we now identify the same stuff as air? If we do, what happens to any distinction between the elements— what name, rather than 'all four names, one after another' (49b), ought to be applied to each? One target Plato has in mind here is the presocratic view that one substance—such as water or air or fire—is primary, but transmutes into the other elements. Why should we consider one element out of the four to be primary? Why should we take, say, water to be primary if it changes into air, fire, and earth, losing all its characteristics as water? A related question is: what stays the same when something changes? If all the perceptible characteristics change, can we say that the thing we started with is the same thing we end up with? So perhaps there is some substrate, something that underlies the perceptible changes, that does not itself change. Another related question is how we refer to things that are changing. Ought we to give names that imply stability to things that change? Perhaps we should not call perceptible fire 'fire' at all, but some other name that reflects its transient nature. Only things that do not change can have names which imply stability.

There are several difficulties with the receptacle, and Timaeus is aware that he is talking about something difficult to describe. One difficulty is what we can know of it: the receptacle has to be characterless, so as not to distort what comes to be in it: if something is so characterless, what can be said about it? Timaeus struggles to say anything positive about the receptacle, and of course there will be serious epistemological problems with anything so utterly characterless. At *Timaeus* 49a it is something difficult and obscure, at 52b it is grasped without sensation by 'a kind of bastard reasoning' and is the subject of a dream. Something that cannot be explained in terms of anything more basic and has no character seems in itself inexplicable.

Is the receptacle supposed to be space, or matter, or some combination of the two? Plato uses a range of metaphors to describe it, without being entirely clear. The evidence for the receptacle as matter is that, in the gold analogy, the receptacle is that out of which shapes are formed (specifically 'out of gold', 50a). So too it is referred to as a plastic base (50c) or soft material (50e), and as mother (50d, 51a) and nurse (49a, 52d). It is like an odourless base for perfumes (50e). The receptacle is also that which is partly ignified and liquefied (51b; cf. 52d) to produce phenomenal fire and water, and so would seem to be a material constituent. A further question here is whether this collection of material metaphors can be made to yield a consistent account of a material receptacle.

On the other hand, the evidence for the receptacle as space is that the receptacle is specifically or implicitly referred to as space (52b, 52d, 53a; cf. 58a) and as a seat or place (52b, 53a) and as that 'in which' things occur (49e, 50d, 50e, 52a, 52b). It is also referred to as a winnowing-basket (52e; cf. 57c, 88de), the motion of which sorts the particles it contains. This is a particularly strong spatial metaphor, as it would suggest that the particles are independent of, but contained by, the winnowing-basket.

Whether all the descriptions that Plato uses for the receptacle are compatible with one another is an open question. It is possible to fuse matter and space together in this way, as Descartes did in the seventeenth century when he argued for an equivalence of matter and extension. Whether Plato manages an entirely coherent account here is debatable, though in relation to this difficult topic we must remember that Timaeus is giving us a likely tale, has warned us that his account may not be entirely consistent, and has issued special warnings about the difficult nature of the receptacle. That something beyond forms and their likenesses is required is relatively easy to argue for. The nature of what is required, whether it is space, matter, or some combination of the two is a rather more difficult issue.

Geometrical Atomism

Timaeus provides us with a new take on atomism. The atomism of Leucippus and Democritus supposed that atoms had an infinite variety of shapes, and an infinite variety of sizes too. Plato offers a much more definite, structured, and geometrical approach. Each of the four elements of earth, water, air, and fire is assigned a three-dimensional shape. Earth consists of cubes, water of octahedra, air of icosahedra, fire of tetrahedra. These are a special set of solids, often known as the 'Platonic solids'. They are constructed from two-dimensional figures of the same shape and size. So the cubes of earth are made from six identical squares, and the tetrahedra of fire from four identical triangles. Plato is aware of a fifth 'Platonic' solid, the dodecahedron, but this does not come into his atomic theory, though there is a vague mention of its being used by the demiurge for the cosmos (55c). The individual solids are too small to be seen by the naked eye, so what we see as fire are many tetrahedra of fire together.

Why does Plato choose these solids, and these triangles to make them up? The claim is that they are the best solids and triangles (53e), so Plato's atomism is, not surprisingly, a teleological one. The size and shape of the basic particles is not accidental, as it was for the early atomists, Leucippus and Democritus. It is a matter of intelligent choice and design by the demiurge. He imposes order on chaotic matter by generating shapes and number (53b).

The elements water, air, and fire can transmute into each other. The solids which constitute them can come apart, as can the planes which constitute the solids. So an octahedron of water can come apart into eight triangular planes, and each of these too can come apart into six basic triangles. These can reform as tetrahedra, and so we have a transmutation of water to fire. Only earth cannot take part in these transmutations, as its faces are squares and its basic particles are of a different type. Plato seeks to explain the characteristic of an element in terms of the properties of its particles. So fire burns because its particles have sharp edges and are good at cutting, and they also move quickly as they are small. Hence the phenomenon of burning is due to the cutting action of sharp, rapidly moving particles. The idea that there is a micro-world beyond our perception, which while it underpins our sense-perceptions can be radically different in its nature from the macro-world, is an enormously significant step forward in the history of science. The idea was not original to Plato, though he developed it in interesting ways.

It is worth considering some of the ways in which Plato's geo-metrical atomism is rather more like modern atomism than that of Leucippus and Democritus. Plato insists that there is a small number of types of ultimate particle, which are mathematically well defined, as opposed to the indefinite number of shapes and sizes of the atomists. Plato's discussion of geometrical atomism stresses that matter has deep structure, in the sense of ultimate particles forming structures which in turn themselves form fur-ther structures, and so on. That is an idea which is absent from Leucippus and Democritus. Although Plato is not specific about how bonding between particles occurs, and indeed this is the major theoretical flaw in the scheme, he is right that this is not an accidental matter based on mechanical interaction but happens in a specific and well-defined manner.

A further important aspect of Plato's thinking on geometrical atomism is the question of irrational numbers and measurement. The Pythagoreans treated geometry arithmetically, by attempting to treat geometrical problems as part of the theory of natural numbers; that is, as numbers composed of indivisible monads. Thus every geometrical length ought to be expressible as the ratio of two natural numbers. If these numbers represent a length, then if we ask how long something is, rather than measure the distance we count the number of monadic lengths involved. So too, according to Aristotle, the Pythagoreans treated physical entities as in some way constituted out of number.[28] The great problem for these projects came with the discovery of the irrationality of the square root of two, for here we have a number/length that cannot be expressed as a ratio of two natural numbers, or as a multiple of a monadic length.[29] That Plato was aware of this not only for lengths but for areas and volumes too is made clear by the Athenian's explicit comments at *Laws* 819d ff.[30] In response to the difficulties of the Pythagorean programme Plato advocated geometrical rather than arithmetical means for the description and explanation of the world. As if to emphasize the overcoming of the difficulties dogging the Pythagoreans, the most basic triangles have sides of root two and root three.

---

[28] See e.g. Aristotle, *Metaphysics* 987b11–13.

[29] Plato is well aware of the irrationality of several numbers; see *Theaetetus* 147c ff., where the square roots of 3, 5, and 17 are mentioned, along with a general term ('oblong numbers') for all numbers with irrational roots.

[30] Cf. also *Epinomis* 990d ff., on numbers and modelling.

There are some difficulties with Plato's geometrical atomism, as Aristotle was quick to point out.[31] When the solid figures of the elements undergo transmutation, and break up into their two-dimensional components, surely there is then empty space, an impossibility in Aristotle's view. When two-dimensional figures come together, why do they do so in a precise manner, to form perfect three-dimensional figures? Why do they join edge to edge, rather than edge to surface, or surface to surface like a pile of sheets of paper?

Critias

Critias follows directly on from *Timaeus*, with Timaeus beginning the work by commenting on the account he has just given in the previous work. Critias then begins to tell the full tale which he had given in outline in the introduction to *Timaeus*. He tells us something of the political order of the city of Atlantis, and gives a description of the city. *Critias* then breaks off abruptly.

There are two sorts of question that we can ask about the origins of the Atlantis myth. First, is it true that Atlantis once existed, or is there at least a basis of fact which Plato has embellished for his own purposes? As far as Atlantis itself is concerned, there is no basis in fact. There is no sunken city in the place he indicates, nor is there any geological remnant (volcanoes, shallow muddy part of the Atlantic), although there are shoals just beyond the Strait of Gibraltar. There are of course undulations in the Atlantic sea floor, but these are caused by tectonic plate movements which force the floor up, rather than by islands having sunk down.

Secondly, is Plato's Atlantis tale based on or derived from some earlier mythological tradition? As far as we are aware, it is not. There is no source for this legend prior to Plato, and no later source that is independent of Plato. Given the ubiquity of the Atlantis story, this may come as a surprise, but it is nevertheless true: Plato is our sole

---

[31] See Aristotle, *On the Heavens* 306b3 ff.

source for the Atlantis myth. It is significant that Plato's tale was believed by many in antiquity who came after him, but they failed to refer to any other source for the myth.

A variation on these possibilities is that Plato was aware of some other disaster affecting an island, and transformed this into the Atlantis myth. The civilization of Minoan Crete, at its height in the fifteenth century BC, has been the focus of attention here. There are some interesting parallels between Minoan Crete and Plato's Atlantis in terms of culture, but nothing compelling. There was a massive volcanic eruption on Thera, 115 km north of Crete, but this has now been accurately dated to around 1640 BC and cannot have anything to do with the decline of Minoan Crete some 200 years later. Should we take the account given by Plato at face value? Was there a record of the demise of Minoan Crete in the written Egyptian records, which somehow came down to Plato? There is nothing in the extant Egyptian records to support this, though it is always possible that the relevant material has been lost. More of a concern is why this information should come to Plato and only to him. One would expect some trace of it in other Greek sources before, during, and after his lifetime, but there is none.

It is likely, then, that Plato's account of Atlantis is largely fictional, though we should take care with the term 'fiction'. This is a modern category, covering a huge diversity of literature, and the distinction between fiction and other forms is by no means sharp, especially with the rise of 'faction'. Even within modern fiction, there is a genre where fictional characters take part in historical events.

If *Critias* is not history as it claims to be, and is not based on any historical event, what is it about? It may be some form of political allegory, with Plato expressing opinions about recent and current politics. The description of ancient Athens can be read as referring to contemporary Sparta rather than to any real ancient Athens. The description of Atlantis can be read as referring to Athens and its recent history. The war between Atlantis and ancient Athens then represents the Peloponnesian war between

Sparta and contemporary Athens.[32] The moral of the tale is that Athens should shun extreme democracy, the growth of the navy, and naval imperialism, and return to the political structures that had served her well in the past, notably in the Persian war. Such a message would be in accord with Plato's known political views. This theory does have the advantage that we can now explain why Plato chooses these particular characters to express this tale: Hermocrates was instrumental in the defeat of the Athenian naval expedition to Sicily, while Solon was the author of the 'ancestral constitution' that the rule of the Thirty Tyrants was supposed to restore.

The fit between Atlantis/ancient Athens and contemporary Athens/contemporary Sparta is interesting, though far from perfect. As *Critias* tells us relatively little, and Athens had a rich political past, it would be surprising if we could not fit some events to the Atlantis myth reasonably well, allowing a Platonic political moral to be drawn. So it cannot be taken as proved that *Critias* ought to be read as a political allegory. Such a reading would also need to explain how such a political allegory fits into *Timaeus/Critias* as a whole. If there is a unified project in *Timaeus/Critias*, how does a political allegory contribute to that? Why, after *Timaeus* has given us an extended account of the origins of the cosmos and mankind, should a political allegory be the next part of the project?

Alternatively, we can take the view that *Timaeus* and *Critias* together have a very strong compositional unity, at least in the sense that *Critias* does precisely what is asked in the introduction to *Timaeus*. Johansen also links *Critias* quite closely with *Republic*,[33] as providing an example of how virtue, construed along the lines of the account in *Republic*, would prevail even under adverse conditions. *Critias* delivers the encomium of virtuous men in action allowed for in *Republic* X 607a and asked for at *Timaeus* 19de. A further link to *Republic* is the allusion to painting in the introduction

---

[32] It might also be read as an Athenian take on the Persian Wars.

[33] T. K. Johansen, *Plato's Natural Philosophy: A Study of the* Timaeus–Critias (Cambridge: Cambridge University Press, 2004).

to *Timaeus*; a similar remark can be found at *Republic* 472d–e in relation to the ideal city. *Critias* also provides something very important for Plato, which *Timaeus* leaves out. While *Timaeus* gives us an account of cosmic order, of the origins of mankind, of how individual men should strive to live, and what can go wrong with their bodies and minds, within this context *Critias* shows us how men should live together in civil society, how civil society was formed, and what can go wrong with such a society. However, since *Critias* is incomplete, no theory about the purpose of the dialogue can be demonstrated to be true.

NOTE ON THE TEXTS

In the case of both the dialogues in this volume, I have translated the Oxford Classical Text of J. Burnet, *Platonis Opera*, vol. 4 (Oxford: Oxford University Press, 1905). The difficulties of *Timaeus* mean that it has suffered over the centuries from quite a bit of textual corruption, and the passages where I differ from Burnet's OCT are listed in the Textual Notes (pp. 162–3), which have been marked in the translations with an obelus (†); the text of *Critias* has required no emendations. Asterisks in the translations refer to the Explanatory Notes (pp. 122–61).

The numbers and letters that appear in the margins of the translations are the standard means of precise reference to passages in Plato. They refer to the pages and sections of pages of the edition of Plato by Stephanus, or Henri Estienne (Geneva, 1578). This edition was published in three volumes, each with separate pagination. Each page was divided into two columns, with the Greek text on the right and a Latin translation on the left. Each column of Greek text contained (usually) five sections, labelled 'a' to 'e' by Estienne. *Timaeus* occupied pp. 17–92 of the third volume of his edition, and *Critias* pp. 106–21 of the same volume.

The Greek of *Critias* is relatively straightforward, with only occasional awkwardness due, perhaps, to its being a work that Plato never revised or even finished. Some of *Timaeus*, however, is written in condensed Greek, the difficulty of which is compounded by Plato's frequent use in this dialogue of artificial sentence structure and word order, which sometimes make his words resemble unmetrical poetry more than anything else, and by his occasionally taking abnormal liberties with the 'rules' of grammar. As one or two previous translations of the work unfortunately testify, it is all too easy to render density as turgidity. I have rarely attempted to imitate Plato's grammatical and syntactical liberties (which can scarcely be reproduced in good English), but only to produce an accurate translation into modern English which preserves both the occasional density, or intriguing opacity, and the moments of dazzling clarity, wit, insight, and figurative language.

My translations of the passages concerned with the Atlantis myth (*Timaeus* 20d–25d, and *Critias* 108e–121c), and many of the notes to these sections, originally appeared in C. Partenie (ed.), *Plato: Selected Myths* (Oxford: Oxford University Press, 2004). They are reproduced here with minor changes. I would also like to thank Professor Vivian Nutton for checking an earlier version of *Timaeus* 81e–86a.

R.W.

SELECT BIBLIOGRAPHY

There is a huge literature concerning *Timaeus* and *Critias*, so this bibliography is very selective. It gives only works in English, and mixes the most useful current work with some important classics in the interpretation of *Timaeus* and *Critias*. In the Introduction and Explanatory Notes I have had to give a single view on many points that are subject to considerable controversy. This bibliography gives some of the important literature to introduce the reader to those controversies. The standard text for Plato in the original Greek is J. Burnet, *Platonis Opera*, 5 vols. (Oxford: Clarendon Press, 1900–7), and all of Plato's works can be found in the Loeb Classical Library series, with Greek text and a facing English translation.

Introductions to Plato

G. Fine (ed.), *Plato*, 2 vols. (Oxford: Oxford University Press, 1999).

R. Kraut (ed.), *The Cambridge Companion to Plato* (Cambridge: Cambridge University Press, 1992).

N. D. Smith (ed.), *Plato: Critical Assessments*, 4 vols. (London: Routledge, 1998).

Kraut is the best single-volume introduction to Plato, and has an extensive bibliography. The other two books contain many classic papers on the interpretation of Plato's philosophy.

Translations of Plato's Complete Works

J. M. Cooper and D. S. Hutchinson, *Plato: Complete Works* (Indianapolis: Hackett 1997).

E. Hamilton and H. Cairns, *Plato: The Collected Dialogues* (Princeton: Princeton University Press, 1989).

Translations of Timaeus and Critias with Substantial Commentary

F. M. Cornford, *Plato's Cosmology* (London: Routledge & Kegan Paul, 1937).

C. Gill, *Plato: The Atlantis Story* (Bristol: Bristol Classical Press, 1980; 2nd edn. in preparation).

D. Zeyl, *Plato:* Timaeus (Indianapolis: Hackett, 2000).

A. E. Taylor, *A Commentary on Plato's* Timaeus (London: Oxford University Press, 1928).

Taylor does not give a running translation, but has many interesting points on specific issues of translation and has a huge amount of background material. His view that *Timaeus* was inspired by Pythagorean theories has now been largely discredited. Cornford's commentary is in many ways the standard work, though it is now a little dated, and is certainly opinionated on several issues.

Translations of Timaeus and Critias

R. G. Bury, *Plato:* Timaeus, Critias, Cleitophon, Menexenus, Epistles (Cambridge, Mass.: 1929 = Loeb Classical Library no. 234; vol. 9 of the Loeb Plato).

P. Kalkavage, *Plato's* Timaeus (Newburyport, Mass.: Focus, 2001).

H. D. P. Lee, *Plato:* Timaeus *and* Critias (Harmondsworth: Penguin, 1971).

Collections of Essays

NB for the sake of economy papers printed in the following collections have not been listed elsewhere in the bibliography.

J. P. Anton (ed.), *Science and the Sciences in Plato* (New York: Eidos, 1980).

T. Calvo and L. Brisson (eds.), *Interpreting the* Timaeus *and* Critias (Sankt Augustin: Academia, 1997).

R. D. Mohr, *The Platonic Cosmology* (Leiden: Brill, 1985); rev. edn. = *God and Forms in Plato* (Las Vegas: Parmenides Publishing, 2005).

G. J. Reydams-Schils (ed.), *Plato's* Timaeus *as Cultural Icon* (Notre Dame, Ind.: University of Notre Dame Press, 2003).

R. W. Sharples and A. Sheppard (eds.) *Ancient Approaches to Plato's* Timaeus, Bulletin of the Institute of Classical Studies, suppl. 78 (London: Institute of Classical Studies, 2003).

M. R. Wright (ed.), *Reason and Necessity: Essays on Plato's* Timaeus (London and Swansea: Duckworth/Classical Press of Wales, 2000).

Books

G. S. Claghorn, *Aristotle's Criticism of Plato's* Timaeus (The Hague: Nijhoff, 1954).

I. M. Crombie, 'Cosmology and Theory of Nature', in *An Examination of Plato's Doctrines*, vol. 2: *Plato on Knowledge and Reality* (London: Routledge & Kegan Paul, 1963), 153–246.

D. Furley, *The Greek Cosmologists*, vol. 1: *The Formation of the Atomic Theory and its Earliest Critics* (Cambridge: Cambridge University Press, 1987).

A. Gregory, *Plato's Philosophy of Science* (London: Duckworth, 2000).

—— *Ancient Greek Cosmogony* (London: Duckworth, 2007), ch. 9 on Plato.

T. K. Johansen, *Plato's Natural Philosophy: A Study of the Timaeus–Critias* (Cambridge: Cambridge University Press, 2004).

R. Patterson, *Image and Reality in Plato's Metaphysics* (Indianapolis: Hackett, 1985).

E. E. Pender, *Images of Persons Unseen: Plato's Metaphors for the Gods and the Soul* (Sankt Augustin: Academia, 2000).

W. J. Prior, *Unity and Development in Plato's Metaphysics* (London: Croom Helm, 1985).

E. S. Ramage, *Atlantis: Fact or Fiction?* (Bloomington: Indiana University Press, 1978).

D. Sedley, *Creationism and Its Critics in Antiquity* (Berkeley: University of California Press, 2007).

A. Silverman, *The Dialectic of Essence: A Study of Plato's Metaphysics* (Princeton: Princeton University Press, 2002).

J. B. Skemp, *The Theory of Motion in Plato's Later Dialogues* (Cambridge: Cambridge University Press, 1942).

P. Vidal-Naquet, *The Atlantis Story: A Short History of Plato's Myth*, trans. J. Lloyd (Exeter: University of Exeter Press, 2007).

G. Vlastos, *Plato's Universe* (Seattle: University of Washington Press, 1975).

M. R. Wright, *Cosmology in Antiquity* (London: Routledge, 1995).

Critias: *General Interpretation*

D. Clay, 'Plato's Atlantis: The Anatomy of a Fiction', *Proceedings of the Boston Area Colloquium on Ancient Philosophy*, 15 (1999), 1–21.

C. Gill, 'The Genre of the Atlantis Story', *Classical Philology*, 72 (1977), 287–304.

—— 'Plato's Atlantis Story and the Birth of Fiction', *Philosophy and Literature*, 3 (1979), 64–78.

G. Gill, 'Plato and Politics: The *Critias* and *Politicus*', *Phronesis*, 24 (1979), 148–67.

K. A. Morgan, 'Designer History: Plato's Atlantis Story and Fourth-century Ideology', *Journal of Hellenic Studies*, 118 (1998), 101–18.

G. Naddaf, 'The Atlantis Myth: An Introduction to Plato's Later Philosophy of History', *Phoenix*, 48 (1994), 189–209.

T. G. Rosenmeyer, 'Plato's Atlantis Myth: Timaeus or Critias?', *Phoenix*, 10 (1956), 163–72.

' Timaeus*: General Interpretation*

S. Broadie, 'Theodicy and Pseudo-history in the *Timaeus*', *Oxford Studies in Ancient Philosophy*, 21 (2001), 1–28.

M. F. Burnyeat, 'Eikos Mythos', *Rhizai* 2 (2005), 7–29.

V. Harte, 'The *Timaeus*: Structures Within Structures', in *Plato on Parts and Wholes: The Metaphysics of Structure* (Oxford: Oxford University Press, 2002), 212–66.

G. E. R. Lloyd, 'Plato on Mathematics and Nature, Myth and Science', in *Methods and Problems in Greek Science: Selected Papers* (Cambridge: Cambridge University Press, 1991), 333–51.

C. Osborne, 'Topography in the *Timaeus*: Plato and Augustine on Mankind's Place in the Natural World', *Proceedings of the Cambridge Philological Society*, NS 34 (1988), 104–14.

—— 'Space, Time, Shape, and Direction: Creative Discourse in the *Timaeus*', in C. Gill and M. M. McCabe (eds.), *Form and Argument in Late Plato* (Oxford: Oxford University Press, 1996), 179–211.

T. M. Robinson, 'Understanding the *Timaeus*', *Proceedings of the Boston Area Colloquium on Ancient Philosophy*, 2 (1986), 103–19.

C. J. Rowe, 'Myth, History, and Dialectic in Plato's *Republic* and *Timaeus–Critias*', in R. Buxton (ed.), *From Myth to Reason? Studies in the Development of Greek Thought* (Oxford: Oxford University Press, 1999), 263–78.

J. G. Lennox, 'Plato's Unnatural Teleology', in D. J. O'Meara (ed.), *Platonic Investigations* (Washington, DC: The Catholic University of America Press, 1985), 195–218.

Dating of Timaeus

H. F. Cherniss, 'The Relation of the *Timaeus* to Plato's Later Dialogues', *American Journal of Philology*, 78 (1957), 225–66; repr. in R. E. Allen (ed.), *Studies in Plato's Metaphysics* (London: Routledge

& Kegan Paul, 1965), 339–78; and in H. F. Cherniss, *Selected Papers* (Leiden: Brill, 1977), 298–338.

G. E. L. Owen, 'The Place of the *Timaeus* in Plato's Dialogues', *Classical Quarterly*, NS 3 (1953), 79–95; repr. in R. E. Allen (ed.), *Studies in Plato's Metaphysics* (London: Routledge & Kegan Paul, 1965), 313–38; and in G. E. L. Owen, *Logic, Science and Dialectic* (Ithaca, NY: Cornell University Press, 1986), 65–84.

D. Nails, *The People of Plato: A Prosopography of Plato and Other Socratics* (Indianapolis: Hackett, 2002).

K. M. Sayre, 'On the Stylometric Dating of the *Timaeus* and the *Parmenides*', in *Plato's Late Ontology: A Riddle Resolved*, 2nd edn. (Las Vegas: Parmenides Publishing, 2005), 256–67.

Astronomy

A. D. Gregory, 'Astronomy and Observation in Plato's Republic', *Studies in History and Philosophy of Science*, 25 (1996), 451–71.

—— 'Plato and Aristotle on Eclipses', *Journal for the History of Astronomy*, 31 (2000), 245–59.

D. L. Guetter, 'Celestial Circles in the *Timaeus*', *Apeiron*, 36 (2003), 189–203.

W. Knorr, 'Plato and Eudoxus on the Planetary Motions', *Journal for the History of Astronomy*, 21 (1990), 313–29.

A. P. D. Mourelatos, 'Astronomy and Kinematics in Plato's Project of Rationalist Explanation', *Studies in the History and Philosophy of Science*, 12 (1981), 1–32.

B. L. van der Waerden, 'The Motion of Venus, Mercury and the Sun in Early Greek Astronomy', *Archive for the History of the Exact Sciences*, 26 (1982), 99–113.

Cosmogony

G. R. Carone, 'Creation in the *Timaeus*: The Middle Way', *Apeiron*, 37 (2004), 211–26.

R. Hackforth, 'Plato's Cosmogony (*Timaeus* 27d ff.)', *Classical Quarterly*, NS 9 (1959), 17–22.

L. Tarán, 'The Creation Myth in Plato's *Timaeus*', in J. Anton and G. Kustas (eds.), *Essays in Ancient Greek Philosophy* (Albany, NY: State University of New York Press, 1971), 372–407.

G. Vlastos, 'Creation in the *Timaeus*: Is it a Fiction?', in R. E. Allen (ed.), *Studies in Plato's Metaphysics* (London: Routledge & Kegan Paul,

1965), 401 – 19; repr. in G. Vlastos (ed.), *Studies in Greek Philosophy*, vol. 2: *Socrates, Plato, and Their Tradition* (Princeton: Princeton University Press, 1995), 265 – 79.

R. Sorabji, *Time, Creation and the Continuum* (London: Duckworth, 1983).

Demiurge

H. F. Cherniss, 'The Sources of Evil According to Plato', *Proceedings of the American Philosophical Society*, 98 (1954), 23 – 30; repr. in G. Vlastos (ed.), *Plato: A Collection of Critical Essays*, vol. 2: *Ethics, Politics, and Philosophy of Art and Religion* (New York: Doubleday, 1971), 244 – 58.

L. P. Gerson, 'Imagery and Demiurgic Activity in Plato's *Timaeus*', *Journal of Neoplatonic Studies*, 4 (1997), 1 – 32.

R. Hackforth, 'Plato's Theism', *Classical Quarterly*, 30 (1936), 4 – 9; repr. in R. E. Allen (ed.), *Studies in Plato's Metaphysics* (London: Routledge & Kegan Paul, 1965), 439 – 47.

R. D. Mohr, 'Plato's Theology Reconsidered: What the Demiurge Does', in J. P. Anton and A. Preus (eds.), *Essays in Ancient Greek Philosophy*, vol. 3: *Plato* (Albany, NY: State University of New York Press, 1989), 293 – 307.

J. B. Skemp, 'The Disorderly Motion Again', in A. Gotthelf (ed.), *Aristotle on Nature and Living Things: Philosophical and Historical Studies Presented to David M. Balme on His Seventieth Birthday* (Pittsburgh and Bristol: Mathesis/Bristol Classical Press, 1985), 289 – 99.

G. Vlastos, 'Disorderly Motion in Plato's *Timaeus*', *Classical Quarterly*, 33 (1939), 71 – 83; repr. in R. E. Allen (ed.), *Studies in Plato's Metaphysics* (London: Routledge & Kegan Paul, 1965), 379 – 99; and in G. Vlastos (ed.), *Studies in Greek Philosophy*, vol. 2: *Socrates, Plato, and Their Tradition* (Princeton: Princeton University Press, 1995), 247 – 64.

Receptacle

H. F. Cherniss, 'A Much Misread Passage in the *Timaeus* (49c7 – 50b5)', *American Journal of Philology*, 75 (1954), 113 – 30; repr. in H. F. Cherniss, *Selected Papers* (Leiden: Brill, 1977), 346 – 63.

M. L. Gill, 'Matter and Flux in Plato's *Timaeus*', *Phronesis*, 32 (1987), 34 – 53.

J. Kung, 'Why the Receptacle Is Not a Mirror', *Archiv für Geschichte der Philosophie*, 70 (1988), 167–78.

E. N. Lee, 'On the Metaphysics of the Image in Plato's *Timaeus*', *The Monist*, 50 (1966), 341–68.

—— 'On Plato's *Timaeus* 49d4–e7', *American Journal of Philology*, 88 (1967), 1–28.

—— 'On the "Gold-example" in Plato's *Timaeus* (50a5–b5)', in J. Anton and G. Kustas (eds.), *Essays in Ancient Greek Philosophy* (Albany, NY: State University of New York Press, 1971), 219–35.

G. R. Morrow, 'Necessity and Persuasion in Plato's *Timaeus*', *Philosophical Review*, 59 (1950), 147–60; repr. in R. E. Allen (ed.), *Studies in Plato's Metaphysics* (London: Routledge & Kegan Paul, 1965), 421–37.

N. H. Reed, 'Plato on Flux, Perception and Language', *Proceedings of the Cambridge Philological Society*, NS 18 (1972), 65–77.

A. Silverman, 'Timaean Particulars', *Classical Quarterly*, NS 42 (1992), 87–113.

D. J. Zeyl, 'Plato and Talk of a World in Flux: *Timaeus* 49a6–50b5', *Harvard Studies in Classical Philology*, 79 (1975), 125–48.

Geometrical Atomism

B. Artmann and L. Schäfer, 'On Plato's "Fairest triangles" (*Timaeus* 54a)', *Historia Mathematica*, 20 (1993), 255–64.

J. Visentainer, 'A Potential Infinity of Triangle Types: On the Chemistry of Plato's *Timaeus*', *Hyle*, 4 (1998), 117–28.

G. Vlastos, 'Plato's Supposed Theory of Irregular Atomic Figures', *Isis*, 58 (1967), 204–9; repr. in G. Vlastos, *Platonic Studies*, 2nd edn. (Princeton: Princeton University Press, 1981), 366–73.

Forms

K. W. Mills, 'Some Aspects of Plato's Theory of Forms: *Timaeus* 49c ff.', *Phronesis*, 13 (1968), 145–70.

W. J. Prior, '*Timaeus* 48e–52d and the Third Man Argument', in F. J. Pelletier and J. King-Farlow (eds.), *New Essays on Plato* (Guelph: Canadian Association for Publishing in Philosophy, 1983 = *Canadian Journal of Philosophy*, suppl. vol. 9), 123–47.

K. M. Sayre, 'The Role of the *Timaeus* in the Development of Plato's Late Ontology', *Ancient Philosophy*, 18 (1998), 93–124.

Unique Cosmos

D. Keyt, 'The Mad Craftsman of the *Timaeus*', *Philosophical Review*, 80 (1971), 230–5.

R. D. Parry, 'The Unique World of the *Timaeus*', *Journal of the History of Philosophy*, 17 (1979), 1–10.

R. Patterson, 'The Unique Worlds of the *Timaeus*', *Phoenix*, 35 (1981), 105–19.

Metaphysics

R. Bolton, 'Plato's Distinction Between Being and Becoming', *Review of Metaphysics*, 29 (1975–6), 66–95.

M. Frede, 'Being and Becoming in Plato', *Oxford Studies in Ancient Philosophy*, suppl. vol. (1988), 37–52.

R. G. Turnbull, 'Becoming and Intelligibility', *Oxford Studies in Ancient Philosophy*, suppl. vol. (1988), 1–14.

Physiology and Psychology

M. J. Adair, 'Plato's View of the "Wandering Uterus"', *Classical Journal*, 91 (1995–6), 153–63.

G. R. Carone, '*Akrasia* and the Structure of the Passions in Plato's *Timaeus*', in C. Bobonich and P. Destrée (eds.), Akrasia *in Greek Philosophy from Socrates to Plotinus* (Leiden: Brill, 2007), 101–18.

D. Frede, 'The Philosophical Economy of Plato's Psychology: Rationality and Common Concepts in the *Timaeus*', in M. Frede and G. Striker (eds.), *Rationality in Greek Thought* (Oxford: Oxford University Press, 1996), 29–58.

J. Kung, 'Mathematics and Virtue in Plato's *Timaeus*', in J. P. Anton and A. Preus (eds.), *Essays in Ancient Greek Philosophy*, vol. 3: *Plato* (Albany, NY: State University of New York Press, 1989), 309–39.

T. Mahoney, 'Moral Virtue and Assimilation to God in Plato's *Timaeus*', *Oxford Studies in Ancient Philosophy*, 28 (2005), 77–91.

J. V. Robinson, 'The Tripartite Soul in the *Timaeus*', *Phronesis*, 35 (1990), 103–10.

T. M. Robinson, *Plato's Psychology* (Toronto: University of Toronto Press, 1970).

R. F. Stalley, 'Punishment and the Physiology of the *Timaeus*', *Classical Quarterly*, NS 46 (1996), 357–70.

C. Steel, 'The Moral Purpose of the Human Body: A Reading of *Timaeus* 69–72', *Phronesis*, 46 (2001), 113–28.

Further Reading in Oxford World's Classics

Plato, *Defence of Socrates, Euthyphro, Crito*, trans. David Gallop.
—— *Gorgias*, trans. Robin Waterfield.
—— *Meno and other Dialogues*, trans. Robin Waterfield.
—— *Phaedo*, trans. David Gallop.
—— *Phaedrus*, trans. Robin Waterfield.
—— *Protagoras*, trans. C. C. W. Taylor.
—— *Republic*, trans. Robin Waterfield.
—— *Selected Myths*, ed. Catalin Partenie.
—— *Symposium*, trans. Robin Waterfield.

SUMMARY OF *TIMAEUS*

TIMAEUS

SOCRATES: One, two, three—but, Timaeus, my friend, where's 17a
the fourth of yesterday's guests* who were to treat me today?

TIMAEUS: He was taken ill, Socrates. He wouldn't have
missed our meeting if he could have helped it.

SOCRATES: Then it's up to you and our friends here to fill in
for the absentee too, isn't it?

TIMAEUS: Of course. We'll do the best we can to make up for b
him. It wouldn't be right for us not to do our best to repay
your hospitality towards us yesterday, when you did everything a host should do for his guests.

SOCRATES: And do you remember the assignment I set you
and the topics you were to address?

TIMAEUS: Only partly,* but you're here to remind us of any
we've forgotten. Or rather, if it's not too much trouble, why
don't you quickly run back over them, from start to finish,
so that they lodge in our minds better?

SOCRATES: All right. I suppose the most important of the issues c
I raised yesterday was the political one,* when I explained my
views on what the best kind of constitution might be and what
kind of citizens should make up such a state.

TIMAEUS: Yes, Socrates, and the political system you described
met with our wholehearted approval.

SOCRATES: Didn't we begin by distinguishing within the citi-
zen body between artisans such as farmers and those who
fight in their defence?

TIMAEUS: Yes.

SOCRATES: And since we were assigning to each person (along
natural lines, of course) just one occupation, one branch of d
expertise—the one that suited each individual in himself—
we said that those whose job it was to defend everyone were
to do nothing more than be guardians of the city against
threats of harm from both outside and inside. They were to

3

deal gently but justly with their subjects and their natural
18a   friends, and severely with those of their enemies who con-
fronted them on the battlefield.

TIMAEUS: Absolutely.

SOCRATES: Yes, because we said, I think, that the guardians had
to have a specific temperament, combining exceptional passion
with exceptional love of knowledge, to enable them to treat each
group with gentleness or severity, as the occasion demanded.

TIMAEUS: Yes.

SOCRATES: And what about their upbringing? Didn't we say
that both their bodies and their minds were to be trained, and
that they were to study all the subjects appropriate to them?

TIMAEUS: Yes.

b   SOCRATES: And we also said that people brought up in the way
we prescribed were never to regard gold, silver, or any other
material possessions as their own. Like professional soldiers,
they were to be paid for their protection by those they kept
safe, but the rate of pay was to be commensurate with modest needs, they were to pool their resources, and they were
to live communally with one another, free from all other
occupations and with excellence their only concern.

TIMAEUS: Yes, so we did.

c   SOCRATES: Then we also touched on the question of the female
guardians, and said that their characters were to be made to
match the men's more or less exactly, and that in every aspect
of life, including warfare, all the women were to be assigned
all the same tasks as the men.

TIMAEUS: Yes, that's right too.

SOCRATES: And what about procreation? Not that we could easily forget what we said on this topic, since it was so unusual.
We stipulated that no marriages were to be exclusive and
that children were to be shared by all the guardians, and we
found ways to make sure that none of them would ever recognize a child as his own. Instead, everyone would consider
d   everyone else his relative—those from the appropriate age-
group as sisters and brothers, those from previous generations

4

as their parents and grandparents, and those from the generations below them as their children and grandchildren.

TIMAEUS: Yes, that's right. There's no difficulty remembering *that*.

SOCRATES: Then again, we had to try to guarantee their excellence right from the moment of their birth, and in order to achieve this we said — I'm sure you remember — that, when it came to bringing people together for sex, our male and female rulers had to make secret use of 'lotteries' to ensure e that bad men and good men would each be paired exclusively with women of the same type. In this way, the measures would arouse no resentment, because they would think that their partner had been chosen for them by chance.

TIMAEUS: How could we forget?

SOCRATES: And we went on to say, didn't we, that the children 19a of good couples were to be brought up, while the children of bad couples were to be quietly sent away to other parts of the city? But we added that the rulers had to be constantly vigilant while these children were growing up, so that they could re-promote those who deserved it and have their places taken instead by those from among their own number who had turned out not to deserve their high rank.

TIMAEUS: Yes.

SOCRATES: So, Timaeus, my friend, have we now covered yesterday's conversation,* or at least gone back over the main points? Is there anything missing, anything we still need to recall?

TIMAEUS: No, that was exactly how the conversation went, b Socrates.

SOCRATES: I'd like you next to hear how I feel about the constitution we described. The best way I can describe the feeling is to compare myself to someone who had gazed on beautiful creatures at rest (either in a picture or real, living creatures*) and conceived the desire to see them in motion, exercising in competition some aspect of what he imagined to be their physical nature. That's how I feel about c

5

the constitution we described: I'd like to hear from someone an account of our city contending against others in typical inter-city contests. I'd like to hear how it does itself proud as it goes to war,* and how in wartime its citizens display qualities appropriate to their education and upbringing, not only in their military achievements, but also in the way they go about negotiating with other cities.

d   Anyway, Critias and Hermocrates, I'm aware that I personally would never be capable of delivering an adequate eulogy of the city and its citizens in these respects.* Now, while this might be hardly surprising in my case, I've come to hold the same opinion about the poets too — poets of past times, as well as our contemporaries. I don't mean any disrespect to poets in general, but it's obvious to everyone that while imitators as a breed have the greatest facility and expertise at reproducing things they've been brought up on, none of them finds it easy to reproduce on stage anything

e   that falls outside his experience, and they find it even less easy to put such a thing into words. As for the sophists,* I believe them to be true experts at making all kinds of wonderful speeches on other subjects, but I'm afraid that, perhaps because they roam from city to city without having made homes for themselves in one particular place, they miss the mark when it comes to describing the many different kinds of things that men who are both philosophers and statesmen achieve in the real world in warfare and on the battlefield, and put into words in their negotiations with other individuals.

    That leaves only people with *your* qualifications,* people

20a   supplied by both nature and nurture with philosophical and statesmanlike characters. Timaeus here, for instance, comes from Italian Locri, an exceptionally well-governed city, where his high birth and great wealth surpass those of any of his compatriots, and where he's been chosen for the most important political offices and posts; and yet at the same time he has gone as far as anyone can, in my opinion, in all intellectual endeavours. As for Critias, all of us here in Athens know that he's no amateur in any of the fields in question. Then there's Hermocrates, whose natural and nurtured competence in all these respects is vouched for by a large number of reliable witnesses.

Even yesterday I was bearing all this in mind, and that b was why I did all I could to satisfy your request that I should describe the constitution. I knew that no one could address the next topics more competently than you, if you agreed to do so, because you were the only people alive today who, now that we've equipped the city with everything suitable for warfare, could go on to display all its qualities. That was why, once I'd delivered the account I'd been instructed to give, I gave you in your turn the assignment I'm now asking you to carry out. You talked it over among yourselves and agreed to pay me back today with treats in the form c of speeches, so here I am, all dressed up for the occasion, and no one could be more ready than I am to receive your hospitality.

HERMOCRATES:* Well, Socrates, we are, as Timaeus here told you, fully committed to the project, and in any case what excuse could we offer for not doing as you say? As a result, even yesterday this was exactly the issue we began to think about as soon as we'd returned from here to the guest-quarters of Critias' house, where we're staying. Actually, the conversation started even earlier, while we were still en route there. Anyway, Critias here brought up a story from ancient d times—but why don't you tell Socrates about it now, Critias, to enable him to judge whether or not it's relevant to the task he's set us?

CRITIAS: Yes, I'd better do so, if the third member of our team agrees. Timaeus?

TIMAEUS: I do.

CRITIAS: All right, then. Socrates, you're about to hear a story which, for all its strangeness, is absolutely true,* with its truth affirmed by Solon, the wisest of the seven sages.* e Now, Solon was a relative of my great-grandfather Dropides,

7

and the two of them were very close, as Solon himself often says in his verses.* Dropides told the story to my grandfather Critias and the old man used to repeat it to us in his turn. He used to tell us that long ago Athens had performed impressive and remarkable deeds, but they had been consigned to oblivion by time and the destruction of human life.* One of these exploits was especially impressive, and recalling it now

21a will be a suitable way not only to repay our debt to you, but also to praise the goddess on the occasion of her festival* with a truthful hymn, so to speak, as she deserves.

SOCRATES: That sounds good. So then, what was it Critias told you? What did he hear from Solon? What was this achievement that was no mere story, but something our city really did, long ago?

CRITIAS: I'll tell you. I heard the ancient tale from a man who was no youngster himself, since Critias was, by his own reck-

b oning, getting on for ninety years old by then, while I was ten at the most. It was the Koureotis of the Apatouria,* and the usual children's event, which happens every time the festival is held, took place then too—which is to say that our fathers set up a recitation contest. Poems aplenty by poets aplenty featured in the recital, but many of the children sang Solon's verses, because they were new then.

One of the members of our phratry remarked (it might just have occurred to him, or he was just trying to please

c Critias) that Solon was not only a great sage in general, but, where his poetry was concerned, was more independent than any other poet. The old man, as I recall, was delighted with this and said with a smile: 'Yes, Amynander, but if only he'd not taken up poetry merely as a hobby, but had worked as seriously at it as other poets do! And I wish that he'd finished the story he brought back from Egypt, and hadn't been forced to neglect it by the feuding and other evils he found here when he got home. If he had, I dare say that he'd

d have become more famous as a poet than Hesiod, Homer, and all the rest.' 'What story was that, Critias?' asked Amynander.

8

'It was about our city's most impressive achievement ever,' Critias replied, 'one which deserves to be better known than any other, but time and the destruction of the people involved have prevented the story from surviving until now.' 'Do please tell us it,' said Amynander, 'from start to finish. What was this story that Solon told? How did he come to hear it? Who told him it was true?'*

'In Egypt,' Critias began, 'around that part of the Delta e where the Nile forks at its crown, there's a district called the Saïtic province, where the largest city is Saïs, famous as the birthplace of King Amasis.* The founder of this city was a deity whose Egyptian name is Neïth, though in Greek, according to the Egyptians, she is Athena. The inhabitants are very pro-Athenian and claim somehow to be related to us. Solon said that he was heaped with honours on his arrival there, but the main point of his account was that, 22a when he once questioned those priests who were experts in history about the past, he discovered how almost completely ignorant about such matters all Greeks were, including himself. Once, he said, he wanted to draw them into a discussion of ancient history, so he launched into an account of the earliest events known here: he began to talk about Phoroneus, who is said to have been the first man, and Niobe; he told the story of the survival of Deucalion and Pyrrha after the b flood, and the tales of their descendants; and he tried, by mentioning the years generation by generation, to arrive at a figure for how long ago the events he was talking about* had taken place.

'Then one of the priests, a very old man, said: "Solon, Solon, you Greeks never grow up. There isn't an old man among you."

'"What do you mean?" Solon replied.

'"None of you have mature minds," the priest replied. "You have no ancient tradition to imbue your minds with old beliefs and with understanding aged by time. The reason for this is that the human race has often been destroyed in c various ways—as it will be in the future too. Though there have been countless causes of briefer disasters, fire and water have been responsible for the most devastating catastrophes. For instance, you have a story of how Phaethon, scion of the Sun, once harnessed his father's chariot, but was incapable of driving it along the path his father took, and so burnt up everything on the surface of the earth and was himself killed by a thunderbolt. This story has the form of a fable, but it alludes to a real event*—the deviation of the heavenly bodies* that orbit the earth and the periodic destruction at long intervals of the surface of the earth by massive conflagrations.

d

' "In one of these conflagrations, all those people who live in mountainous regions and in places that are high and dry are far more likely to die than those who live by rivers and the sea. The Nile, so often our saviour, saves us at these times from disaster by being released.* But when the gods purge the earth with a flood of water, it is the herdsmen and shepherds in the mountains who are spared, while the inhabitants of your cities are swept into the sea by the rivers. Here in Egypt, however, water never rains onto the fields from above—it never has, neither then, nor at any other time. Here it does the opposite: all our water rises up from below.*

e

' "This explains why the legends preserved here are the most ancient, even though the human race is actually continuous, in larger or smaller numbers, everywhere in the world where neither excessive cold nor excessive heat prevents human habitation. But from long ago every impressive or important or otherwise outstanding event we hear about, whether it happens in your part of the world or here or elsewhere, has been written down here in the temples and preserved. What happens in your part of the world and elsewhere, however, is that no sooner have you been equipped at any time with literacy and the other resources of city life than once again, after the usual interval, a heavenly flood pours down on you like a plague and leaves only those who are illiterate and uncivilized. As a result, you start all over again

23a

b

and regain your childlike state of ignorance about things that happened in ancient times both here and in your part of the world.

' "For instance, Solon, the accounts you gave just now within a genealogical framework of events in your part of the world hardly differ from childish tales. In the first place, you remember just the one deluge when there were many before it, and in addition you're unaware that the noblest and most heroic race in human history once existed in your land. You and all your current fellow-citizens are the descendants of what little of their stock remained, but none of you realizes it, because for many generations the survivors died without leaving a written record. But in fact there was a time, Solon, before the greatest and most destructive flood, when the city which is now Athens was outstandingly well governed in all respects, and was unrivalled at warfare too. The noblest achievements and the finest political institutions we've ever heard of on earth are attributed to it."

'Solon told us how astonished he was to hear this, and said that he begged the priests as forcefully as he could to give him next a detailed and thorough account of those fellow citizens of his from long ago. And the priest replied: "I'll do so gladly, Solon, not just for your sake and for Athens, but also and especially for the sake of the goddess who is the patron, nurse, and governess of both our cities. Your city was founded first, when the goddess received your rootstock from Earth and Hephaestus, and ours was founded a thou- sand years later.* The written records in our temples give the figure of 8,000 years as the age of our culture, so it is Athenians of 9,000 years ago whose customs and whose finest achievement I shall briefly explain to you. You and I will consult the written records on some future occasion, when we have time, and go through them thoroughly, in detail, and in order.

' "It's worth comparing their way of life with ours here, because you'll find many current instances here of customs that used in those days to obtain in your part of the world. First, we have the priestly caste, which is kept distinct from all the rest; then we have the artisan caste, each member of which—people such as herdsmen, hunters, and farmers—works at his own business, without involvement in anyone

b else's. Then there's the warrior caste and, as I'm sure you've noticed, they're separated off from all the others, required by law to focus exclusively on military matters. Moreover, their weaponry consists of shields and spears, which we were the first in Asia to adopt, following the example of the goddess,* just as you did first in those regions where you Greeks live. As for intellectual attainments, I'm sure you can see how seriously we here have customarily taken the study of the universe, and how the application of its divine

c principles to human affairs has enabled us to discover everything that contributes towards health, up to and including divination and medicine, and to acquire all the related branches of knowledge.

'"The way things are organized and set up here was in fact formerly the way the goddess arranged things among you Athenians, when she founded your state at the time I'm talking about. She chose the region in which you had been born because she realized that the temperate climate there would produce men of outstanding intelligence.* Because

d the goddess loves both war and wisdom, she chose this region as the one that would produce men who would most closely resemble herself and founded a city there first. And so your people began to live there and to adopt customs such as those I've described. In fact, you had an even more stable culture than ours, and your all-round excellence had no rivals, which is hardly surprising since you were the offspring and the wards of gods.

'"Our records contain many impressive and admirable exploits performed by your city, but there's one above all

e that stands out for its importance and courage. Our documents record how your city once halted an enormous force

that was marching insolently against not just the whole of
Europe, but Asia as well, from its base beyond Europe in the
Atlantic Ocean. I should mention that in those days the
ocean there was navigable, since there was an island in front
of the strait which, I've heard you say, your people call the
Pillars of Heracles.* The island was bigger than both Asia
and Libya combined, and travellers in those days used it to
get to the further islands, from where they had access to the
whole mainland over on the other side, the mainland which 25a
surrounds that genuine sea.* Everything this side of that strait
is like a narrow-mouthed harbour, but that is the true sea, and
the land which completely surrounds it truly deserves the
name 'mainland'.

'"On this island of Atlantis a great and remarkable
dynasty had arisen, which ruled the whole island, many of
the other islands, and parts of the mainland too. They also
governed some of the lands here inside the strait—Libya up
to the border with Egypt, and Europe up to Etruria.* Once b
upon a time, then, they combined their forces and set out en
masse to try to enslave in one swoop your part of the world,
and ours, and all the territory this side of the strait. This was
the occasion, Solon, when the resources of your city, its courage and strength, were revealed for all to see; it stood head
and shoulders above all other states for its bravery and military expertise. At first it was the leader of the Greek cause, c
and then later, abandoned by everyone else and compelled
to stand alone, it came to the very brink of disaster,* but it
overcame the invaders and erected a trophy, thereby pre-
venting the enslavement of those who remained unenslaved
this side of the boundaries of Heracles and unhesitatingly
liberating all the rest.

'"Some time later appalling earthquakes and floods
occurred, and in the course of a single, terrible day and night d
the whole fighting-force of your city sank all at once beneath
the earth, and the island of Atlantis likewise sank beneath the
sea and vanished. That is why the sea there cannot now

13

be navigated or explored; the mud which the island left behind as it settled lies a little below the surface† and gets in the way."'

There you have it, Socrates. That was a brief version of the story told me by old Critias, who heard it from Solon. Yesterday, of course, as I listened to the description you were giving of the constitution and its citizens, I recalled the story I've just told and was surprised to notice how closely your description matched most of Solon's tale, by some miraculous coincidence. But I chose not to say anything straight away, because a lot of time had passed and my recollection of the story was imperfect. I thought it would be better for me first to get the whole thing up to the mark in my own mind before telling it out loud.

So I readily agreed yesterday to the assignment you set us because I was expecting us to be reasonably well placed to propose a theme that suited our purposes, which is always the most difficult thing to find in such cases. To that end, as our friend here told you, as soon as we left here yesterday I began to relate the story to them as I recalled it, and after I left them I spent the night going over it until I'd recovered pretty much everything. There's a saying, as you know, that lessons learnt young endure amazingly well. How true it is! Speaking for myself, I'm not convinced that I could recall everything I heard yesterday, but I'm absolutely certain that not the slightest detail of this story has escaped me, even though I heard it such a long while ago. The story amused and entertained me at the time I heard it, and the old man enjoyed teaching me it, because I asked him about it again and again, until it became lodged in my mind as securely as painted colours heat-fixed for permanence.* Besides, I began telling our friends here the story at daybreak today, so that they too would have material to contribute to the speech.

So, to get to the point of what I've been saying: Socrates, I'm in a position to tell the story in exact detail, not just the summary version. We shall now proceed to transfer the citizens and the city you described for us yesterday from your fable into fact and locate that city right here, as Athens; d we shall claim that your imaginary citizens are in fact our ancestors, the ones the priest spoke about. The match will be so perfect that no discordant note will be struck if we identify your citizens with the men of that past era. We'll divide the task up among us and all do our best to discharge the assignment you set us as we should. What you have to do, then, Socrates, is consider whether this account of ours will meet with your approval, or whether we need to come up with another project instead.   e

SOCRATES: How could we prefer any speech to the one you're proposing, Critias? Its relevance to the goddess makes it the perfect speech for the present occasion, her festival, and the fact that it isn't a made-up story but a true historical account* is of course critically important. If we turn down this speech, what are the chances of our coming across others? None at all. So do, please, give your speeches — and I wish you all good luck — while I now relax and listen, instead of being the speaker as I was yesterday.   27a

CRITIAS: See if you approve of how we've divided up our treats for you, Socrates. Since Timaeus knows more than the rest of us about the heavenly bodies and has specialized in natural science,* we decided that he should speak first, and should start with the origin of the universe and end with the creation of human beings. It will be my turn next, and I'll inherit from him the human race as a whole, now created in his speech, and from you* a particular group of exceptionally well-educated humans. Then, in keeping not just b with Solon's story but also with his legislation, I shall introduce them before us, as if we were a panel of judges, and make them citizens of this city of ours, on the grounds that they are in fact Athenian citizens from an earlier epoch who've been rescued from oblivion by the hieroglyphic record; and from then on we can assume that the people we're talking about are fellow citizens, fellow Athenians.

SOCRATES: It looks as though I shall lack for nothing—as though I'm in for a brilliant feast of words in return for mine of yesterday. Apparently, then, Timaeus, it will be your job to speak next, once you've invoked the gods as custom requires.

c TIMAEUS: Of course, Socrates: anyone with even a slight amount of sense always calls on the gods at the start of any enterprise, great or small. And we are people who plan to talk, somehow, about the creation of the universe, or whether it might even be uncreated, so if we're to avoid going wildly wrong, we really have no choice: we must call on gods and goddesses and pray that our account meets with their approval—with *their* approval above all, but then also d with ours. As far as the gods are concerned, let this be our invocation; but we also need to call up our own resources, to reduce the chances of any failure of understanding on your part and to enable me to express my thoughts on the matters before us as clearly as possible.

Our starting-point lies, I think, in the following distinction: what is it that always is, but never comes to be, and what is it that comes to be† but never is?* The former, since it is 28a always consistent, can be grasped by the intellect with the support of a reasoned account, while the latter is the object of belief, supported by unreasoning sensation,* since it is generated and passes away, but never really is. Now, anything created is necessarily created by some cause,* because nothing can possibly come to be without there being something that is responsible for its coming to be. Also, whenever a craftsman takes something consistent as his model, and reproduces its form and properties, the result is bound in every case to be a thing of beauty, but if he takes as his b model something that has been created, the product is bound to be imperfect.

The whole universe or world (or whatever: let it be called by whatever term it finds acceptable)... well, the first question to be asked about it is the perennial first and fundamental question: did it always exist, in which case it was not created and has no beginning, or has it come to be, in which case there was something that began it in the first place?* It has come to be. After all, it is visible, tangible, and corporeal, and everything with these properties is perceptible, and we have already demonstrated that everything perceptible— which is to say, everything that is grasped by belief with the c support of sensation—is subject to creation and belongs to the class of things that have come to be.

Now, we've already said that anything created is necessarily created by some cause. But it would be a hard task to discover the maker and father of this universe of ours, and even if we did find him, it would be impossible to speak of him to everyone. So what we have to ask is, again, which of those two kinds of model* the creator was using as he constructed the universe. Was he looking at what is consistent 29a and permanent or at what has been created? Well, if this universe of ours is beautiful and if its craftsman was good, it evidently follows that he was looking at an eternal model, while he was looking at a created model if the opposite is the case—though it's blasphemous even to think it. It's perfectly clear, then, that he used an eternal model, because nothing in creation is more beautiful than the world and no cause is better than its maker. The craftsman of this universe, then, took as his model that which is grasped by reason and intelligence and is consistent, and it necessarily follows b from these premises that this world of ours is an image of something.

It is, of course, crucial to begin any subject at its natural starting-point. Where an image and its original are concerned, we had better appreciate that statements about them are similar to the objects they explicate, in the sense that statements about that which is stable, secure, and manifest to intellect are themselves stable and reliable* (and it's important for statements about such things to be just as irrefutable

c and unassailable as statements can possibly be), while statements about things that are in fact images, because they've
been made in the likeness of an original, are no more than
likely, and merely correspond to the first kind of statement: as
being is to becoming, so the truth of the one kind of account
is to the plausibility of the other.* So, Socrates, you shouldn't
be surprised if, when discussing gods and the creation of the
universe, we often find it impossible to give accounts that
are altogether internally consistent in every respect and perfectly precise. We'll have to be content if we come up with
statements that are as plausible as anyone else's,* and we
should bear in mind the fact that I and all of you, the speaker
d and his judges, are no more than human, which means that
on these matters we ought to accept the likely account and
not demand more than that.

SOCRATES: Excellent, Timaeus! You're absolutely right:* we
must, as you suggest, be satisfied with that. We're impressed
and delighted with your preamble, so do please go on to
develop your theme.

TIMAEUS: I should explain, then, how this created universe
e came to be made by its maker. He was good, and nothing
good is ever characterized by mean-spiritedness over anything; being free of jealousy,* he wanted everything to be as
similar to himself as possible. Wise men tell us that there
30a is no more important precondition for the created world
than this, and we could not go wrong if we were to accept
it. For the god wanted everything to be good, marred by as
little imperfection as possible. He found everything visible
in a state of turmoil, moving in a discordant and chaotic
manner,* so he led it from chaos to order, which he regarded
as in all ways better.*

What is perfectly good can accomplish only what is perfectly beautiful; this was and is a universal law. So the god
b took thought and concluded that, generally speaking, nothing
he made that lacked intelligence could ever be more beautiful than an intelligent product, and that nothing can have

intelligence unless it has soul. And the upshot of this thinking was that he constructed the universe by endowing soul with intelligence and body with soul, so that it was in the very nature of the universe to surpass all other products in beauty and perfection. This is the likely account, and it follows that we're bound to think that this world of ours was made in truth by god as a living being, endowed thanks to his providence with soul and intelligence.*

c

Since this is so, the next question to ask is which living being the maker made the universe in the likeness of.* We're bound to rule out anything condemned by its nature to be partial, because nothing touched by imperfection can ever be beautiful. But we shall affirm that there is nothing more similar than the universe to the whole of which all other living beings, individually and collectively, are parts—that whole which encompasses within itself all *intelligible* living beings, just as this world is made up of us and all other *visible* beings.

d

For by choosing as his model the most beautiful of intelligible beings, perfect and complete, the god made the world a single, visible, living being, containing within itself all living beings that are naturally akin to it.

31a

Now, we've been speaking of a single universe, but is this right? Or would it be more correct to speak of a plurality, even an infinite plurality,* of universes? No, there can be only one, if it is to have been created by the craftsman-god so as to correspond to its model. For the whole which encompasses all intelligible living beings can never be one of two, with another alongside it, because then there would have to be another living being for them both, of which they both would be parts, and then it would be more correct to speak of this universe as having been made in the likeness of that one, the one that includes both, rather than in their likeness. So, to ensure that this universe of ours resembled the com-

b

plete and perfect living being in respect of its uniqueness, the maker did not make two or an infinite plurality of worlds, but this world of ours is and always will be a unique creation.*

Anything created, then, is bound to be corporeal — visible and tangible. But fire is required for the creation of anything visible, and solidity for anything to be tangible, and earth for solidity. It follows that the god began to form the body of the universe out of fire and earth. But it's impossible for any two things to form a proper structure without the presence of a third thing; there has to be some bond to mediate between the two of them and bring them together. The best bond is the one that most effectively unifies itself and the things it is joining, and nothing does this better than correspondence. For whenever among three numbers (or, for that matter, three solids or three powers*) one is a mean, such that as the first in the series stands to the mean, so the mean stands to the final number of the series (or, conversely, as the final number stands to the mean, so the mean stands to the first), then the mean can also be treated as first or last (or, alternatively, the first and last terms can be treated as means), and so all of them will of necessity turn out to be identical; and since they are all identical, they are all one.

Now, if for some reason the body of the universe had been created as only a plane surface, without depth, a single mean would have been enough to bind together both the mean itself and the other terms involved. In fact, however, solidity was the only appropriate form for the universe, and it always takes two means, not just one, to make a good fit between solid terms. Hence between fire and earth the god placed water and air, and he made them all stand in the same ratio to one another (in so far as that is possible), so that as fire is to air, so air is to water, and as air is to water, so water is to earth; and so he bound together and structured the visible and tangible universe. This was how the body of the universe was created from these constituents, four in number, with correspondence making it a concordant whole. And as a result affinity came to be a property of the world, and affinity unified it so thoroughly with itself that it can be taken apart only by him who bound it together.*

The formation of the world occupied each of the four in its entirety; the maker made it out of the totality of fire, water, air, and earth, leaving unused no part or property of any of them. His purpose was to ensure, first, that the world d should be as complete a living being as it possibly could be, a totality consisting of the totality of its parts. Second, he 33a wanted it to be one, and so he ensured that there was nothing left over from which another similar universe could be created. Third, he wanted it to be unageing and free from sickness, because he realized that when things that are hot, cold, and so on — things with strong properties — surround a compound body and strike it from outside, they break it up before its time, bring on disease and old age, and waste it away. This was the god's thinking, and this was why and how he ensured that the structure he made was single, a totality consisting of all totalities, complete, unageing, and untroubled by disease.*

The shape he gave it was the one that was both appropriate b and natural to it. The appropriate shape, for the living being that was to contain all living beings within itself, would be the one that includes all shapes within itself. And so he made it perfectly spherical,* equidistant in all directions from its centre to its extremes, because there is no shape more perfect and none more similar to itself — similarity being, in his opinion, incomparably superior to dissimilarity.*

He gave it a perfectly smooth finish all over, for a number c of reasons. It had no need of eyes, since there was nothing visible left outside it, nor of ears, since there was nothing to hear either. There was no air around it to require breathing in, nor did it need to be equipped with organs for the intake of food and, once the goodness had been extracted from it, its subsequent evacuation. For there was nowhere for anything that might leave it to go, and nowhere for anything that might come to it to come from. Rather, it fed itself from its own waste and was so designed that every process and action happened within it and by its own agency, since its creator d believed that the universe would be more perfect if it were self-sufficient than if it needed things other than itself.

34a Then again, he thought it would be redundant to equip it with hands,* since there was nothing for it to hold or ward off, and equally redundant to fit it with feet or any other means of getting around. It did have motion, but the motion he assigned to it was the one that was natural to its body and that, of all the seven kinds of motion, has the most to do with reason and intelligence. And so he gave it circular movement, by starting it spinning at a constant pace in the same place and within itself. This freed it from the imbalance involved in all the other six kinds of motion,* and since its circular movement did not require feet, he created it without legs and feet.*

b So the god who exists for ever took thought for the god that was to be,* and for all these reasons he made for it a body that was smooth, uniform, equal in all directions from its centre, and a complete totality, made up of bodies that were also complete totalities. And once he had set in the centre a soul, which he then stretched throughout the body and with which he also coated the outside, he set the body spinning and made it a single, unique universe, capable, thanks to its perfection, of keeping its own company, of needing nothing and no one else, since it was enough for it that it had familiarity and affinity with itself. This, then, was how he created it to be a blessed god.

c As for its soul, despite its delayed appearance in this account of ours, it was not designed by the god to be younger than the body. How could he have wedded them to each other and then let the older be ruled by the younger? It's just that the things we say reflect the coincidence and contingency that characterize our lives.* But in fact he made soul prior and senior, in terms of both birth and excellence, since it was to be the mistress—the ruler, with the body as its subject. And now I shall explain how he made soul and what materials he used.

22

He combined the two kinds of substance—the one indi- 35a
visible and never changing, and the other the divided and
created substance of the physical world—into an intermediate, third kind of substance,* and then again, in the case
of† both identity and difference, he likewise formed inter-
mediates between, in each case, that aspect of them which is
undivided and that aspect of them which is divided in the
physical realm. Then he took these three ingredients and
made out of them a single, homogeneous mixture, though
getting difference to be compatible with identity took force,
since difference does not readily form mixtures.* But once
he had mixed identity and difference with substance and cre- b
ated a single blend out of the three ingredients, he divided up
the whole mixture again, this time into as many portions as
he needed, with each portion being a blend of identity,
difference, and substance.

He began the division by first taking a single portion from
the mixture; next he took a portion which was double the
quantity of the first, and then a third portion, which was
one-and-a-half times the quantity of the second and three
times the quantity of the first; then he took a fourth portion
which was double the quantity of the second, and a fifth which
was three times the quantity of the third, and a sixth which was c
eight times the quantity of the first, and then a seventh portion which was twenty-seven times the quantity of the first.*
After this, he filled up the double and triple intervals by cut- 36a
ting off further portions from the mixture and inserting
them into the gaps, so that in each interval there were two
means, a mean that exceeded one of its extremes by the same
fraction of the extremes as it was exceeded by the other
extreme, and another mean that exceeded one of its extremes
by the same number as it was exceeded by the other extreme.*
These links created, within the first set of intervals, further b
intervals of 3 : 2, 4 : 3, and 9 : 8, and then he filled up all the
4 : 3 intervals with the 9 : 8 interval, leaving in each case a
portion, and the portion that remained was an interval whose

23

terms, expressed numerically, were 256:243.* And so at this point the mixture, from which he was cutting these portions, was all used up.*

He then split this whole structure lengthwise into two, joined the two halves to each other middle to middle (like the letter *chi*, X), bent them round in a circle until they met, and attached each half to itself and to the other at a point opposite their original junction.* He invested them† with the motion that spins at a constant pace in the same place, with one of the rings inside the other; the outer revolution he named the revolution of identity, and the inner one the revolution of difference. He made identity move around towards the right, as if along a side, and difference towards the left, as if along a diagonal, and he gave sovereignty to the revolution of identity and constancy. For he left it single and intact, but he sliced the inner one in six places into seven unequal rings,* in conformity with the three double and the three triple intervals. And he ordained that these rings would move in contrasting ways, with three of them being similar in speed,* but the other four moving at rates that differed both from one another and from the other three, while remaining proportionate to one another.

Once the whole structure of the soul had been created to the satisfaction of its creator, he next made the whole corporeal world inside it, and then joined their centres and fitted them together. Then the soul, which was interwoven throughout the entire fabric from the centre to the furthest limits of the universe, and coated the outside too, entered as a deity upon a never-ending life of intelligent activity, spinning within itself for all time. The soul is invisible (as opposed to the body of the universe, which is visible), and since it is characterized by reasoning and harmony, it is the supreme creation of the supreme intelligible and eternally existing being.

The soul was blended together out of identity, difference, and substance (its three ingredients); the principle of its partition and bonding was rational proportionality; and it circles back on itself. For all these reasons, when it comes into contact with things, whether their substance is scattered or undivided, it is moved throughout the entirety of its being and it states rationally and precisely with what, in what sense, in b what manner, and at what time anything that is the same as or different from something is the same or different,* and is qualified in either of these ways in relation to both things in the world of creation and to that which is eternally consistent.* The statement that arises and is carried silently and noiselessly along within the self-moving soul is equally true whether it concerns difference or identity, but when its subject is the realm of sensations and it is the ring of difference, moving unerringly, that makes the declaration to the whole of the creature's soul, beliefs and opinions (albeit reliable and true ones) are the result,* as opposed to when the subject of the statement is the realm of reason and when it is the c ring of identity, running smoothly, that makes the declaration, in which case understanding and knowledge cannot fail to follow. But if anyone were to name anything other than the soul as the place where belief and knowledge arise,* he would be completely and utterly wrong.

When the father-creator saw that his creation had been set in motion and was alive, a gift to please the immortal gods, he was pleased and in his joy he determined to make his creation resemble its model even more closely. Since the d model was an ever-living being, he undertook to make this universe of ours the same as well, or as similar as it could be. But the being that served as the model was eternal, and it was impossible for him to make this altogether an attribute of any created object. Nevertheless, he determined to make it a kind of moving likeness of eternity, and so in the very act of ordering the universe he created a likeness of eternity, a likeness that progresses eternally through the sequence of numbers, while eternity abides in oneness.*

This image of eternity is what we have come to call 'time',* since along with the creation of the universe he devised and e created days, nights, months, and years, which did not exist before the creation of the universe.* They are all parts of time, and 'was' and 'will be' are created aspects of time which we thoughtlessly and mistakenly apply to that which is eternal.* For we say that it was, is, and will be, when in fact only 'is'

38a truly belongs to it, while 'was' and 'will be' are properties of things that are created and that change over time, since 'was' and 'will be' are both changes. What is for ever consistent and unchanging, however, does not have the property of becoming older or younger with the passage of time; it was not created at some point, it has not come into existence just now, and it will not be created in the future. As a rule, in fact, none of the modifications that belong to the things that move about in the sensible world, as a result of having been created, should be attributed to it; they are aspects of time as it imitates eternity and cycles through the numbers.

We use other inaccurate expressions too, such as 'What

b has been created *is* what has been created' and 'What is being created *is* being created', and also 'What will be created *is* going to be created' and 'The non-existent *is* the non-existent.' But perhaps now is not the appropriate moment* to cover these matters in detail. In any case, time was created along with the universe, and since they were created together, they will also perish together, if they do ever perish. And the creation of the universe conformed to the model of eternity, so as to

c be as similar to it as possible. For the model exists *for all eternity*, while the universe was and is and always will be *for all time*.*

This was how the god reasoned and planned for the creation of time. As a result, in order that time might be created, the sun and the moon and five other heavenly bodies—the so-called planets—were created to determine and preserve the numbers of time.* Once he had made bodies for each of them, he put them into the orbits within the circuit of differ-

d ence, seven bodies for seven orbits. He put the moon into the first circle around the earth, he put the sun into the circle second closest to the earth,* and the Morning Star and the planet which is said to be sacred to Hermes he put into circles with the same speed as the sun, but assigned them tendencies that oppose it.* Consequently, the sun, Hermes' planet, and the Morning Star constantly overtake and are overtaken by one another.* As for the other three planets, a thorough account of where and why he located them as he did would make this supposedly subordinate discussion longer and more troublesome than the main discussion it's meant to be e serving. There might perhaps be time for a proper explanation of these matters later.

Anyway, when all the heavenly bodies whose shared task it was to produce time had attained their appropriate movements, and when they had been created as living beings, their bodies fastened with bonds of soul, and when each of them had understood its instructions, they began to revolve in conformity with the oblique movement of difference, which 39a crosses the movement of identity and is subject to it.† The circles they made ranged from larger to smaller, and those with smaller circles revolved faster than those with larger circles. Thanks to the movement of identity, however,† the heavenly bodies with the fastest revolution appeared to be overtaken by those which moved more slowly, though in fact they were overtaking them.* This happens because the faster speed of the movement of identity twists all the orbits into spirals, since they progress simultaneously in two contrasting directions, and so makes the heavenly body that falls b behind it the most gradually appear to be the closest to us.

In order that there might be a clearly visible way to measure their relative speeds as† they journey on their eight revolutions, the god ignited a light in the circuit that is second closest to the earth, and we have come to call this light the sun. He created it to illuminate as much of the universe as it could and to enable all suitably endowed creatures to become numerate by studying the revolution of identity and sameness. This is how and why night and day were created, which make c

27

up the circuit of the most intelligent revolution, the undivided one. A month is when the moon has completed a circuit of its circle and caught up with the sun, and a year when the sun has completed a circuit of its circle.

The revolutions of the other heavenly bodies have not been taken into consideration by people, or by so few that they have not been labelled or had their relative speeds examined and measured in numerical terms. This means

d   that people in general fail to appreciate that the wanderings of these five planets, which are bewilderingly many and amazingly complex, do constitute time.* All the same, it's still possible to understand that the perfect number of time makes up a perfect year* at the moment when all the eight revolutions, with their relative speeds, attain completion and regain their starting-points when measured against the movement of the ring of identity and sameness. And so this is the reason for the creation of all those bodies which turn as they travel across the heavens: they exist in order that this

e   universe of ours might, by imitating the eternity of the perfect, intelligible living being, be as similar as possible to it.

So far, up to the creation of time, the universe had been made in all respects to resemble its model, but there was still a point of dissimilarity: it did not yet contain all living beings, which remained to be created. In carrying out this final task of his, the god, of course, took the model as the exemplar he was to copy. He thought, then, that the universe should contain exactly the same number and kinds of living beings as are discerned by mind within that which is the living being par excellence. And so there are four kinds of living beings in the universe: the heavenly gods, winged

40a   creatures that travel through the air, those that live in water, and finally those that go on foot on dry land.

The gods he formed mostly out of fire,* to make them as visible and as beautiful as they could be; he made them spherical, after the fashion of the universe as a whole; he placed them within the movement† of the sovereign ring, to follow in its train; and he distributed them all around the heaven, to be a true adornment for it, arrayed in complex patterns throughout the whole ring. He endowed each of the gods with two kinds of motion: even rotation in the same place, to enable them always to think the same thoughts about the b same things; and forward motion, under the sovereignty of the revolution of identity and sameness. But with respect to the other five kinds of motion, they were to be stable and unmoving, so that each of them might be, to the fullest extent, as perfect as possible. And so all the fixed stars were created as divine, ever-living beings, spinning evenly and unerringly for ever. And I have already described how those heavenly bodies which turn and wander, in precisely the way the fixed stars don't, were created.

As for the earth, our nurse, winding around†* the axis that had been run straight through the universe, he designed c it to be the preserver and creator of night and day, and the first and eldest of the gods that were created within the universe. But what about the dancing of these gods and the ways they pass by one another? What about the ways their revolutions turn back on themselves and go forward again?* What about which of them come into conjunction and opposition with one another,* and in what order they pass in front of one another, and at what times any of them are veiled from our sight and then reappear,* to frighten those who are capable† of calculation and to send them signs of the future? d To describe all this without visible models* would be labour spent in vain. This will do as an account of the nature of the visible, created gods, so let's end it here.

As for all the other divinities, it's beyond our abilities to understand and explain their creation, so we had better trust the accounts of our predecessors, who were, or so they claim, descendants of the gods and can therefore be expected to know all about their forefathers. There's no way for us not to believe the gods' children, even when what they say is implausible e and illogical;* no, we must follow custom and trust their

claim to be proclaiming matters that are familiar to them. So
let's accept their account of the creation of these gods and
simply repeat it: Earth and Heaven gave birth to Oceanus
and Tethys, who in their turn were the parents of Phorkys,
Cronus, Rhea, and all the gods of that generation; then from
41a   Cronus and Rhea came Zeus, Hera, and all those well-
known beings who are said to be their siblings and who then
gave birth to further offspring.*

Once all the gods had been created—both those that
traverse the heavens for all to see and those that make themselves visible when they choose—the creator of this universe
of ours addressed them as follows: 'Gods, divine works of
which I am the craftsman and father, anything created
by me is imperishable unless I will it.†* Any bond can be
b   unbound, but to want to destroy a structure of beauty and
goodness is a mark of evil.* Hence, although as created
beings you are not altogether immortal and indestructible,
still you shall not perish nor shall death ever be your lot,
since you have been granted the protection of my will, as a
stronger and mightier bond than those with which you were
bound at your creation.

'Now mark my words and apprehend what I disclose to
you. Three kinds of mortal creature remain yet uncreated,*
c   and while they remain so the universe will be incomplete,
for it will not contain within itself all kinds of living creatures, as it must if it is to be perfect and complete. If I were
to be directly responsible for their creation and their life, they
would have the rank of gods. To ensure that they are mortal,
and that this universe is truly whole, it is you who must, in
fulfilment of your natures, imitate the power that I used* in
creating you and turn, as craftsmen, to the creation of living
creatures. Now, there is a part of them that deserves to share
with us the title of immortality—the part which is called
divine and which rules in those of them who are ever prepared to follow justice, to follow in your train—and it is my
job to sow the seed and get the process under way. But then

I shall hand things over and the rest is up to you. Interweave d
the mortal with the immortal, create living beings and give
them their birth; give them food for their growth, and when
they waste away receive them back again.'

After this speech, he turned once more to the bowl he had
used previously to mix and blend the soul of the universe.
He poured into it what was left of the ingredients he had
used before and mixed them in the same way, with the only
difference being that they were no longer as unfailingly pure
as before, but were a grade or two lower in the scale of
purity.* Once he had a complete mixture, he divided it up
into as many souls as there are stars and he assigned each
soul to a star. Then, with each soul mounted on its chariot, e
so to speak, he showed it the nature of the universe. He told
them the laws of their destinies—how it was ordained that
the first incarnation they would undergo would be the same
for all of them, so that none of them would suffer any disad-
vantage at his hands, and how, after he had planted each of
them in the appropriate instrument of time,* they were to be
born as the most god-fearing of creatures. And he explained 42a
that human nature comes in two forms, and that the superior kind was that which would subsequently come to be
called 'male'.*

Because the bodies in which they had been implanted
were inevitably subject to comings and goings, there were,
he went on, certain necessary consequences: the first innate
capacity, shared by them all, would be perception, caused by
the action on them of powerful properties;* the second
would be desire, a mixture of pleasure and pain; the third,
fear and passion, and all the emotions that either follow in b
their train or stand opposed to them. And he explained that
whether they lived moral or immoral lives would depend on
whether they were in control of these things or were controlled by them.* Any soul which made good use of its allotted
time would return to dwell once more on the star with which
it had been paired, to live a blessed life in keeping with its

character; but any soul that fell short would, for its second
c incarnation, become a woman instead of a man.* If under
these circumstances it still didn't refrain from wickedness, it
would become, on each subsequent incarnation, an animal
of a kind determined by the principle that it should resemble
the kind of wickedness it displayed. And it would continue
to change, with no end to its trials and tribulations, until it
had drawn its burdensome mass of fire, water, air, and earth,
filled with unrest and irrationality, into alignment with the
revolution of identity and sameness within itself—which is
d to say, until it had gained control of this encrustation by
means of reason and had re-attained its original, best state.*

Once he had gone through all these decrees for them,
which freed him of responsibility for any wickedness any of
them might subsequently perform, he set about planting
some of them in the earth, some in the moon, and others in
the other instruments of time. After this, he handed over to the
younger gods the task of forming their mortal bodies. When
they had also created any further attributes a human soul
e might require, and whatever went along with such attributes,
he left it up to them to govern† and steer* every mortal creature as best they could, so that each one would be as noble and
good as it might be, apart from any self-caused evils.

With these arrangements in place, he resumed his life in
his proper abode,* while his children attended to their
father's orders and set about obeying them. They took the
immortal principle of a mortal creature and, in imitation of
the craftsman-god who had made them, withdrew from the
43a world, as a temporary loan, portions of fire, earth, water, and
air, and fastened them together. However, they didn't use
the indestructible bonds with which they themselves were
held together, but joined the portions together with countless rivets,* too minute to see, and made each body a unified
whole consisting of all four ingredients. Then they bound
the revolutions of the immortal soul into the body with its
ebbs and flows.

These revolutions neither dominated nor were dominated by the mighty flood within which they had been bound, but sometimes they were forced to fall in with its motion, and sometimes they forced it to do the same. The result was that the entire creature was in motion, but it was disorderly b movement, chaotic and irrational progress involving all six kinds of motion. It travelled erratically in every one of the six directions—forward and back, right and left, down and up. For it was a mighty wave that washed over it and ebbed away from it, a mighty food-supplying wave, but even greater was the disturbance caused by the properties of things as they struck the body—as any given body met and collided c with fire from outside and elsewhere, or with a solid mass of earth, or with liquid streams of water, or when it was overtaken by a gust of air-driven wind—and when the motions caused by all these things passed through the body and struck the soul. In fact, that is why these motions came collectively to be called by the name they still bear: 'sensations.'*

Moreover, just then, at the time we're speaking of, these motions produced their strongest and most powerful impulse. Their movement coincided with that of the ever-flowing current and vigorously shook the circuits of the soul. d With their contrary flow opposing the circular movement of identity, they prevented it from getting going, and they also threw the revolution of difference into confusion. The upshot was that they twisted and distorted all three double and all three triple intervals, and the intervening means and bonds ($3:2$, $4:3$, and $9:8$)—which could not be completely unbound except by him who bound them together—and caused all kinds of disruption and corruption in the e rings, wherever and however they could. As a consequence, the rings became only tenuously linked to each other, and although they remained in motion, their movements were irrational: they sometimes went in reverse, at other times from side to side, and at other times upside down.

Think, for instance, of a man who is upside down, with his head resting on the ground and his feet up in the air, supported against something: as long as these circumstances last, both he, the person in that position, and any spectators perceive his right as his left and his left as his right, and he sees their right and left the wrong way round too. Extreme versions of this, and other experiences of the same kind, are undergone by the revolutions, and whenever they encounter 44a from outside anything that belongs to the class either of identity or of difference, they call it the same as something or different from something, but get things completely the wrong way around and prove themselves to be deluded and stupid. At that time there is no sovereign circuit in them, no rulership, and so some of the sensations that sweep in from outside and strike the revolutions also draw the whole chamber for the soul along with them, and then, for all that the revolutions appear to be in control, they're actually being controlled. And these experiences are responsible for the fact that even today, as well as at the beginning, a soul lacks b intelligence when it is first bound into a mortal body.

But eventually the stream of growth and nurture abates, and with the passage of time the circular motions regain tranquillity and return to their proper courses, and things increasingly return to normal.* From then on, as each of the rings regains its normal shape, their revolutions become less erratic, begin to identify difference and identity correctly, and make their possessor intelligent. Also, if proper nurture c is supported by education, a person will become perfectly whole and healthy, once he has recovered from this most serious of illnesses; but if he cares nothing for education, he will limp his way through life and return to Hades unfulfilled and stupid.

But I've got ahead of myself. We do need to go into the matters before us in more detail, but first there are some preliminaries. We need to discuss the creation of human bodies, part by part; we need to discuss the soul; and we

34

need to discuss what the gods were thinking of and intending when they created the body and soul. Where these matters are concerned, we had better keep to the most plausible account d and let it guide our steps.

In imitation of the rounded shape of the universe,* the gods bound the two divine circuits into a spherical body, which we now call the head. The head is the most divine part of us and the ruler of all the rest of our parts, and once they had assembled the body as a whole, they handed it over to the head, to be its servant, because they realized that the body's capacities included all the movements there were to be. In other words, not wanting the head to roll around on the ground without the ability to climb over the various rises e and out of the various dips, they gave it the body to be its vehicle and means of transport.* This is why the body is elongated and why it sprouted four limbs which can be stretched and flexed; it was the gods' way of devising a form of transport. By using these limbs to hold on to things and to support itself, the body became capable of crossing every kind of terrain, while carrying our most divine and sacred 45a part in its lofty home.

So that's why we have legs and arms attached to us. Now, the gods considered the front more valuable and more authoritative than the back, so they made forward the main direction in which we travel. It then became necessary for the front of a human being to have specific differences from the back, and so, taking first the head-box, they positioned the face there, fixed on the face organs to enable the soul to be b fully aware,* and ordained that this part, our natural front, should be the leader.

The first of the organs they constructed were the light-bearing eyes, and the reason they attached the eyes to the face was as follows. They found a way to make a distinct stuff out of that portion of fire which has the ability to shed gentle light without burning, and to make it the property of each passing day. Then they made the pure fire within us, which is

35

naturally akin to this daylight, flow through the eyes,* and they compressed the whole of the eyes, but especially the central part, until they were smooth and dense, so that they
c would block everything that was more coarse and let only something with this kind of purity filter through. So whenever the ray that flows through the eyes issues forth into surrounding daylight, like meets with like and coalesces with it, until a single, undifferentiated stuff is formed, in alignment with the direction of the eyes, wherever the fire from inside strikes and pushes up against an external object. The similarity between the fire from within and the fire outside means that the stuff is completely homogeneous,
d and whenever it touches or is touched by anything else, it transmits the object's impulses right through itself and all the way up to the soul, and the result is the perception we call 'seeing'.

At nightfall, however, with the departure of its cognate fire, the visual ray is interrupted. It issues forth, but, encountering something dissimilar to itself, fades and dies out, since it can no longer attach itself to the fireless air adjacent to it. The upshot is that it not only stops seeing, but also encour-
e ages sleep. For the internal fire, which gets trapped inside by the closure of the eyelids (the gods' way of protecting the organ of sight), disperses and smooths out any internal impulses, and the result of this smoothness is a state of quiet. When the state of quiet is profound, the sleep that ensues is almost dreamless, but when some relatively large impulses remain trapped inside, they produce images whose nature and number depend on the nature and location of the move-
46a ments; and although these images are internal copies, when awake we recall them as events that occurred outside us.

It should now be easy to understand what happens in the formation of images by mirrors or any other reflective surface.* As a result of the interaction between the fire from inside and the fire from outside, and because a single, though much-distorted, substance is formed on each occasion by

the surface, things necessarily appear as they do. When the b
fire from your face coalesces with the fire from my organ of
sight on something that is smooth and bright, left appears to
be right, because the opposite parts of the visual ray make
contact with the opposite parts of your face, contrary to the
way they usually impact on each other. On the other hand,
right appears as right and left as left whenever light changes
sides as it coalesces with the other light, and this happens
when the mirror's surface is curved up on either side, so that c
the right side of the visual ray is deflected over to the left,
and vice versa. But when just such a mirror is turned until
it is vertical in relation to the face, it makes everything
appear upside down, since the bottom of the ray is deflected
to the top and the top to the bottom.

Now, all these factors count as contributory causes,* used
by the gods to serve their work of achieving the best possible
result. Most people, however, take them to be not contribu- d
tory causes, but the actual causes of everything, because of
the various effects they have, such as cooling things down
and heating them, or thickening and thinning them.* But
none of them can possibly possess rationality or intelligence.
We are bound to affirm that the only existing thing which
can properly possess intelligence is soul, and soul is invisible, whereas fire, water, earth, and air are all visible substances. So anyone who desires understanding and knowledge
must look for his primary causes to that which is essentially
intelligent, and look for his secondary causes in the domain e
of things that are moved by other things and in their turn
move others by automatic necessity. We should do the same
as well: we should discuss both kinds of causes, but keep
those which fashion good and beautiful products with the
help of intelligent craftsmanship separate from those which
produce random and disorderly results, with no part played
by intelligence.

Anyway, I've said enough about the accessory causes that
enabled the eyes to gain the power they now possess, and I'd

better go on to explain why the gods endowed us with
47a eyes — what the eyes do that does us so much good. It follows
from what I've been saying that sight is enormously beneficial for us, in the sense that, if we couldn't see the stars and
the sun and the sky, an account such as I've been giving of
the universe would be completely impossible. As things are,
however, the visibility of day and night, of months and the
circling years, of equinoxes and solstices, resulted in the invention of number, gave us the concept of time, and made it possible for us to enquire into the nature of the universe. These in
b their turn have enabled us to equip ourselves with philosophy
in general, and humankind never has been nor ever will be
granted by the gods a greater good than philosophy.

This is, in my opinion, the greatest benefit we gain from
the eyes — and why should we celebrate all the lesser benefits,
the loss of which would cause a non-philosopher who had
lost his sight to wail and grieve in vain? Instead, let's simply
state that the reason and purpose of this gift is as follows: the
gods invented and supplied us with vision to enable us to
observe the rational revolutions of the heavens* and to let them
affect the revolutions of thought within ourselves (which are
c naturally akin to those in the heavens, though ours are turbulent while they are calm). That is, the gods wanted us to
make a close study of the circular motions of the heavens, gain
the ability to calculate them correctly in accordance with
their nature, assimilate ours to the perfect evenness of the
god's,* and so stabilize the wandering revolutions within us.

The same account goes for sound and hearing too:* they
were given to us by the gods for the same purpose and the
same reasons. Speech, for instance, was designed for exactly
the same purpose, and in fact makes a major contribution to
it; and then as much of the domain of the Muses as can be
d employed for the hearing of sound† was given for the sake
of attunement. And attunement, whose movements are
naturally akin to the circular motions of our souls, is useful
to the man who makes intelligent use of the Muses not for

mindless pleasure (which is nowadays taken to be the point
of melody), but for the disharmony of the soul's revolutions
that has arisen in us: attunement is an ally, provided by the
Muses for the soul in its fight to restore itself to order and
harmony. Rhythm also was given for the same purpose by
the same benefactors, to support us because for the most e
part our internal state is inconsistent and graceless.

Well, so far, apart from a brief digression,* my whole presentation has been concerned with the products of intelligent craftsmanship, but since the creation of this world of
ours was the result of reason and necessity together, I should
also serve up an account of the creations of necessity.* 48a
Reason prevailed over necessity by persuading it to steer the
majority of created things towards perfection,* and this was
how the universe was originally created, as a result of the
defeat of necessity by the persuasive power of intelligence.
Since this was the manner and means of the creation of the
universe, then an account of how it actually came into existence has to include the wandering cause as well,* and how it
is in its nature to cause movement and change. So we'd better retrace our steps, find a different starting-point this time, b
one that exactly suits these facts, and start again from the
beginning, to take account of this, just as we did earlier with
the facts before us then.

What we have to do is see what fire, water, air, and earth
were like in themselves before the creation of the universe,
and what happened to them then. No one before has ever
explained how they were created.* People talk as if it were
clear what fire and so on are and take them to be the principles
and† letters, so to speak, of the universe, when in actual fact
they shouldn't even be compared to syllables.* Only someone of slight intelligence is likely to make such a comparison. c
So let's take the following as our position: where all four are
concerned, we should not talk of their 'origin' or their 'principles', or follow whatever conception of them is currently

popular, above all because it's hard for us to keep to our present explanation and at the same time to clarify such a conception.* You shouldn't expect me to speak in that way, and I'd find it impossible to persuade myself that it would be the right way for me to go about the major undertaking
d before us. Instead, I'll stick to what I originally said about the value of likely accounts, I'll start again from the beginning, and I'll try to come up with an account of them, individually and collectively, that is at least as plausible as what I said before, and is more thorough.† So, as we embark on this account, let's call on the saviour god on this occasion too to preserve us from odd and outlandish explanations and to guide us towards a conclusion based on likelihood. And then
e let's start again from the beginning.*

For this fresh start of ours, we need to take account of more than we did before. Earlier we distinguished two types of things, but now we have to disclose the existence of a third kind, different from the others. Our earlier discussion required no more than the two—the model, as we suggested, and the copy of the model, the first being intelligible and ever-
49a consistent, the second visible and subject to creation—and we didn't distinguish a third at the time, on the grounds that these two would be sufficient. But now the argument seems to demand that our account should try to clarify this difficult and obscure kind of thing.*

How, then, should we conceive of it? What is its nature— what capacity or capacities does it have? We wouldn't be at all far from the mark if we thought of it as the receptacle (or nurse, if you like) of all creation.* This is a true statement, but it doesn't tell us everything we need to know about it. That degree of clarity is difficult, however, and not least
b because achieving it necessarily requires the raising of a prior problem about fire and its companions. The point is that it's hard to say, with any degree of reliability and stability, that any of them is such that it should really be called 'water' rather than 'fire', or that any of them is such that it should

be called by any particular name rather than by all four names, one after another.* Given this difficulty, then, how can we plausibly say exactly what one of them is? What terms should we use to describe it, and what are we to say?

In the first place, we apparently see what we've just been calling 'water' solidifying and turning into stones and earth, and we also apparently see it decomposing and ex- c panding, becoming wind and air. Ignited air appears to be fire and, conversely, contracted and extinguished fire seems to change back to air. Again, when air shrinks and thickens it appears to become cloud and mist, and when these are further compressed water flows from them, and water in turn gives rise to earth and stones.* In other words, it looks as though there's a cyclical process whereby they generate one another.

Since it seems, then, as though none of them ever retains d its identity, how could one insist without qualms and without making a fool of oneself that any of them is 'this' rather than something else? It can't be done. By far the safest course is to treat them and speak about them as follows. Whenever we see something—fire, for instance—that is constantly changing, we should not label it 'this' fire, but 'something of this sort'.* Likewise, we should never say 'this' water, but 'something of this sort', and the same goes for everything else that we indicate by means of expressions such as 'that' e and 'this', under the impression that we're designating some particular thing and that these things have the slightest stability. The point is that they run away rather than face expressions such as 'that' and 'this' and 'just so',† and every form of speech that makes them out to be stable entities.

We had better not speak of any of them like that. Instead, it would be safest to say 'something of this sort', an expression which can be used to describe each and every one of them, and is similarly applicable at every stage of the cyclical process. So, for example, we should refer to fire as 'something that is regularly of this sort',* and so on for everything that is subject

50a   to creation. The only safe referent of the expressions 'this' and 'that' is that within which each created thing comes into existence and puts in an appearance, and from which it subsequently passes away,* but anything that is of such-and-such a quality—warm or white or any of the opposites, or any combination of opposites—should never have that terminology used of them.

    I'd better go back over what I've been saying and try to make it even clearer. Imagine someone who moulds out of gold all the shapes there are, but never stops remoulding each form and changing it into another. If you point at one

b   of the shapes and ask him what it is, by far the safest reply, so far as truth is concerned, is for him to say 'gold'; he should never say that it's 'a triangle' or any of the other shapes he's in the process of making, because that would imply that these shapes are what they are, when in fact they're changing even while they're being identified.* However, he'd be content if you were, after all, also prepared to accept, with some degree of assurance, the reply 'something of this sort'.

    By the same argument, the *same* term should always be used in speaking of the receptacle of all material bodies, because it never is anything other than what it is: it only ever acts as the receptacle for everything, and it never comes to

c   resemble in any way whatsoever any of the things that enter it. Its nature is to act as the stuff from which everything is moulded—to be modified and altered by the things that enter it, with the result that it *appears* different at different times.* And whatever enters it and leaves it is a copy of something that exists for ever, a copy formed in an indescribably wonderful fashion which we'll look into later.*

    Anyway, for the time being we should think of there being

d   three kinds: the created world, the receptacle of creation, and the source, in whose likeness the created world is born. And it would not be out of place to compare the receptacle to a mother, the source to a father, and what they create between them to a child. We should also bear in mind that in order for there to exist, as a product of the moulding stuff, something that bears the whole multifarious range of visible qualities, the moulding stuff itself, in which the product is formed and originates, absolutely must lack all those characteristics which it is to receive from elsewhere, otherwise it could not perform its function. After all, if it were similar to any of the e things that enter it, it would be no good at receiving and copying contrary or utterly different qualities when *they* enter it, because it would leave traces of its own appearance as well. That is why, if it is to be the receptacle of *all* kinds, it must be *altogether* characterless.* Think, for instance, of perfumery, where artisans do exactly the same, as the first stage of the manufacturing process: they make the liquids which are to receive the scents as odourless as possible. Or think of those whose work involves taking impressions of shapes in soft materials: they allow no shape at all to remain noticeable, and they begin their work only once they've made their base stuff as uniform and smooth as possible.

The same goes, then, for that which repeatedly has to 51a accept, over its whole extent, all the copies of all intelligible† and eternally existing things: if it is to do this well, it should in itself be characterless. This explains, then, why in speaking of the mother and receptacle of every created thing, of all that is visible or otherwise perceptible, we shouldn't call it earth or air or fire or water, or any of their compounds or constituents. And so we won't go wrong if we think of it as an invisible, formless receptacle of everything, which is in some highly obscure fashion linked with the intelligible b realm. It's almost incomprehensible,* but in so far as we can use what we've been saying to arrive at a conception of its nature with some degree of accuracy, the best we can do is say that fire is the impression we receive when some part of it has been ignited, and water is the impression we receive when some part has been moistened, and earth and air are the impressions we receive in so far as it is the receptacle for copies of earth and air.

But we need to apply rational thought to achieve more clarity about these matters, by asking the following questions. Is there such a thing as fire which is just itself?* And what about all the other things we constantly describe in the same way, as each being just itself? Or is this kind of reality found only in things that are visible or otherwise perceptible by the bodily senses, and is the perceptible world, then, all that exists? If so, our repeated assertion that there are intelligible versions of individual things is foolish, and turns out to be empty talk. Well, the issue is too important for me just to insist that we're right and leave it untried and untested, but at the same time I don't want to load a lengthy digression onto an already long speech. It would be best by far, under the present circumstances, if we could make a major distinction obvious in a few words.

Speaking for myself, this is how I cast my vote: if knowledge and true belief are two distinct kinds of thing,* then these entities absolutely do exist in themselves, even though they are accessible only to our minds, not to our senses; but if, as some people think, true belief is no different from knowledge, then we must count all the things we perceive with our bodily senses as the most reliable things in existence. But we're bound to claim that knowledge and true belief are different, because they occur under different circumstances and are dissimilar. In the first place, the former is a result of instruction, the latter of persuasion; in the second place, the former is always accompanied by a true account, while the latter cannot explain itself at all; in the third place, the former is unmoved by persuasion, while the latter can be persuaded to change; and finally, we have to claim that the former is the property of the gods, but of scarcely any human beings, while the latter is something every man has.

This being so, we have to admit that there exists, first, the class of things which are unchanging, uncreated, and undying, which neither admit anything else into themselves from elsewhere nor enter anything else themselves, and which are

imperceptible by sight or any of the other senses. This class
is the proper object of intellect. Then, second, there is the
class of things that have the same names as the members of
the first class and resemble them, but are perceptible, created,
and in perpetual motion, since they come into existence in a
particular place and subsequently pass away from there.
This class is grasped by belief with the support of sensation.
Then, third, there is space,* which exists for ever and is
indestructible, and which acts as the arena for everything b
that is subject to creation. It is grasped by a kind of bastard
reasoning, without the support of sensation, and is hardly
credible.* In fact, when we take space into consideration we
come to suffer from dreamlike illusions, and to claim that
every existing thing must surely exist in some particular
place and must occupy some space, and that nothing exists
except what exists on earth or in the heavens.

This dreaming keeps us asleep and makes it impossible
for us to determine the truth about these and other related c
matters; we find it impossible to speak the truth even about
the realm of true being, where illusion plays no part. And the
truth is this: since even the conditions of an image's occurrence lie outside the image itself—since it is an ever-moving
apparition of something else—it *has* to occur in something
other than itself (and so somehow or other to cling on to
existence), or else it would be nothing at all; anything that
genuinely exists, however, is supported by the true and rig-
orous argument that neither of two distinct entities can ever
occur in the other, because that would make them simultan- d
eously one and two. So there we have, briefly argued, the
position that gets my vote: there were three distinct things
in existence even before the universe was created—being,
space, and creation.

As if it were not enough that the nurse of creation presents
a complex appearance (as a result of being moistened and
heated, of assuming the characters of earth and air, and of e
acquiring all the qualities that follow from all this), it is also

45

thoroughly imbalanced (as a result of being filled with dissimilar and imbalanced powers), and not only is it shaken by the things it contains, so that it lurches haphazardly all over the place, but its motion in turn further shakes them. This stirring causes them to be constantly moving in different directions and to become separated. It's like when things are shaken and sifted by sieves or other devices for cleaning grain: the heavy, dense material goes one way, while the light, flimsy material goes and settles elsewhere. Likewise, when these four were shaken at that time by the receptacle (which was itself in motion, like an implement for shaking stuff), the least similar among them ended up the furthest apart, and those that were most similar were pushed the closest together.*

53a

This explains, of course, how they came to occupy different locations even before they had become the constituents of the orderly universe that came into existence. Not only were they disproportionate and erratic, however, before that event, but even when the organization of the universe was first taken in hand, fire, water, earth, and air, despite displaying certain hints of their true natures, were still wholly in the kind of state you'd expect anything to be with no god present.* Finding them in that condition, then, the first thing the god did, when he came to organize the universe, was use shapes and numbers to assign them definite forms;* and we can take for granted, as the principal axiom affirmed by us, that the god did not leave them in the condition he found them, but made them as beautiful and as perfect as they could possibly be.*

b

So what I have to do now is try to explain to you the composition and origin of each of them. It will take an unusual argument, but you'll be able to follow it, because you're familiar with the intellectual disciplines I shall draw on in my account. The starting-point is, of course, universally accepted: that fire, earth, water, and air are material bodies. Now, this means that, like all bodies, they have depth, and anything with depth is necessarily surrounded by surfaces, and any rectilinear surface consists of triangles.* There are

c

two basic triangles from which all triangles are derived, and d
each of them has one right angle and two acute angles. On
one of the two basic triangles, the two acute angles are each
half of a right angle which has been divided by equal sides;*
on the other basic triangle, the two acute angles are unequal
portions of a right angle which has been divided into two
parts by unequal sides.* These, then, are the principles of
fire and the other bodies, or so we assume, since we are continuing to let likelihood, supported by logical necessity,
guide our account; if there are any principles more ultimate
than these, they are known only to the god and to men who
are dear to him.

We have to decide, then, which are the most beautiful e
bodies that can be created. There should be four of them,
and they must be dissimilar to one another, but capable (in
some cases) of arising out of one another's disintegration. If
we succeed at this task, we'll know the truth about the generation of earth, fire, and the bodies that act as proportionate
means between these two extremes. For we will never agree
with anyone who claims that there are or could be more
perfect visible bodies than these four,* each after its own
kind. So we should do our best to construct our four substances, each of outstanding beauty, and to reach a position
where we can claim to have adequately understood what
they are like.

Of our two triangles, the isosceles one is essentially single, 54a
whereas there's an infinite number of right-angled scalene
triangles. What we have to do, then, if we're to start properly, is select the most beautiful of this infinite plurality of
scalene triangles. If anyone can demonstrate that his choice
creates more beautiful structures, we'll welcome our defeat,
not resent it. But until then our position is that there is one
that is the most beautiful, and surpasses† all other scalene
triangles, and that is the one which is a constituent of the
equilateral triangle, with two triangles making the equilateral one as a third. It would take rather a long time to explain

47

b   why, but if anyone challenges our claim and finds that we were wrong,† we won't resent his victory. So these are our choices for the two triangles from which the bodies of fire and the rest were constructed—the isosceles, and the one whose essential property is that the square of the longer side is triple the square of the shorter side.*

I had better, just for a moment, clarify something that was not clearly expressed earlier. We were thinking that all four substances issued from one another and turned into one another, but this was wrong. Although there are indeed four

c   substances that are produced by the triangles we've selected, three of them are assembled from the one that has unequal sides, while only the fourth is assembled from the isosceles triangle. It follows that they are not all capable of arising out of one another's disintegration, in the sense of forming a small number of large entities from a large number of small ones or vice versa. Only the three can do that,* since they are all made up of a single type of triangle, and so, when the larger bodies fall apart, a large number of small bodies, in their appropriate shapes, are formed from them, and conversely, when many small bodies are resolved into their con-

d   stituent triangles, they might even, if they become numerically one, produce a single, large entity with a single mass.

That's all that needs to be said about the generation of the four substances from one another, but the next questions would be: what shape was each of them made with, and how many constituents combine to produce each of them? Let's start with the first and smallest composite figure and its factor, which is the triangle whose hypotenuse is twice as long as its minor side. If you join two such triangles at their hypotenuses and do this three times, so that all the hypot-

e   enuses and the short sides converge at the centre, you get a single equilateral triangle made up of six triangles.* If you put four of these equilateral triangles together in such a way that they form a single solid angle at the point where three

55a   plane angles meet, this solid angle is the angle that comes

48

straight after the most obtuse possible plane angle. Four of these solid angles form the first solid figure,* the one which divides the whole surface of a surrounding sphere into equal and similar zones. The second figure is made up of the same triangles, but this time they form a set of eight equilateral triangles and use four plane angles to make a single solid angle. Six of these solid angles complete the second body. The third figure is made up of 120 of the elementary triangles, made into a solid, and twelve solid angles, with five equilat- b eral triangular planes contributing to each solid angle. It has twenty faces consisting of equilateral triangles.

Once it had generated these figures, one of our two elementary triangles was absolved of further responsibility. Next, however, the isosceles triangle set about generating the fourth body: it formed itself into sets of four triangles, had their four right angles meet at the centre, and so produced a single equal-sided rectangle. Six of these rectangles joined together made eight solid angles, each made up of c three plane right angles fitting neatly together. The resulting construct had the shape of a cube,* with six faces consisting of equal-sided rectangular planes. There remained one further construct, the fifth; the god decorated it all over and used it for the whole.*

Now, suppose someone took all this into consideration and wondered whether it would be right to say that there is an infinite number of worlds, or a finite number. This wouldn't be an outrageous question to ask, but he would conclude that only a man of boundless ignorance of matters he should know d about could think that there is a boundless plurality.* It would be more reasonable, however, for someone to linger over the question whether in actual fact there are, strictly speaking, one or five worlds.* Our view, based on likelihood, asserts that the world is a single god, but someone else might take different points into consideration and draw a different conclusion.

But we had better not engage with him at the moment. We should allocate the figures whose generation we've just described to fire, earth, water, and air. Let's begin by assigning the cube to earth, because, of the four bodies, earth is the

e   most inert—the hardest to move and the readiest to hold its shape—and this description must above all fit the figure with the most secure faces. To put it in terms of our fundamental triangles, the most secure face must be the one consisting of triangles with equal sides, because it is naturally more secure than a face consisting of triangles with unequal sides. Besides, of the plane figures constructed out of our two kinds of triangle, an equal-sided square necessarily offers more stability than an equal-sided triangle. So not only do the square's constituent triangles offer more stability than those of the equilateral triangle, but also as a whole a square is more stable than a triangle.*

56a   In assigning this figure to earth, then, we are preserving the likelihood of our account—as also if we assign the most inert of the remaining figures to water, the most mobile to fire, and the figure that is intermediate in terms of mobility to air; the smallest to fire, the largest to water, and the one in between to air; and the most angular to fire, the second-most angular to air, and the least angular to water. Of them all, then, the one with the fewest faces is bound to be the

b   most mobile, since it is altogether the sharpest and the most angular of the three figures; and it is also bound to be the lightest, since it consists of the smallest number of identical parts. Then the one that comes second is the one that comes second in all these respects, and the one that comes third is the one that comes third in all these respects.

So, on grounds of both logic and likelihood, we can assume and affirm that the solid which was created in the form of a pyramid is the element and seed of fire, and the one we generated second is the element and seed of air, and the third one is the element and seed of water. Now, we must of course think of all these elements as being so small

c   that we cannot see any individual one, whichever of the four categories it belongs to; what we see are lumps made up of a

lot of them all at once.* And, as regards the correspondences
that obtain for their sizes, their relative mobility, and all their
other properties, we should appreciate that, whenever and
wherever necessity allowed itself to submit to persuasion, the
god always seized the opportunity to make them correspond
precisely with one another and be perfectly compatible in all
such respects.

On the basis of everything we've said up until now about
the four substances, it's highly likely that the facts are as
follows. When earth encounters fire and is broken up by its d
angularity, it will be swept away (just as it would also be if it
were a mass of air or water, rather than fire, within which it
underwent disintegration), until its particles meet up some-
where and recombine as earth — and only as earth, because
earth's constituents cannot play a part in any other figure.
On the other hand, when water is broken up into its parts by
fire or air, there's the possibility that, when they come
together again, the result might be one bit of fire and two
bits of air; and the fragments of air produced by the disinte- e
gration of a single bit of air could become two bits of fire.
Conversely, when a little fire is surrounded by a lot of air or
water or even earth, its motion brings it into conflict with the
movement of the surrounding matter, and if the fire loses the
battle, it disintegrates, and two bits of fire combine to make
one air-figure. And when air is overcome and broken up,
two-and-a-half bits of air join together into a single complete
water-figure.*

Let's make a fresh set of calculations here. When one of
the other bodies is cut up by the sharpness of the angles and 57a
edges of surrounding fire, if it recombines as fire, the process
of disintegration stops, because nothing that is homogeneous and self-identical can change or be changed at all by
something that has the same constitution; but disintegration
continues as long as the process of transformation pits something weaker against something stronger. Then again, when a
few smaller bits, surrounded by a lot of larger bits, are being

b broken up and extinguished, the process of extinction stops
if they're capable of recombining as the figure of the victorious body, so that fire turns into air, or air into water.* But if
the smaller bits confront and resist the larger bits, or even
any one of the other bodies,† the process of disintegration
continues either until the smaller bits have been forced to
withdraw, disintegration is complete, and they've taken ref-
uge with a body to which they are naturally akin; or until the
smaller bits have been defeated and have turned into a single
body of the same kind as the victorious body, in which case
they stay and live alongside the victorious body. In addition,
c while these processes are going on, all four substances are
exchanging places. Most of each kind of substance was dis-
pelled into its own region by the movement of the receptacle,*
but any bits that are in the process of changing and taking
on a different identity are moved by the shaking of the
receptacle towards the region of the substance to which they
are now assimilated.

So much for the origin of the primary bodies in their
original, unalloyed state. But the fact that they come in a wide
variety of types is attributable to the structure of each of the
d two elementary triangles: neither structure originally engendered a triangle of just a single size;* the triangles could be
smaller or larger, and numerically as many as there are versions of all the four bodies. And so, of course, the variety of
ways they can interact, either just with themselves or with
one another, is infinite—and this is the variety that has to
be observed by those of us who intend to rely on likelihood
in our accounts of the way things are.

What about movement and rest? Either we agree on how
they begin and what factors are involved, or our subsequent
e discussion is going to be faced with many obstacles. I've
already addressed the issue to a certain extent, but I have to
add that uniformity and motion are incompatible. After all, it's
difficult, not to say impossible, for there to exist something to
be moved if there's no mover for it, or for a mover to exist if

there's nothing to be moved. In the absence of a mover and a moved, there's no such thing as motion, and mover and moved cannot possibly be uniform with each other. It follows that we should always associate rest with uniformity and attribute motion to diversity. And diversity is due to inequality, the 58a cause of which we've already discussed.*

We have not, however, explained why the four bodies haven't become completely separated from one another, in which case the changes of quality and place that occur as a result of their interactions would have ended. So we had better retrace our steps and address the issue now. Once the vault of the universe has gathered the four bodies together inside itself, it compresses everything and squeezes out every last bit of void,* because, being spherical, it is in its nature to want to be close to itself. This explains why fire b permeates everything the most, then air (as the second most subtle body), and so on. For the larger the constituent parts of a body, the more gaps remain in its structure, and the smaller the constituent parts, the fewer the gaps, and so the reduction caused by the compression pushes the small bodies into the gaps within the large bodies.* The result is that, with small bodies next to large ones, the smaller ones cause the larger ones to expand, while the larger ones cause the smaller ones to contract, and so they all change place and move, upwards or downwards, towards their proper regions. For as each of them changes size, it also changes location. And c so a state of uniformity is never achieved, and diversity, now and in the future, keeps these things in perpetual motion.

Next, we need to take note of their varieties. Fire comes in many forms: there's flame, for instance, and the non-burning emanation from flame that sheds light for the eyes, and the residue of fire that coals retain after the flames have been extinguished. The same goes for air, which in its purest d form is called 'aether', and when it is particularly foul 'fog' and 'darkness'. There are other kinds of air too, nameless ones, that occur as a result of its triangles' differences in size.

As for the varieties of water, they fall initially into two groups: the liquid and the liquefiable. Liquid water has particles that are small but unequal, and so, because of this unevenness and the shape of its figure, not only is it mobile in itself, but it can easily be moved by something else.

e Liquefiable water, however, consists of large, uniform particles, which make it more stable than the liquid version, and heavy, since its uniformity concentrates it. But when fire enters it and begins to break it up, it loses its uniformity, and with that destroyed it admits more motion. Once it has become mobile, it spreads out over the ground thanks to the pressure of the adjacent air. Each of these processes has its own name: we call the reduction of its bulk 'melting', and the spreading out over the ground 'flowing'.

59a What about the opposite situation, when fire is being driven out of it? Given that the fire doesn't pass into a void, the air adjacent to it comes under pressure and then compresses the liquid mass, which is still mobile, into the places previously occupied by fire and so makes the liquid homogeneous. The compression of the liquid and its recovery of uniformity (since fire, the cause of its lack of uniformity, is in the process of leaving) return the liquid to its normal state. The release of the fire is called 'cooling', and the reduction that happens when the fire leaves we regard as 'solidification'.*

b To take a few of all the varieties of what we've called liquefiable water, there's one that is extremely dense (because it consists of the most subtle and uniform parts) and unique of its kind, and has been endowed with a shiny, yellow colour: this is our most highly prized possession, gold, the solidity of which is due to its having been filtered through rocks. And gold also has an offshoot, dark in colour and so dense that it is very hard: this is adamant. Then there's a kind which is gold-like in terms of its particles, except that its particles are not uniform; in terms of density it is more dense than gold (and it also contains a small proportion of fine earth, which makes it harder), but it is lighter because

c

there are large gaps in it. This is the structure of copper, a bright, solid kind of water. When its constituent earth and water* begin to age and to separate once more from each other, the earthy part appears by itself on the surface and is called 'verdigris'.

We wouldn't now find it at all complicated to work out the details of all the other similar varieties; all we'd have to do is keep our gaze fixed on plausibility. If someone needed a break from accounts of eternal things, and put them to one side in favour of the innocent pleasure of exploring likely accounts of created things, he would create within his life a d source of modest, intellectual amusement. So, since we've just indulged in this diversion, we shall carry on with further likely accounts on the same topic.

All water of a light and liquid variety has an admixture of fire and air,† and is called 'liquid' because of its mobility and the way it rolls over the ground. It owes its softness to the fact that its faces are less stable than those of earth and so yield to pressure. But when fire and air are extracted from this kind of water and leave it on its own, the departure of these bodies makes it more uniform and concentrated, e which is to say that it solidifies. Water that fully undergoes this process above the ground is called 'hail', while the same phenomenon on the ground is called 'ice'; water that undergoes less of this process and remains only semi-solidified above the ground is called 'snow', while the same phenomenon on the ground, with dew in the process of solidification, is called 'frost'.

Most varieties of mixtures that involve water are known collectively as 'saps' or 'juices', since they are filtered through 60a soil-based plants. There are so many different ways in which they can form mixtures that many remain nameless, but there are four which are particularly conspicuous (they have fire in them) and so have been named. The first of these is wine, which heats body and soul together. The second kind is smooth and, because it expands the visual ray, it is bright

and shiny to look at, with an iridescent appearance: this class consists of the oils, such as pine resin, castor-oil, olive-oil of course, and everything else that has the same attributes. The
b   third kind restores the constrictions in the mouth to their normal, loose-textured state,* and thanks to this action produces sweetness: the general term by which this kind is known is 'honey'. The fourth kind is caustic (that is, it attacks flesh) and frothy: it is different from all the other saps, and is called 'verjuice'.

Now for some varieties of earth. One kind is filtered through water and turns into a stony body, as follows. The interaction of earth and water wears out the water, which changes into air,
c   and then the air tries to rush up to its proper region. But there is no void above the mixture, and so the new air pushes at the adjacent air.* This adjacent air is heavy, and so, when pushed, it spreads out over the mass of earth, and crushes and compresses it into the places that are being left empty by the rising of the new air. The earth, compressed by the air, forms stone, which is insoluble in water. Two varieties of stone are formed: the more beautiful kind* is made out of equal, uniform particles and is transparent, the less beautiful kind is the opposite.

Another kind of earth has been deprived of all moisture
d   by brief contact with fire and therefore has a more brittle composition than stone. We have come to call this variety of earth 'pottery'. In another instance, some moisture is left behind, and the result is earth which, once it has cooled down, is liquefiable by fire, and this is the dark-coloured millstone.†*

Then there are the two kinds of earth that have similarly had all the water extracted from the mixture, but consist of fairly light portions of earth and are briny; they are semi-solid and can be dissolved again in water. One is soda, good for cleaning off oil and soil, and the other is the substance
e   which interacts well with the sense-organ in the mouth — salt, proverbially† beloved of the gods.

56

The explanation for why some compounds of earth and water are the kinds of solids that are not soluble in water, but are liquefiable by fire, is somewhat as follows. Fire and air don't usually decompose lumps of earth, because fire and air have smaller particles than the gaps in the structure of earth; so, since they have plenty of room to move and don't have to use force, they leave the earth intact and undissolved. Water, however, causes earth to disintegrate and dissolve, because the particles of water are larger, and so they force an opening. 61a But water dissolves earth only when no pressure was involved when the earth was put together, while nothing but fire dissolves earth that was put together under pressure, because then only fire can make its way into the structure of the earth. The same goes for water too: only fire causes the disintegration of water that has been reduced by extreme pressure, but both fire and air disperse water which was put together under less pressure—air by acting on the gaps and fire by acting also on the triangles. However, air that was put together under pressure cannot be broken apart except into its elements, and if no pressure was involved only fire can dissolve it.

To return to bodies which are compounds of earth and water: as long as the gaps in the earth, even if they are being b forcibly compressed, are occupied by the compound's original water, any particles of water approaching from outside fail to gain entrance and leave it undissolved; all they can do is flow around the whole lump. However, when particles of fire penetrate the gaps in the water, fire acts on water† as water does on earth, and so it is only these particles of fire that cause the compound body to be dissolved and to melt. Among such compounds, those which contain less water than earth include all kinds of glass and every variety of liquefiable stone (to use that expression), and those which c contain more water than earth include all wax-like solids and those whose structure makes them usable as incense.

This will have to do as a presentation of the complexities involved in how the four substances interact and change into

one another thanks to their shapes. I should next try to explain how they came to have their qualities. A first point to note is that I'll be talking throughout about things that are perceptible, but we haven't yet discussed the formation of flesh, or of the properties of flesh, or of the mortal part of the soul. In actual fact, it's impossible to give an adequate account of
d these things without also discussing sensible qualities, and vice versa, but it's also more or less impossible to do both simultaneously. We must first assume the existence of one or the other of them, and then later check our assumptions. And so let's take for granted certain facts about the body and the soul, so that next, now that we've dealt with the four bodies, we can discuss their qualities.

First, then, let's see what we mean when we call fire 'hot'. We should do so by paying attention to fire's ability to open
e up and cut into our bodies. Almost all of us identify the experience as sharp, but all the factors that make fire intense and keen enough to pierce whatever it encounters — the thinness of its edges, the sharpness of its angles, the smallness of its constituent parts, and the speed of its motion — need
62a to be taken into account. We need to bear in mind the kind of shape it has, which is more perfectly designed than any other for opening up and lacerating our bodies, and so gives us not only the experience of what we call 'heat', but also its name.*

The opposite experience is obvious, but I don't want my speech to be deficient in any way. For, of course, when the larger particles of moisture outside the body enter the body, they try to push out the smaller ones, but are incapable of occupying the places formerly occupied by the smaller particles. What they do, then, is compress the moisture within our bodies and solidify it, changing its state from
b one of diversity and movement to one of rest, induced by uniformity and concentration. But anything that is forcibly compressed naturally resists by pushing itself out in the opposite direction, and the name given to this resistance and

this vibration is 'shivering' or 'ague', while both the experience as a whole and the cause of it are called 'cold'.

Something is 'hard' if our flesh yields to it, and 'soft' if it yields to our flesh; the terms are relative in this way. In order for something to yield, it has to rest on a small base, but the figure that consists of square faces is especially resistant, c because it rests on a very secure base. The more something attains maximum concentration and density, the more rigid it is.

The best way to gain the clearest possible understanding of 'heavy' and 'light' is to consider the nature of 'down' and 'up' at the same time. For the idea that the universe is essentially divided up into two opposite regions — a lower one, defined as that towards which everything that has some physical bulk moves, and an upper one, defined as that towards which anything moves only if forced to do so — is altogether incorrect.* The universe is spherical, and so all its d extremities, being equally far from the centre, must equally be extremities; and the centre is the same distance away from the extremities, and so should really be regarded as directly opposite all of them. Since this is how the world is, which of the regions mentioned could one classify as 'up' or 'down' without exposing oneself to justified criticism for improper use of words? It's wrong to say that the central region is, in itself, either 'down' or 'up': it's just in the centre.* And the periphery is not of course the centre, but neither can parts of it be distinguished on the grounds that one of them has more of a relation to the centre than any of the parts directly opposite it.

How can one use the terminology of opposition for something that is entirely undifferentiated? How could anyone think that was right? After all, if there were some solid body 63a equally poised in the centre of the universe, it couldn't possibly drift off to any extremity, because there'd be nothing to differentiate one extremity from another. No, if a man were to journey all around its surface, he would often find himself standing at his own antipodes and so he would call the same spot both 'down' and 'up'. The point is, to repeat what I said a moment ago, that the universe is spherical, and so it's impossible for an intelligent person to talk of one part of it as 'down' and another as 'up'.

But how did these terms arise? In which circumstances do they really apply—that is, as a result of which phenomena have we become accustomed to divide the entire universe in this way? In order to answer these questions, we need to make the following thought-experiment. Suppose the surface upon which a man was treading were that region of the universe which has been assigned principally to fire (which is to say, the region which contains the largest collection of the stuff towards which fire tends to move), and suppose he had the ability to remove portions of the fire, put them in scales, and weigh them. When he lifted the beam and drew the fire into the air (which would take force, because air is not fire), it's surely obvious that he would have to use less force for the lesser amount of fire than he would for the greater amount. For when a single effort is used to raise two things at once, the object that resists less is bound to follow the force more readily than the object that offers more resistance, and so the large amount is said to be 'heavy' and to tend 'downward', and the small object is said to be 'light' and to tend 'upward'.

This is exactly what we have to detect ourselves doing where we are now. When we stand on earth and weigh a couple of earthy things (sometimes even some earth itself), we draw them into the air, and this takes force, because air is not earth, and we're going against the natural tendency of earth. Both our objects try to rejoin their cognate earth, but the smaller follows the force we exert more readily and more quickly than the larger into the alien medium. And so we call the smaller one 'light', we describe the place we force them into as 'up', and we use 'heavy' and 'down' for the opposite property and place.*

It follows that these properties necessarily stand in different relations to each other, because of the opposition that obtains between the regions occupied by the majority of each of the four bodies. For when we compare what is 'light' in one region with what is 'light' in the opposite region, what is 'heavy' with what is 'heavy', and likewise for 'up' e and 'down', we'll find them all in the process of becoming, or actually being, opposite to one another, and at an angle to one another, and utterly different from one another. But the one and only point to bear in mind about them all is this: it is its tendency towards its cognate mass that makes the object with the tendency 'heavy' and makes the region into which it is moving 'down', and the other set of terms is reserved for when things move in the other way. This will do as an explanation of these properties.

As for smoothness and roughness, however, I'm sure that anyone could understand what causes them and could explain them to someone else. Something is rough if it combines hardness with unnevenness, and something is smooth if it is uniform and dense.   64a

We've been discussing experiences in which any and every part of the body may be involved, and there's a very important matter that still remains to be explained, namely the feelings of pleasure and pain that such experiences entail — that is, all those experiences which involve not only perception, gained by means of bodily parts, but also accompanying pains and pleasures. Now, in the case of every property, whether or not it is perceived, if we are to understand its causes we need to remember the distinction we b made earlier between mobility and inertness, because that will help us find answers for everything we intend to understand. For when any body that is naturally mobile is exposed to even a slight modification, its parts spread the change all around by passing it on to other parts, until they reach the intelligent part and inform it of the action of the modifying agent. Conversely, a stable body merely receives the change,

without creating any ripple effect; it doesn't move any of its
c   neighbours, and so, with the various parts failing to transmit
the effect to other parts, the original modification remains in
them, without moving on to the creature as a whole, and
leaves the body unaware of any modification. This is what
happens with all the predominantly earthy parts we have in
our bodies, such as bones and hair,* whereas the former case
applies especially to the organs of sight and hearing, because
they are characterized especially by the presence in them of
fire and air.

So here is how we should conceive of pleasure and pain.
d   Any modification that is unnatural (that is, forced) and sudden is painful, while any modification that restores our
normal condition and is sudden is pleasant; and any modification that is gentle and gradual is imperceptible, but the
opposite kind of modification is perceptible.

Unimpeded modifications, however, certainly cause sensation, but involve no pain or pleasure. This is what happens
with sight, for instance, which I described earlier as a substance that becomes attached to ours in the daytime. For
nothing that modifies sight, not even something sharp and
caustic, causes pain, nor again, when it recovers its original
e   state, is there any pleasure involved, despite the fact that its
perception of whatever modifies it, of everything it meets
and makes contact with, is as thorough and clear as it could
be. And the reason for the lack of pleasure and pain in sight
is that there's no force involved in its contraction and expan-
sion. Any body whose constituent parts are larger, however,
does not readily yield to the modifying agent, and so the
impulse is transmitted throughout the body, and pleasure or
pain occurs—pain when unnatural change is involved, pleas-
65a   ure when its normal state is restored.

Any body that undergoes a gradual departure from its
normal state, a gradual depletion, but an overwhelming and
sudden replenishment, has no perception of the depletion
but only of the replenishment, and therefore gives the most

intense pleasure to the mortal part of the soul, without any perception of pain. This is easy to see in the case of pleasant scents. On the other hand, any body that experiences a sudden modification, and regains its normal state only gradually and slowly, provides the mortal part of the soul with the completely opposite experience. This too can be readily observed, when the body is burnt and cut.* b

That will have to do as a description of those processes in which any and every part of the body may be involved, and as an account of what the agents of these processes are called. We must next turn to processes which happen in particular parts of us and try, if we can, to explain what they are and how they are caused by their agents. Now, our earlier discussion of sapidity was incomplete, and we should first explain, as best we can, those processes which are specific to the tongue. It looks as though they too, along with most others, happen as a result of certain things contracting and expanding, but they also seem to depend, more than any other kind of sensory experience, on roughness and smoothness. c

When particles of earth enter the mouth and encounter the moist, supple flesh in the region of the tiny veins which are the tongue's taste-samplers, so to speak, and run from the tongue to the heart, the particles are dissolved. If in the process of dissolution they make the veins more compact and dry, then those particles that are quite rough taste astringent, and those that are less rough taste harsh. Some solutions, however, rinse the veins and scrub the whole tongue: those that do so to excess and even inflict enough damage to decompose a layer of the tongue (this is the action of soda, for instance) are called 'bitter', while those that are weaker than soda and whose scrubbing action is less severe are called 'salty'; they lack the harshness of bitter things and produce quite an agreeable sensation. d e

On the other hand, when the particles combine with the warmth of the mouth and have the edge taken off their roughness by it, and then are made as fiery as the source of the heat and in their turn heat it up, they become light enough to rise up towards the sense-organs in the head, and on the way they cut into whatever they encounter. All the particles that do this are called 'spicy'.

And when these same particles† have been lightened by decomposition and enter the narrow veins, those of them that are proportionate both with the earthy particles lying inside the veins and with those that contain a portion of air stir them into random movement around one another. In their random movement the particles of earth and air are dislodged and change places, and thus they create pockets that are wrapped around the particles that are entering from outside. So when a pocket of moisture (earthy or pure, as the case may be) is wrapped around air, moist containers of air, hollow spherical bits of water, are created. Those that consist of pure moisture surround their contents as transparent 'bubbles', as they are called, while the agitation and rising of those that consist of earthy moisture are called 'effervescence' and 'fermentation'. And what causes all these processes is called 'acid'.

The opposite explanation is needed for the quality that has precisely the opposite description to the one just given for acidity. When the composition of the particles that enter, once they are within their liquid surroundings, approximates to the condition of the tongue, it smears a smooth surface over the rough bits, tightens up those bits which have become unnaturally diffuse and relaxes those which are unnaturally tight, and restores everything as much as possible to its normal state. Everyone finds such a remedy for abnormal tightness and looseness pleasant and enjoyable, and it is called 'sweet'.

That's enough on that topic, and now for the nostrils and what they do. There are no specific figures involved, because every scent is a 'half-breed': no single figure, as it turns out, has the proportions that would give it a scent. Our scent-veins are too narrow for earth and water, and too broad for fire

and air,* which means that no one has ever smelled any of
them. Scents occur when things are damp or decomposing
or dissolving or giving off smoke or vapour. That is, they
occur in an intermediate stage, when water is changing into e
air, and air into water, and all scents are vapour or mist—
mist being what effects the transition from air to water and
vapour the transition from water to air. It follows that all
scents are more subtle than water and more gross than air.
The best opportunity for understanding scents is when your
nose is blocked and you have to make an effort to breathe in.
On such occasions, no scent filters through; the breath is
drawn in by itself, without any scent. And so† all the various 67a
scents are nameless, because there aren't a specific number
of types of scent nor are they straightforward. But let's here
draw the only obvious distinction there is, between pleasant
and unpleasant scents, and let's say that unpleasant scents
roughen and assault the whole of the trunk between the head
and the navel, and that pleasant scents mollify the trunk and
restore it, with a feeling of contentment, to its normal
state.

The third part of us that is involved in sense-perception
is the organ of hearing, and we must next investigate and b
explain its experiences. Broadly speaking, let's take sound to
be a blow delivered by air, through the ear, on the brain and
the blood, and transmitted to the soul; and let's say that
hearing is the movement, beginning at the head and ending
in the region of the liver, caused by the impulse. When this
movement is rapid the pitch of the sound is high, and the
slower the movement the lower the pitch; a steady movement produces a uniform, smooth sound, and the opposite
kind of movement produces a harsh sound; and loud or soft
sounds are produced respectively by great and small move- c
ments.* As for harmonious sounds, we must leave them for
a later stage of the discussion.*

The fourth and final* kind of perception contains so many
varieties that we must divide it up. We call them all 'colours',

and each of them is a flame that flows from individual bodies and whose particles, being compatible with the organ of sight, produce vision. I've already explained how sight occurs,* but no more than that, and so now it makes excellent sense for us to cover colours. The following account would seem to be reasonable. The particles that travel from external objects and encounter the visual ray are of various sizes—some smaller, some larger, and some the same size as the particles of the visual ray itself. Those that are the same size are imperceptible—in fact, they are precisely those things that we call 'transparent'. Those that are larger contract the visual ray, while the smaller ones expand it, and so these larger and smaller particles are close kin to the hot and cold particles that act on flesh, and to the astringent particles and also those heating ones we called 'spicy' that act on the tongue. The particles we call 'black' and 'white', then, are the same as those qualities, but in a different category, and they appear different from each other for the reasons given. And so we should use the names accordingly: 'white' is what expands the visual ray, and 'black' is the opposite.*

When a different kind of fire, with a faster movement, strikes the visual ray and expands it all the way up to the eyes, it forces apart and decomposes the actual openings in the eyes, and expresses from them a flood of mixed fire and water, which we call 'weeping'. Since this fast-moving force is itself fire, when it meets fire from the opposite direction—the one leaping out from the eyes like a flash of lightning, and the other forcing its way in and being extinguished in the moisture—the ensuing turmoil creates all sorts of colours, and we call the experience 'dazzling', and what causes it 'bright' and 'shiny'.*

There is also a kind of fire which is intermediate between these last two. It reaches the moisture of the eyes and blends with it, but it doesn't dazzle; and to the gleam of the fire through the moisture with which it is mixed, which produces the colour of blood, we give the name 'red'. When bright is mixed with red and white, the result is orange-yellow,* but it would be foolish to try to state the precise proportions of the mixture, even if they were knowable, because one couldn't, with any degree of plausibility, come up with either a proof or a likely account of them.

Red mixed with black and white makes magenta, and vio- c let is the result when this mixture is further burnt and more black is mixed in. The mixture of orange-yellow and grey produces yellow ochre, while grey is a blend of black and white. Yellow comes from the mixture of white and orange-yellow. The combination of bright and white, steeped in deep black, produces dark blue; dark blue mixed with white makes light blue; and yellow ochre blended with black makes green.

As for the rest, it should be more or less clear from these d examples what mixtures we must say they are equivalent to, if we're to preserve our likely story. But if one were to investigate these matters by actually putting them to the test, he would be displaying ignorance of the difference between human beings and gods. It is a divine matter to possess sufficient knowledge, and at the same time sufficient competence, to mix a plurality into a oneness, and conversely to break a oneness up into a plurality; there is not now nor will there ever be any human being who is up to either of these tasks.

All this was the effect of necessity on our four substances, e and this was the condition in which the craftsman-god, who made all that is perfect and best in this world of becoming, found them, at the time when he turned to fathering the self-sufficient, perfect god.* To serve him in his work, he made use of causes and their necessary effects, but he took personal responsibility for fashioning the goodness in all created things. And that is why we should distinguish two kinds of cause, the necessary and the divine, and should search in everything for the divine cause, if we are to attain 69a as blessed a life as our nature permits. But our concern with divine causes should lead us not to ignore necessary causes either, because it is impossible to discern the divine causes that interest us on their own, apart from necessary ones,* or to understand them, or in fact to have anything to do with them.

Now that the two kinds of cause, sifted and sorted like a builder's timbers, lie ready for our use, as the materials from which we're to stitch together the rest of our account,* let's go back to the beginning for a moment and swiftly make our way up to the point from where we embarked on the journey that brought us here. Let's try at last to bring our story to a close and to round it off in a way that fits in with what we've already said.

b

To repeat, then, one of my original assertions, the god found the four bodies we've been talking about in a chaotic state and made each of them compatible with itself and with the others, in as many ways and respects as they could be proportionate and compatible.* For at that time none of them had its characteristics, except by chance,* and in fact none of them had the slightest right to be called by the names that are now used of it and the others — 'fire', 'water', and so on. So he first imposed order on them all, and then he created this universe of ours out of them, as a single living being containing within itself all living beings, both mortal and immortal. He himself was the craftsman and creator of the divine beings, and he gave his own offspring the job of creating mortal beings. In imitation of their father, once they had received from him the immortal seed of soul, they proceeded to fashion a mortal body in which to enclose it, and to assign the whole body to be its vehicle.

c

They also housed within the body another type of soul, a mortal kind, which is liable to terrible, but inevitable, experiences. Chief among these is pleasure, evil's most potent lure;* then pain, fugitive from good; and then those mindless advisers confidence and fear, and obdurate passion, and gullible hope. Into the mix they added unreasoning sensation

d

68

and ever-adventurous desire, and so, constrained by necessity,* they constructed the mortal soul. Piety kept them from polluting the divine soul with these things, short of the direst emergency, and so they lodged the mortal soul in separate quarters, elsewhere in the body; and they built an e isthmus to distinguish the region of the head from that of the chest, by placing the neck between them, to keep them apart. So they bound the mortal soul within the chest—the thorax, as it is called.

Since there are better and worse parts of the mortal soul, they also created a partition within the thoracic chamber (much as the women's quarters are separated from the 70a men's quarters in a house) by setting the diaphragm as a barrier between them.* They housed the competitive part of the soul, the part that is characterized by courage and passion, closer to the head, between the diaphragm and the neck, so that it would be within hearing of reason and would share with it the task of forcibly restraining the appetitive part whenever it completely refused to obey the dictates of reason issuing from the acropolis,* unless forced to do so. So they established the heart there in the guardhouse. The reason they did so is that the heart is the node of the veins and b the source of the blood that circulates vigorously throughout the body.* So suppose reason reports that the body is being injured by something from outside, or possibly even by an internal appetite: on receiving the message, passion flares up and transmits its inducements and threats through all the body's alleyways, so that every sentient part of the body becomes aware of them. And then all the parts become perfectly submissive and obedient, and so allow the best part to be the ruler in their midst.

Now, when frightening events are anticipated and when c passion is being stirred, the heart leaps, but the gods knew in advance that it was fire that was going to be responsible whenever any part of the body that is subject to passion swells like this, and so, as a remedy, they had implanted the

lung in the body. For the lung is not only soft and bloodless, but it also has pores drilled inside it, like a sponge, and so, as the recipient of breath and drink, it cools the heart down
d   and provides relief and comfort from the heat.* This is why they bored the windpipe through to the lung, and why they wrapped the lung around the heart like a kind of cushion, so that when passion is most active there, the heart has something soft and cooling to leap against. For the calmer the heart is, the more it can join passion in serving reason.

They lodged the appetitive part of the soul—the part that wants food, drink, and everything the nature of the
e   body makes it feel it lacks—between the diaphragm and its boundary at the navel, building in this general area a kind of trough for the nourishment of the body. They tethered it there as if it were a wild animal, but one they were bound to look after, once it had been attached, if human beings were ever to exist. And the reason they stationed it there was to ensure that it was kept so busy feeding at the trough, and lived so far away from the deliberating part, that it would
71a raise as little disturbance and din as possible, and so would allow the sovereign part to deliberate in peace about what was best for them all, collectively and individually.*

The gods knew that this part of the soul would never understand reason, and they knew that even if it did somehow have some dim awareness of any of them, it was not in its nature to pay attention to anything reasoned they said. They knew that it would much more readily be bewitched by images and phantasms,* whether they appeared at night or in the daytime. But the gods had planned for exactly this eventuality, and had
b   formed the liver and put it in the place where this part of the soul lived. They made the liver dense, smooth, bright, and sweet (but with some bitterness), so that it could act as a mirror for thoughts stemming from intellect, just as a mirror receives impressions and gives back images to look at.*

And so these thoughts can frighten this part of the soul, when they come down hard on it and threaten it, by exploiting

something of the liver's innate bitterness. By rapidly suffus-
ing the entire surface of the liver with gall, the image they
cast on it is one of bilious colours; they make the liver all
compressed, wrinkled, and uneven, and induce pain and c
nausea by warping and shrinking a lobe, or by blocking up
and closing cavities and portals. Alternatively, when some
breath of mildness wafts down from the thoughts and paints
the opposite kind of images on the surface of the liver, they
afford a respite from bitterness by refusing to stir up or
involve themselves with something alien to them. Instead,
by exploiting the sweetness inherent throughout the liver
for their own purposes,† they straighten all its parts until
they are free of distortions, wrinkles, and blockages, and d
they make the part of the soul that has been housed in the
same part of the body as the liver gracious and cheerful, so
that at night it can indulge in the modest entertainment of
divination by dreams, which it has to rely on since it lacks
the ability to reason and to apply intelligence. For the gods
who created us bore in mind that their father had ordered
them to make the human race as good as possible, and so
they organized even our base part so that it might have some
kind of contact with truth,* and established the seat of div- e
ination in it.

There's good evidence that divination was a gift from the
gods to compensate for human stupidity. For true, inspired
divination is out of the question for anyone who has his wits
about him; sleep or illness has to have fettered and weakened
his intellect, or he has to be possessed, in an altered state of
consciousness. However, he needs to be in command of his
intelligence not only to recall and reflect upon the messages
conveyed to him by divination or possession, whether he was
asleep or awake at the time, but also to subject to rational
analysis all the visions that appear to him, and to decide in 72a
what sense and for whom they signify some future, past, or
present trouble or benefit.* But it's not the job of someone
who has been out of his mind and remains so to assess by

himself the visions and the voices; no, it's an old, true saying that only a man of sound mind possesses the ability to do what pertains to himself, and to know himself.* That's why

b it's usual for interpreters to be appointed to assess the omens of those who are possessed. These interpreters are occasionally called 'diviners', but that just displays utter ignorance of the fact that they're really translators of riddling sayings and seeings, and should properly be thought of not as diviners, but as interpreters of omens.

Divination, then, is the reason why the liver is as it is and where it is—the location we mentioned. It should also be said that while a creature is still alive the signs to be found on its liver are fairly clear, but once the creature has been deprived of life the liver becomes opaque and its omens too

c faint to give any clear indications of meaning.* Moreover, the internal organ which lies just to the left of the liver was designed to serve it and was put there to do so: like a cloth which is kept beside a mirror so as to be always available and ready, it keeps the liver always bright and clean. Whenever the surface of the liver gains some impurities, as a result of physical ill-health, the spleen with its porousness—its pitted and bloodless fabric—cleans them all up.* Hence, as it

d absorbs the matter it has cleaned off the liver, it swells up and festers; but then, once the body has been purged, the swelling goes down and it reduces back to its normal size.

So much for the extent of the mortal and immortal parts of the soul, and where, in what company, and why they were given separate residences. Is our account true? We could be certain if and only if it met with the gods' endorsement. But that it is at least likely I think we can safely affirm, not only now, but even after we've examined the issues further. So let it stand.

e The same principle should guide us as we set about the next topic, which was the formation of the rest of the body.* It would be best to attribute its construction to some such reasoning as follows. The gods who formed the human race knew that we would lack self-control over food and drink, that our greed would make us consume far more of them than was either moderate or necessary. They wanted to ensure that the human species was not rapidly killed off by diseases and did not come to an end straight away, without having attained 73a its proper end. As a result of this prescience, then, they put the so-called 'abdomen' in place as a receptacle to hold excess food and drink, and they looped the intestines to and fro to stop food passing so quickly through us that before very long the body would necessarily need more, and so generate a cycle of insatiability. For gluttony would prevent any of us from being interested in philosophy and culture, as a result of being incapable of attending to the most divine part of us.

As for bones, flesh, and everything of that sort, this is b what happened. All of them depend for their existence on the formation of the marrow, because as long as the soul is bound to the body, the bonds of life, the roots of human-kind, are set fast in the marrow.* The marrow itself was created out of different constituents. What the god did was set to one side, away from all others of their kinds, those of the primary triangles which were rectilinear and smooth enough to be capable of producing perfectly precise versions of fire, water, air, and earth, which he then blended together in due proportion to come up with a seed-bank for the entire c human race—which is to say that he used them as the con-stituents of the marrow. And then he planted the different kinds of soul firmly in the marrow.

He set about dividing the marrow into the same number and variety of shapes as the number and particular varieties of soul that it was going to hold. (This was actually the very first stage of the process of assigning parts of the soul to different locations.) That is, he formed into a perfect sphere the field, so to speak, that was to be sown with the divine kind of seed, and he called this portion of the marrow the 'brain', because in a complete creature the container for this d portion of marrow would be the 'head'.* But the portion of the marrow that was to confine the remaining kind of soul, the mortal kind, he divided into cylindrical shapes, to all of which he gave the name 'marrow'. He used this cylindrical marrow, like an anchor, as a foundation for the bonds of the whole soul, and finally he set about making the human body to surround this marrow, with the first of his constructions being a protective covering for it, made out of bone.*

e   This was his recipe for bone. He sieved all the impurities and roughness out of earth, kneaded and moistened it with marrow, put the mixture into fire, and dipped it in water. He then put it back into fire and then into water again, and did this swapping from one to the other often enough for it to become indissoluble by both of them. Drawing on this mixture, he fashioned from it a sphere in which to enclose

74a   the brain, but left a narrow opening; and then he used more of the mixture to make the vertebrae to enclose the marrow for the neck and the back, and lined the vertebrae up one under another, like hinges,* starting at the head and continuing through the entire trunk. And so he kept the full quota of seed penned safe inside a stony enclosure, into which he introduced joints, using in their case the quality of difference that had been inserted between them, like a mean, to ensure movement and flexibility.

b   Bone, however, was still too brittle and inflexible for the god's liking, and he also thought that it wouldn't take long for exposure to extreme heat and then subsequent cold to mortify the bone and so destroy the seed inside. So he created ligaments and flesh. He used the ligaments to link all the limbs, and to allow the body to bend and straighten around its pivots as the ligaments tightened and relaxed. And he made flesh as a defence against the burning heat of summer and a shield against winter's cold, and also to protect the

c   body against accidents by softly and gently yielding to solid matter, much as felted materials do. He also made it contain warm moisture, so that in the heat of summer the moisture of its sweat† would enable it to cool the whole surface of the body from its own resources, and conversely, in winter, it would have this fire within itself to provide at least some defence against the assault and encroachment of the freezing cold from outside.

With these plans in mind, the god who shaped us mixed water, fire, and earth well together, stirred in a leaven of acidity and salt, and so made flesh, sappy and soft. And he made d ligaments from a blend of bone and unleavened flesh, which produced a single substance intermediate between the two of them, to which he applied an orange-yellow colour. This is why ligaments have a more rigid and cohesive texture than flesh, and are softer and moister than bones. The god wrapped these ligaments around the bones with their marrow, and used them to join the bones to one another; and then over the whole frame he draped the canopy of flesh.

He used very little flesh, however, to enclose those bones e that have the most soul, while he used a lot of especially thick flesh for those that contain very little soul. He even made a little flesh for the points where bones make contact with one another, where there was no rational requirement for there to be any; but he didn't want the joints to seize up and make bodies too stiff for ease of movement. He also didn't want sensitivity to be impeded and the mind made less retentive and more obtuse in intellectual matters by thick layers of flesh packed densely together. So that is why all the parts of the body that lack joints (such as the thighs, lower legs, and 75a waist, and the bones of the upper arms and forearms)—that is, all the bones that have so little soul within their marrow that they lack intelligence—were well supplied with flesh. And the reason why all the intelligent parts have less flesh is invariably as stated—with the exception, of course, of any fleshy part that was made just as an organ of sense, such as the tongue. For any part whose creation and development are governed by necessity cannot possibly have dense bone and a b lot of flesh at the same time as acute sensitivity.

After all, if these two properties were prepared to coincide in a single structure, the head would have been the prime candidate for possessing them, and human beings, with heads on their shoulders strengthened by flesh and ligaments, would live twice as long, or even more, and would have gained healthier and less painful lives than now. But as things are, the craftsmen-gods who made us weighed up whether they should create a worse but longer-lived race, or a better one that didn't live as long, and decided that the shorter life was in every conceivable respect better than the longer one. And so they covered the top of our head with just a thin layer of bone, though not with flesh (or ligaments, because it doesn't have joints). For all these reasons, then, every man's head is more vulnerable than the body to which it is attached, but more sensitive and intelligent.* And this was also why the god provided only the edge of the head with ligaments—the ones he wound around the neck and, with the help of the principle of identity, glued in place. He joined the ends of the jaw-bones to these ligaments behind the face, and he distributed the rest of the ligaments here and there throughout the body, connecting joint to joint.

The gods responsible for such things equipped the mouth with its orderly array of teeth, tongue, and lips, and gave them their present arrangement, because this was both necessary and in our best interests. They were guided by necessity in making the mouth an entrance, but by what is best for us in making it an exit. For everything that enters the body as nourishment is necessary, while no stream could be more beautiful or better than the stream of words that flows out of us in the service of intelligence.

The seasonal excesses of either heat or cold meant that they couldn't allow the head to be nothing but bare bone, but at the same time they couldn't let it be so screened by a mass of flesh that it became obtuse and insensitive. So a superfluous piece of crust—or 'skin', as we now call it—was removed from the body's flesh, and, thanks to the moisture of the brain,

76

shrank and spread until it clothed the entire circumference of the head. The moisture seeped up through the sutures, watered it, and sealed it at the crown of the head, as if it were tying a knot. And the fact that there are various kinds of suture is due to the circular motions and to food: the more these two forces conflict with each other, the more sutures there are, and the less they do so, the fewer the sutures.

The divine part of the soul now set about pricking the skin b of the head with fire all over and on every side, until the skin had been punctured enough for the moisture to begin to pass outside through it. All that was purely wet and purely warm left, while that which was a compound, of the same constituents as the skin, was pulled up by the motion and elongated outside, each bit of it being just as fine as its puncture-hole. This took so long, however, that the surrounding air outside had time to push it back inside again under the skin, where it curled around and took root. These were the c processes, then, that provided the skin with hair. Hair is a wiry form of the same ingredients as the skin, though harder and denser, because it became compressed as it cooled down. (It was during the process of detachment from the skin that each hair cooled down and became compressed.) So this was how the creator god matted our heads with hair: hair was the result of the processes I've mentioned, and in making use of them the god's thinking was that this, rather than flesh, was the appropriate covering to protect the brain's chamber, since it was light, provided adequate shelter and protection d in all seasons, and didn't impede and obstruct the brain's sensitivity at all.

Then there's the mixture formed at the fingers by the intertwining of ligament, skin, and bone, a single compound made up of all three of them, which dries to become hard skin. These three were the contributory causes of its formation, but responsibility for its creation really lay with the ability to think about the future.* For our creators were aware that among the future incarnations of men would be not just women, but all e

77

the various animal species, and they knew that many of these creatures would need nails for many practical purposes, and so they created rudimentary nails as soon as human beings came into existence. So much for the reasoning and thinking that led the gods to cause skin, hair, and nails to grow at the extremities of the body.

77a Once the mortal creature had been equipped with its full complement of parts and limbs ... well, its circumstances were such that it necessarily spent its time exposed to fire and air, and they were melting and eroding it away. The gods therefore came up with a scheme to help it. They engendered a compound with a constitution that was naturally akin to the human constitution, but which was so different in appearance and awareness that it was in fact a different living being. These living beings are now cultivated trees, plants, and seeds, which have been reclaimed by agriculture for our use from their original wild state, before they were ever cultivated.

b I call them 'living beings' because there can be nothing wrong or incorrect in calling everything that is characterized by life a 'living being', but the kind of living being that we're talking about at the moment possesses only the third kind of soul, the one we located between the diaphragm and the navel. This kind of soul knows nothing of belief, reasoning, and intelligence, but is aware only of the pleasures and pains that accompany its appetites. Passivity is its constant and only mode of existence; it was not created with the gift of a natural capacity for self-consciousness or for rational thought about any aspect of itself (which are properties only of that c which spins within itself and around its own centre, repelling external impulses while drawing on its own power of movement). And so, although it is certainly alive and counts as a living being, it is fixed and rooted in one place, without the ability to move itself.*

Once the gods, who are as superior to us as we are inferior to them, had engendered all these species to nourish us, they bored pipes through the human body, like those irrigation

channels you find in orchards, so that the body might be
watered, so to speak, by onrushing streams. The body's channels, however, were hidden under the junction of skin and d
flesh. They first cut two veins for the back, which, since the
left and right sides of the body match, they ran down either
side of the spine, with the life-giving marrow between them
to ensure that it flourished. Thanks to its downhill course, the
downpour could flow easily enough to pass from there evenly
through its channels to all the other parts of the body.* They
next split these veins at the head, plaited them together, and e
sent them over to opposite sides, crossing the veins from the
right side of the body to the left, and those from the left to the
right, to help the skin join the head to the body (given that
there were no ligaments surrounding the head at its crown and
holding it in place), and at the same time to make sure that the
whole body might be fully aware of sense-impressions from
both sides.

After that, they constructed the irrigation system. We'll
find it easier to see how it works if we can first agree that 78a
everything that consists of smaller particles is impermeable
by larger particles, while anything that is made up of larger
particles is permeable by smaller particles.* This explains
why fire, which has the smallest constituent parts, cannot
be blocked by anything; it passes through water, earth, air,
and anything that consists of them. The same principle will
help us to understand what goes on with our abdomens.
When food and drink fall into the abdomen, it keeps them
in, but it can't keep in fire and the air we breathe, because b
they consist of smaller particles than the particles of the
abdomen itself. And so, for channelling stuff from the abdomen to the veins, the god made use of air and fire, which he
wove into an object that looked rather like a fish-trap.*
It had a pair of tubes at the entrance, for one of which he
wove a further fork; and from the tubes he ran cords, so to
speak, which coiled throughout the whole structure from
one end to the other. All these inner parts of the 'basket' he c

79

made out of fire, while the tubes and the container were made from air.

He then took this artefact and wrapped it around the living being he had formed, somewhat as follows. He inserted the tube system by way of the mouth, letting one of the two tubes fall down the windpipe and into the lung, while the other descended alongside the windpipe into the abdomen.* It was the one that went into the lung that he split, and he sent a branch each in tandem along the channels of the nose, so that if the other tube, the one at the mouth, ever failed to function, this one would replenish all its streams too, as well as its own.

d He enveloped the entire trunk of the human body within the main container, and he initiated an alternating sequence whereby the whole thing first flowed gently together and into the tubes (gently, because the tubes are made from air) and back out of the tubes again; and at the same time the artefact sank inside through the body (which was possible because of the body's open texture) and then out again. Since rays of fire were bound fast inside the container, they e followed the motion of the air in either direction. This process never ends as long as the mortal creature subsists and is, of course, the one the inventor of names called 'breathing in and out'.

The sole reason for the creation of the artefact, the sole purpose of this whole process, is so that the human body may be nourished and stay alive, by being watered and refreshed. For as the air goes in and out, it is accompanied by the fire inside it, which is attached to it. The fire surges to and fro and enters the body by means of the abdomen, where it finds 79a food and drink. It decomposes them, of course, and breaks them down into small pieces, which it then conducts through the channels on its route. Just as water flows from spring to irrigation channels, so fire draws the pieces to the veins and creates streams that flow through the veins as if the body were a conduit.

Let's take another look at the process of breathing, to see how it has come to be as it is now. Given that there's no void to be entered by any of the moving bodies, it obviously follows b that, when our breath moves outside and away from us, it doesn't enter a void, but pushes whatever is adjacent to it out of its place. Each body that is pushed in this way dislodges its neighbour, and so on, until, as a result of this automatic process, they are all necessarily driven around, following the breath, to the place originally occupied by the breath before it left, which they enter and fill up again. This all takes place instantaneously, as when a wheel goes around, because there's c no void. So the chest and the lung no sooner expel some air than they are refilled by the air around the body, which is being driven around and sinks inside through our porous flesh.* And conversely, when the air goes the other way and leaves through the body, it propels the breath around and in through the openings at the mouth and nostrils.

We should assume that the whole process first started as follows. In every living being, the hottest internal parts are d those that are close to the blood and the veins; it's as if we have our own innate fire-spring. In fact, this is the thing that, in our image of the fish-trap, we said was woven out of fire and ran through the inside of the 'basket' (while all the outside parts were made of air). Now, it's indisputable that what is hot naturally tries to join up with the matter to which it is naturally akin, and so it tends out of the body towards its own region. There are two passages through which it can leave, either via the body or via the mouth and the nostrils, and e whenever it rushes towards one of these openings, it propels air around towards the other. The air that was subject to this propelling-around is heated by its exposure to the internal fire, and cools down once it is outside the body. Given this change in temperature, and the fact that bits of air are now being heated at one or other of the openings, the heated stuff becomes more inclined to return by the route it came in by, since it tends towards what it is naturally akin to, and so it propels whatever is at the other of the two openings around towards the first one. By constantly receiving and returning the same impulse, then, air creates a cyclical churning back and forth, and the result is breathing in and out.

80a This is also where we need to look if we're to explain certain other phenomena too, such as the cupping-glasses that doctors use,* and swallowing, and the way things that are thrown keep moving after their release through the air or on the ground. Then there are also all those sounds we hear as high or low in pitch because their speed is fast or slow. Sometimes their motion makes them sound discordant because of the unevenness of the movement they generate in us. At other times, however, they sound sweet because of the uniformity of the movement in us: slower sounds catch up with the movements generated by faster sounds that had gone before, just as the impulses are dying away and have reached a speed similar to that which the new arrivals impart; this means that, when they catch up, the slower sounds don't throw the movements into turmoil with the new impulse they impose on them, but initiate an extra, slower motion, which fits in with the motion of the faster one which is coming to an end, and so create a single experience which is a blend of high and low pitch.* This, a source of mere pleasure to the mindless, delights the intelligent as a representation of divine harmony in mortal movements.

Then there are also all the different ways that water flows, and the descent of a thunderbolt, and the amazing way that amber and magnetite 'attract' things. In reality, as anyone conducting a proper investigation would see, there's no attraction involved in any of these cases and there's no void involved either;* these things propel parts of themselves around against other parts, and their movement is always due to the tendency of the parts to move from wherever they are towards their own proper site as they expand and contract. In short, he would see that all these 'miracles' are due to the ways in which things are entwined with one another.

Breathing, which is what we started out to investigate, is d just another example of the same principles and processes, as I've already shown. The fire chops up the foodstuffs and, as it rocks back and forth inside us along with the breath, it fills the veins from the abdomen; its surge draws the chopped-up pieces from there into the veins. This is how the streams of nourishment keep flowing throughout the bodies of all living creatures. Now, the streams consist of freshly cut fragments of food from things which are naturally akin to the human constitution (cereals, fruit, and greens, planted by the god for this specific purpose, to be our food) e and the mingling of all these foodstuffs means that the streams take on a wide variety of different hues, but the predominant one in their case is red, the colour that is produced by fire as it cuts through and stains a moist environment. This, as we explained earlier,* is why what flows through the body, which we call 'blood', looks as it does. It is food for the flesh and the entire body, and by irrigating each part of the body, it enables it thoroughly to replenish 81a anything that is being depleted.

Both replenishment and wasting occur in conformity with the general principle of movement in the whole universe— that everything moves towards that with which it has natural affinity. It's not just that the things around us are constantly wearing our bodies down and scattering us in various directions by sending bits off towards the bulk of the stuff to which they are naturally akin. It's also that the contents of our blood, which have been chopped up inside us and have become surrounded by the 'universe' that any living crea- b ture constitutes for them, necessarily imitate this universal movement.* In other words, it is by moving towards what is cognate with it that each of the pieces inside us replenishes any part which stands in need of replenishment at that time.*

Wasting happens, then, whenever more is leaving a creature's body than is coming in on the bloodstream, and growth is the opposite. When the structure of any creature is new, with the elementary triangles of the four bodies still fresh from the stocks, so to speak, the triangles are securely connected to one another, and the composition of the whole

c structure is supple, because it is newly made from marrow and fed on milk. Now, the triangles that enter the creature from outside (the triangles from which its food and drink are made) are older and weaker than the creature's own triangles, and so, once inside, they're overpowered and cut up by the fresh triangles; and this is what causes the creature to grow, since it is being nourished by plenty of assimilable substances. With each passing year, however, many such battles are fought by a creature's inner triangles against many such

d adversaries, and as a result the triangles' roots start to lose their grip—which is to say that they lose the ability to cut up incoming food into assimilable structures, and instead they themselves are easily broken up by the invaders from outside. When this happens, all creatures waste away and experience what we call 'old age'.

Eventually, the marrow's triangles, for all their tight connection, can no longer hold out against the stress and they come apart. In so doing, they loosen the bonds of the soul too and, since it has been freed under natural circumstances, it

e flies joyfully away.* For everything that is contrary to a thing's nature causes it pain, while everything that corresponds to its nature is pleasant. So, by the same principle, death that is caused by illness and wounds is painful and unnatural, while there's no death less troublesome than the one which accompanies old age on its journey to a natural end. Such a death comes with more pleasure than distress.

I'm sure everyone is perfectly well aware of the causes of

82a sickness. Since the components of a creature's body are four— earth, fire, water, and air—disorders and diseases occur as a result of abnormal predominance and deficiency among them,* and when one of them moves from its proper location to that of one of the others, and when any part of the body

84

acquires a form of fire or one of the other substances (all of which come in a plurality of forms) that is inappropriate for it, and so on and so forth. The reason is that each of these unnatural situations and shifts makes things change from cold to hot, from dry to wet, from heavy to light, and so on b for all such qualitative changes. In fact, it is only, I dare say, the approach or departure of something that is identical with a given part of the body, corresponding to it in all aspects and qualities, that leaves it unchanged, sound and intact, while the departure or approach of something that is out of tune, something that fails to meet these conditions, is going to produce countless changes and no end of illness and decay.

Now, there are of course also structures which are bound to be second in order of construction, and so anyone want- c ing to understand disease has to take a second look at it. Marrow, bone, flesh, and ligament are all compounds of the primary structures, and so is blood (though in a different way). Even though most diseases happen in the way I've already said, the worst and most severe diseases occur when the processes that lead to the formation of these secondary structures reverse, and they start to decay.

What I mean is this. In the normal course of events, flesh and ligament are made out of blood—ligament from its fibres (with which it is cognate), and flesh from thickened blood (the d part of it that thickens when the fibres are removed). Then from ligaments and flesh there is secreted something sticky and oily which not only glues the flesh to the bones, but also actually feeds the bone that surrounds the marrow and causes it to grow. Some of this substance filters through the bones—though, because of the density of the bones, only those triangles that are so pure as to be exceptionally smooth and oily get through—and once inside it trickles and drips from the bones, and so irrigates the marrow.

When the process happens like this, the result is generally e health, but when it's reversed, the outcome is invariably disease. For whenever decomposing flesh sends its putrefied matter back into the veins, the blood, that courses copiously and with its varied constituents in the veins along with the air we breathe, becomes mottled with various hues, qualified by a complex mixture of bitterness, acidity, and saltiness, and contaminated by all kinds of bile, serum, and phlegm. The main havoc all these curdled and spoiled substances wreak is on the blood, which loses its ability to nourish the body, as it carries these agents of destruction through the veins all around the body, without keeping any more to the natural order of circulation. And these substances are not only inimical to one another (since none of them does any of the others any good), but they are also hostile to any part of the body that has managed to stay intact and stand firm, and they set about destroying and decomposing it.

83a

When it is very old flesh that decomposes, it resists assuagement and gains a darker hue (as a result of the prolonged burning it has undergone), and because it has been thoroughly corroded, in its bitterness it launches a severe attack on every part of the body that remains undamaged. Sometimes its bitterness becomes more attenuated than usual, and then the dark-hued matter gains an acid quality instead; at other times the bitter stuff gains a reddish hue, from having been steeped in blood, and the combination of this and the dark hue gives it a green colour. And when it is new flesh that is decomposed by the fire of the inflammation, the mixture includes an orange-yellow colour along with bitterness. Whatever its appearance, it has the same name— 'bile'—which was given to it either by some healers, or by someone capable of discerning within a plurality of things with dissimilar appearances a single generic form that deserves a single name. And each of the other things that we take to be a kind of bile has gained its own specific definition, depending on its colour.*

b

c

There are two kinds of serum, a harmless kind when it is a watery discharge of blood, and an aggressive kind when it derives from black, acidic bile and gains a salty quality by being heated. This latter kind is called 'acid phlegm'. Then there's the stuff that's produced along with air by the decomposition of new, supple flesh. When this stuff is inflated by d air and the whole package is enclosed within moisture, bubbles form, each of which is too small to be seen, but collectively they have enough bulk to be visible, in which case they appear as white in colour because of the froth that forms. The name we give to the totality of the matter deriving from the putrefaction of supple flesh and the air that is involved with it is 'white phlegm'. Moreover, the watery discharge of newly formed phlegm is what we call 'sweat', 'tears', and so on — whatever other similar substances there might be that e are routinely purged from the body.

All these substances, then, become agents of disease when blood is not enriched, as is normal, by food and drink, but instead is augmented by pernicious substances, contrary to the normal course of events. Now, provided that the foundations that secure any part of our flesh that is being decomposed by disease remain secure, the effect of the affliction is halved, because the flesh can still easily recover. However, when the 84a glue that binds flesh to bone is so diseased that it becomes detached simultaneously from flesh, bone, and ligament† — when bone is no longer being fed, and flesh and bone become disconnected, because as a result of an unhealthy way of life the glue has dried up and become harsh and salty instead of oily, smooth, and sticky — then all the stuff that this is happening to crumbles back inside the flesh and the ligaments as it becomes separated from the bone, and at the same time the flesh parts from its roots and leaves the ligaments bare and b covered in salt. Also, the flesh itself collapses back into the bloodstream, where it intensifies the problems I've already mentioned.

Severe as these physical conditions are, there are more basic ones that are even worse; they occur when flesh is so dense that an insufficient quantity of breath gets through to it. The bone turns mouldy, the mould heats the bone up until

it mortifies, and then, so far from taking in food, bits that
c have crumbled off it go in the wrong direction and enter the
food themselves. The food then enters the flesh, and bits of
flesh collapse into the bloodstream and aggravate all the diseases I've already mentioned. But the very limit of severity in
this category of disease is reached when the marrow becomes
diseased, as a result of some specific deficiency or excess.
This produces the most serious diseases, those that are more
or less guaranteed to be fatal, as *all* the bodily processes
necessarily reverse the direction of their flows.*

There is also a third category of diseases, which needs to
d be considered under three headings: those caused by the air
we breathe, those caused by phlegm, and those caused by
bile. When the lung, whose job it is to dispense the air we
breathe to the body, is so clogged with fluxes that its channels are contaminated, the air fails to reach some parts of the
body, and enters other parts of the body in unduly large
amounts. In the first case the outcome is decay, brought on
by lack of ventilation, while in the second case the air pushes
its way through the veins so forcefully that it distorts them,
until it reaches the midriff, the part with the diaphragm,
where it gets trapped, and so the body begins to waste
e away. These conditions cause countless painful ailments,
which are often accompanied by copious sweat. Also, the air
that is produced inside the body by the disintegration of
flesh often can't escape. This causes the same degree of
acute distress as when air has come in from outside and got
trapped, but the worst pain comes when the air produced
inside the body settles around the ligaments and the tiny
veins there and accumulates until its swelling forces both the
tendons and the ligaments attached to them to stretch backwards. This state of tautness is, of course, what has given
these ailments their names of 'tetanus' and 'opisthotonos'.*
It's hard to find a remedy for these diseases, and in fact a
fever, should one occur, is the most effective way of bringing
them to an end.

88

Thanks to the air in its bubbles,* white phlegm is danger- 85a
ous when arrested, and although less harmful if it finds a vent
to the outside of the body, it still stipples the body with its
offspring—white pustules and cysts, and similar skin conditions. However, if a mixture of it and black bile is splashed
onto the circuits in the head, the ones that are most divine, it
throws them into confusion. This is less harmful if it happens
during sleep, but harder to shake off if the attack comes while
a person is awake. As a disorder of our sacred part, it is per- b
fectly named the 'sacred disease'.* Phlegm that is acid and
salty is the source of all those ailments that involve fluxes from
the head, the names of which vary according to the places into
which they flow.

Whenever any part of the body is said to be 'inflamed'—
that is, when it is hot and burning—the reason is bile, which
causes either all sorts of itchy eruptions, if it finds a vent to
the outside of the body, or a range of inflammatory condi- c
tions, if it remains shut up inside. The worst situation, however, is when bile infects pure blood and disrupts the usual,
orderly arrangement of the fibres. These fibres are spread
throughout the blood, with the job of ensuring that it remains
in an equilibrated state between thinness and thickness—
that it becomes neither so hot and runny that it flows out of
the body's pores, nor too thick and inert to circulate readily
in the veins. The fibres were created and constituted to pre- d
serve a fine balance in this context. Even after death, when
the blood is cooling down, if the fibres are gathered together
all the rest of the blood becomes runny, while if they are left
in place the combined action of the fibres and a cool environment soon causes the blood to clot.*

In the situation under consideration, bile has been dissolved out of flesh and back into the blood from which it was
originally formed. At first, its invasion of the blood is gradual, and being hot and wet, it's thickened by the action of the
fibres, since this is their job in the blood; and as it congeals, e
with its heat being forcefully quenched, it produces internal

chills and shivering. But as more of it pours in, the heat it gives off overpowers the fibres, and its seething agitates them and throws them into disarray. If there's enough of it to see its victory through to the end, it penetrates the marrow, where in short order its heat loosens the soul's cables (to use a nautical image) and sets the soul free.* If there's too little of it, however, and the body resists the process of dissolution, the bile suffers defeat and is either driven out onto the surface of the body as a whole, banished from the body like an exile from a feuding city,† or is compressed through the veins and into the upper or lower abdomen, where it causes diarrhoea, dysentery, and all similar complaints.

Ill-health in the body may be due mainly to an excess of fire (which causes continuous burning and fevers), or to an excess of air (which causes quotidian fevers*), or to an excess of water (which causes tertian fevers, because it's more sluggish than air or fire), or to an excess of earth (which, as the most sluggish of the four, causes quartan fevers, which are hard to shake off).

So much for physical disorders and their causes, and now for diseases that affect the soul as a result of a physical condition. This is how they occur. It's indisputable that mindlessness is a disease of the soul, and since there are two kinds of mindlessness — madness and ignorance — it follows that everything which happens to a person that causes him to become either mad or ignorant must be called a disease. So we should count excessive pleasures and pains as the most serious diseases that can afflict the soul, because when a man is overjoyed or, conversely, suffering from pain, he's so immoderately concerned to gain the one or lose the other that he's incapable of seeing or hearing anything aright. In short, he's in a state of frenzy and, for as long as it lasts, he completely loses the ability to think rationally.*

When there's a build-up of seed in a man's marrow, and it becomes copious and profuse, like a tree overladen with fruit, his desires and their satisfaction bring him agony and pleasure, time after time. The pleasures and pains are so intense that he spends most of his life in a crazed state, but although his soul has been infected with mindlessness by his d body, he's not generally held to be ill, but to be a bad man, by his own choice. In actual fact, however, sexual incontinence is a soul-sickness caused largely by the presence in the body, thanks to the porousness of the bones, of just a single substance, in profuse enough quantities to moisten it. And indeed, hardly any of the bad behaviour which is commonly attributed to lack of control in the face of pleasure and is said to be shameful, as if it were freely chosen, should really be held against a person. For no one is bad of his own choice:* e an unhealthy body and a vulgar upbringing are what make a bad man bad, and these are afflictions that no one *chooses* to have.

Where pain is concerned as well, the same principle applies: a poor state of the soul is often due to the body. A person's acid and salty phlegm, or† his bitter and bilious fluids, can get trapped inside the body, without finding an outlet, and then they roam around the body. If they encoun- 87a ter the motion of the soul and interaction takes place between it and the vapours they give off, all kinds of diseases arise, which vary in severity and frequency. These diseases might be carried to any of the soul's three locations* and, depending on which one they assault, they create a complex syndrome either of obstinacy and gloom, or of rashness and hesitancy, or of forgetfulness and mental dullness.

In addition, when men who are constitutionally unsound, b as I've been describing, live in cities with pernicious political systems and hear correspondingly pernicious speeches at home and in public, and when, moreover, what they learn from childhood onwards does nothing at all to remedy all this, these two factors, which have nothing whatsoever to do with one's own choice, are responsible for the badness of those of us who become bad. We should always blame the sowers rather than the seed, and the teachers rather than the taught, but we should still do our best to ensure that our environment, our occupations, and our education help us to prefer good to bad.

c   This topic belongs to another kind of speech, but now it is right and proper that we should discuss in its turn the counterpart to these issues, namely how to tend to our bodies and minds to keep them safe and sound. After all, good has more of a claim on our attention than bad. Now, anything good is beautiful, and nothing beautiful lacks proportion, so we are bound to expect a healthy creature to be a well-proportioned creature. But although we discern and think rationally about trivial cases of proportion, we're incapable of reasoning when it comes to the most important and significant cases. For

d   instance, the factor that has the most bearing on health and sickness, and on moral goodness and badness, is whether or not there's proportion between soul and body, but we don't consider these things at all. We fail to see that when a relatively weak and frail body is the vehicle for a soul that has no weakness or pettiness in it, or when the combination of the two of them is imbalanced in the opposite way, the creature as a whole lacks proportion in the most important respects, and therefore lacks beauty. However, for those capable of seeing it, a creature whose soul and body are in balance is a vision of the utmost beauty and attractiveness.

e   Think, for example, of a body which is out of proportion with itself, in the sense that it has one leg longer than the other or some other abnormality: it's not just that it's ugly, but also that it makes a lot of trouble for itself in a work context, as its lurching gait exhausts it and makes it liable to all sorts of injuries and accidents. The same goes, we're bound to think, for the complex of soul and body that we call a living creature. Suppose its soul is stronger than its

88a   body. When the soul gets abnormally passionate, it makes the whole body quiver from within and fills it with illnesses; and when it's intent upon study and research, it causes the body to waste away. Or again, when it's involved in teaching or disputation, in public or in a private house, surrounded by arguments and competitiveness,† it heats the body and churns it up, and induces fluxes, which fool most so-called healers into blaming the innocent party. On the other hand, the balance of power might lie with the body rather than the soul, so that a strong body has a petty, weak mind attached to it. If so, of the two fundamental desires that human beings b possess — the bodily desire for food and the desire of the most divine part of us for knowledge ... well, when the impulses of the stronger part win and reinforce their favourite, they turn the soul into something obtuse, dull, and forgetful, and give it the worst of all diseases, ignorance.

There's only one way to protect oneself against both these situations, which is not to exercise the soul to the exclusion of the body, nor the body to the exclusion of the soul. Then, evenly balanced and healthy, each is able to resist the other. So the mathematician or the enthusiastic cultivator of any c other intellectual pursuit has to pay his debt of physical exercise by attending the gymnasium, and someone concerned with developing his physique has to compensate with exercises for the soul by addressing all kinds of cultural and philosophical pursuits. There's no other way for a man to come to have a genuine claim to both the two epithets 'beautiful' and 'good' at once.*

The same principle also holds good when it comes to treating parts of the body, where the body of the universe should be our model. The inside of the human body is heated d and chilled by things that enter it, while its outside is dried and moistened by external objects. If the body, which is affected in these and related ways by impulses from both inside and outside, is subjected to these changes while unmoving, it is overpowered and ruined. On the other hand, if someone takes what we called the nurse and the nurturer of the universe as his model, and allows his body to be still as rarely as possible, by keeping it constantly and thoroughly stirred up by exercise, he provides it with a natural means of resistance to the inner e and outer impulses. By keeping the qualities and fragments that roam according to their natural affinities around the body in a state of moderate agitation, he orders and organizes them in relation to one another, along the lines of what I was saying before about the universe.* By separating enemies he stops discord and disease arising in the body, and by grouping friends together instead he creates a sound constitution.

89a   Now, the best kind of movement is one that is generated by oneself within oneself, because there's no movement that has more natural affinity with the movement of the thinking part and of the universe as a whole. Somewhat worse than this is any externally generated movement, but worst of all is the one that affects only parts of a supine, still body, and uses substances that are different from the bodily parts affected. It follows, where means of purging and restoring the body are concerned, that the best is exercise, and the second-best is being rocked on a boat or some other vehicle that isn't an exhausting ride. The third kind of change, however, should

b be a last resort in dire emergencies and never otherwise accepted by a man of intelligence. This is the medical use of drugs to purge the body.*

The point is that, except in cases of grave danger, diseases should not be exacerbated by the use of medicines. All illnesses structurally resemble living creatures, in the sense that the composition of creatures lasts for an ordained number of years, not only as members of a given species, but also as individuals: each individual creature comes into existence with a

c predetermined lifespan, leaving aside unavoidable accidents. This is because, right from the start, every creature's triangles are put together with the capacity for lasting a certain amount of time,† beyond which it cannot possibly remain alive. Diseases have analogous structures, and so if one tries to eliminate a disease by the use of drugs before its time, problems are liable to increase both in severity and number. Hence, control of this whole area should be achieved by means of regimen, to the extent that one has time to do so, and one

should avoid exacerbating an obstinate nuisance by the appli- d
cation of drugs.*

So much for both the composite living creature and the
part of it that consists in the body; we've spoken enough
about what a person has to do, in terms of controlling and
being controlled by himself,* to give himself the best chance
of living the life of reason. But it's even more important that
we should first do all we can to ensure that the controlling
part itself is in the finest and best possible condition for the
task of exercising control. It would be a hard enough job to
discuss this topic in detail on its own, without covering any- e
thing else, but a casual treatment along the lines of what's
already been said might not go amiss as a way for me to bring
my speech to a conclusion.

So let's look at it this way. As we've already said a number
of times, there are three kinds of soul lodged within us. Since
each of them has its own movements, it will take us no time
at all to follow the same principle as we did just now and assert
that whichever of them passes its time in idleness, with its
own movements stilled, is bound to be the weakest of them,
while the one that constantly exercises is bound to be the
strongest. And from this it follows that we should take care
to ensure that they keep their movements in proportion with 90a
one another.*

As far as the most important type of soul we possess is
concerned, we are bound to identify it with the personal deity
that was a gift of the god to each of us. This, of course, is the
kind of soul that dwells, as we said, in the summit of our body,
and it raises us up from the earth towards the heavenly
region to which we are naturally akin, since we are not soil-
bound plants but, properly speaking, creatures rooted in
heaven. For it is from heaven, where our souls originally came
into existence, that the gods suspended our heads,* which are
our roots, and set our bodies upright.   b

When a man is caught up in his appetites or his ambitions
and devotes all his energies to them, the mental processes

that go on inside him are bound to be restricted entirely to mortal beliefs, and he himself is bound to be completely and utterly as mortal as a man can be, since that is the part of himself that he has reinforced. But anyone who has devoted himself to learning and has genuinely applied his intelligence — which is to say, anyone who has primarily

c exercised his intellect — cannot fail to attain immortal, divine wisdom, if the truth should come within his grasp. He achieves the full measure of immortality that is possible for a human being, and because he always takes care of the divine part of himself and maintains the orderly beauty of his companion deity, he is bound to be exceptionally blessed. But there is only one way that anyone can take care of anything, and that is by giving it food and exercise that is congenial to it.* So, since the movements that are naturally akin to our divine part are the thoughts and revolutions of the universe, these are

d what each of us should be guided by as we attempt to reverse the corruption of the circuits in our heads, that happened around the time of our birth, by studying the harmonies and revolutions of the universe. In this way, we will restore our nature to its original condition* by assimilating our intellect to what it is studying and, with such assimilation, we will achieve our goal: to live, now and in the future, the best life that the gods have placed within human reach.*

e And so it looks as though we have now pretty much achieved the target originally set us of explaining the creation of the universe from the beginning up to the origin of human beings. But we should just briefly mention how all other creatures came to exist; it won't mean prolonging the speech much, and we'll be able to judge ourselves to have given a more balanced account.

We may take the following, then, as our account of this topic. Some men, once they had been incarnated, lived unmanly or immoral lives, and it's plausible to suggest that they were reborn in their next incarnation as women. That,

91a therefore, was when the gods invented sexual desire,* a living being that they formed, though different in men and in women, and endowed with a soul. Here's how they made each of these creatures. At the point where the channel for drink receives liquid (once it has passed through the lung, behind the kidneys, and into the bladder) and discharges it under pressure from air, they bored a channel into the marrow they had constructed, that extends from the head, down through the neck, and through the spine—that is, the marrow we b described earlier as seed. The marrow, as something endowed with soul and now granted an outlet, generated, in the part where the outlet is, a lively appetite for emission and the result was the male yearning for procreation. And this is why men's sex organs, like a creature which is incapable of listening to reason, are disobedient and headstrong, and, goaded by their frantic appetites, try to have everything their way.

To turn to women and the 'womb' or 'uterus' they pos- c sess: there exists inside the womb, for the same purpose, a living being with an appetite for child-making, and so if it remains unproductive long past puberty, it gets irritated and fretful. It takes to wandering all around the body and gener-ating all sorts of ailments, including potentially fatal prob-lems, if it blocks up the air-channels and makes breathing impossible. This goes on until a woman's appetite for child-bearing and a man's yearning for procreation bring the two of them together and they strip the fruit from the tree, so to d speak. They sow in the field of the womb tiny creatures, too small to be seen. At first not fully formed, these creatures then become articulated, while the womb nourishes them until they've grown enough to emerge into the light of day. The result of this process, then, is the creation of living creatures.

So this is how women and females of any species were created. Birds, however, are a mutant tribe, sprouting feath-ers instead of hair; they are reincarnations of men who had no badness in them, but were lightweight, in the sense that although they studied the heavens,* they were foolish enough

97

e   to think that their arguments would never be perfectly secure unless they personally witnessed the phenomena.

Land animals, a brutish race, are reincarnations of men who never applied themselves to philosophy and never pondered the nature of the heavens, because they stopped making use of the circuits in their heads and instead followed the lead of those aspects of the soul that reside in the chest. This way of life bowed their upper bodies and heads down, by the principle of natural affinity, until their forelimbs rested on the ground, and their heads became elongated or otherwise

92a   oddly shaped, depending on how an individual's revolutions shrank from disuse. This explains why animals of this kind have four or more legs, and the more mindless they were, the more such underpinning the gods gave them, to draw them even closer to the ground. As for the most mindless of them,* the ones with their whole bodies level with the ground, the gods made them without feet, since they no longer needed them at all; these are the creatures that crawl along the ground.

b   Aquatic creatures make up the fourth kind, and they are reincarnations of especially stupid and ignorant men. In transforming them into these creatures, the gods decided that they no longer deserved even to breathe pure air, since their tasteless behaviour had sullied their souls with impurities, and so, instead of letting them breathe fine, pure air, they forced them down into the murky depths of water, to do their breathing there. This is how all aquatic creatures came into existence, such as fish and shellfish, and they have been assigned the lowest realm as a penalty for having plumbed the

c   lowest depths of ignorance. These principles apply just as much now as then, and they determine the interchangeability of creatures and how their changes are influenced by their losing or gaining intelligence.*

So now we may say that our account of the universe is at last complete, since we have explained how this world of ours

obtained its full complement of mortal and immortal creatures. It was created a visible living being, encompassing
within itself those creatures that are visible; it was created a
perceptible god, made in the likeness of the intelligible god.
This universe of ours is single, the only one of its kind: there
is none greater or better, none more beautiful, none more
perfect.

CRITIAS

TIMAEUS: How pleased I am to have come to the end of my 106a
account, Socrates! I feel as relieved as someone resting after
a long journey, now that I've finished with it. And my prayer
to the god who has just been created in my speech (though of
course he was created long ago, in fact) is that for our sakes
he may keep safe everything that was well said, and that if we b
inadvertently struck a false note he will impose the appropriate penalty—and the right penalty when someone is out of
tune is to make him harmonious. I pray, then, for the gift of
knowledge, the most perfect and most effective medicine,* so
that in the future any account we give of the creation of gods
may be accurate. And with this prayer I make way for Critias,
as we agreed: it's his turn to speak now.
CRITIAS: Well, Timaeus, I'm ready, but first I have a request
to make—the same one that you relied on at the beginning c
of your speech, when you asked for leniency given the
immensity of the topics you were going to address. In fact,
I think I have even more of a right to leniency, and to more 107a
of it, for what I'm about to say. And despite being pretty
sure that, in making the request, I'll seem more than a little
self-important and unduly rude, I still have to make it. I'm
not suggesting that anything in your speech was less than
excellent—how could anyone in their right mind presume
to do so?—but I do want to try to show that what remains
to be said is actually more difficult, and therefore calls for
more leniency. You see, Timaeus, it's easier for someone to
give an impression of competence in speaking to us humans
about gods than it is when the subject of his speech is mortal b
men. When the audience's situation is one of inexperience
and downright ignorance of a topic, that makes it rather easy
for someone to address it—and, of course, we know how
we're placed when the topic is the gods.

I can make my meaning clearer if you'll just bear with me for a while. Our words are never going to be more than images and representations of things, I'd say, so let's look at how painters go about creating images of divine and human

c figures, in terms of how easy or difficult they find it to get the viewers to think that they've produced an adequate representation. Take things like the landscape, or mountains, rivers, and woodland, or the sky as a whole, as well as the bodies that exist and move in it. We shall find, first, that we're satisfied if an artist is capable of representing any of these things in a way that even vaguely resembles them, and also that, since our knowledge of such things is inexact, we don't criticize or challenge the painted images, but in these

d cases are content with an imprecise and deceptive outline.* When an artist tries to represent human bodies, however, our constant familiarity with them means that we quickly spot any flaws, and we turn into harsh critics of anyone who fails to produce perfectly exact likenesses.

We're bound to think that the same phenomenon applies to speeches too: we're content with discussions of divine, heavenly bodies if they bear no more than a slight resemblance to the originals, whereas we subject discussions of

e mortal, human affairs to detailed critical scrutiny. So allowances should be made if in the improvised speech I'm about to give I prove incapable of producing an account that does justice to its subject in all respects, because we ought to think it hard, rather than easy, to produce a likeness of humans and their affairs that satisfies people's expectations.

108a Anyway, my reason for saying all this, Socrates, is not just that I wanted to remind you all of these facts, but to ask you to show more leniency, not less, towards the speech I'm about to make. If you think my request for this favour is fair, do please grant it, without any further prompting from me.

SOCRATES: Of course we will, Critias—and let's make the same allowance for Hermocrates too, our third speaker, since it's plain to see that before long he's going to be asking

for the same favour as you two, when it's his turn to speak. b
To help him come up with a different preamble, rather than
feeling compelled to use the same one, he may speak, when
the time comes, knowing that he already has our forbearance.
But I should warn you, my dear Critias, of your audience's
state of mind: the playwright who preceded you went down
amazingly well with it, so you'll need a very great deal of
leniency if you're to prove yourself a competent successor.*

HERMOCRATES: Your warning applies to me as much as to our
friend here, Socrates. All the same, Critias, no trophy was ever c
set up by faint-hearted men: you must advance courageously
to your speech and, with an invocation to Apollo Paean* and
the Muses, demonstrate that these fellow citizens of yours from
long ago were men of virtue, and sing their praises.

CRITIAS: Hermocrates, my friend, the reason you still feel bold
is that you've been positioned in the rear, with someone else
before you; but you'll find out soon enough what the front
line is like. Be that as it may, I shall do as you say, spurred on
by your encouragement and advice. I had better invoke not d
only the gods you mentioned, but all the rest of them as well,
especially Memory, as the deity responsible for all the most
important aspects of my account. If I can remember and
report with sufficient accuracy the tale once told by the priests
and brought here by Solon, I'm pretty sure that this audience
here will judge me to have fulfilled my task well enough. So
that's what I had better do now, with no further delay.

Let's recall, first, that in all 9,000 years* have passed since e
war was declared between those who lived beyond and those
who lived within the Pillars of Heracles. This is the war
whose course I shall now describe. It is said that one side was
led right through to the end of the fighting by Athens, while
the other side was commanded by the kings of Atlantis—an
island which, as we said, was once larger than Libya and
Asia, though by now earthquakes have caused it to sink and
it has left behind unnavigable mud, which obstructs those 109a

who sail out there into the ocean.* As our tale unfolds, so to speak, along its course, there will be opportunities to reveal details of the many non-Greek peoples and all the Greek communities that existed then, but first we must start with an account of the resources and the political systems of the Athenians of the time and their opponents in the war. And of the two sides, Athens had better go first.

b   Once upon a time, the gods divided the whole earth among themselves, region by region. There were no disputes involved;* after all, it makes no sense for the gods not to know what is appropriate to each of them and, since they do have such knowledge, it is illogical to believe that they would dispute claims and try to gain what properly belonged to another one of them. So each gained by just allocation what belonged to him, established communities in his lands, and, having done so, began to look after us, his property and creatures, as a shepherd does his flocks, with the difference

c   that they did not use physical means of compulsion. Shepherds use blows as they tend to their flocks, but the gods focused on that part of each creature which makes it most easy to steer, like helmsmen steering from the stern; they took hold of its mind, employed the rudder of persuasion as they saw fit, and in this way guided and led every mortal creature as a whole.

    As a result of the allocation, various gods gained various regions to govern, and Hephaestus and Athena (who are very similar in nature, not just because they are brother and sister, with a common father, but also because their love of education and of craft give them the same goals) gained Athens here as their shared allocation, since the nature of the district was such that it was suitable for courage and

d   intelligence.* So they created men of courage, who were born from the ground,* and implanted in their minds the outline of their political system.

    Although the names of these first Athenians have been preserved, their achievements have been obliterated by the destruction of their successors and the long passage of time. I've already mentioned the reason for this: those who survived on each occasion were illiterate mountain-dwellers, who had heard only the names of the rulers of the land and knew hardly anything about their achievements. They were happy to name their children after their predecessors, but were unaware of their acts of courage and their customs, e except for the occasional obscure rumour about this or that. For many generations, they and their children were short of essentials, and this problem was what occupied their minds 110a and their conversations, rather than events of the distant past. After all, storytelling and enquiring about the past arrive in communities along with leisure, when and only when they see that some people have been adequately supplied with the necessities of life.

Anyway, this is how the names but not the achievements of those men of old came to be preserved. My evidence for saying this is that, according to Solon, the account those priests gave of the war of that time included not only most of the names of Cecrops, Erechtheus, Erichthonius, Erysichthon, and the other predecessors of Theseus,* but also attributed b most of their achievements to each of them by name, and did the same for their wives too. And another point, relevant to the way the goddess is portrayed, is that, according to Solon, in those days military training was undertaken by women as well as by men, and that it was in accordance with this practice that people in those days began to display the goddess in armour. It was a token of the fact that all gregarious ani- c mals, female and male, have been equally equipped by their natures to practise the virtue peculiar to their species.

In those days, most of the inhabitants of this land — most classes of citizens — were occupied with the crafts and with agriculture, but the warrior class, which from the very beginning had been separated off by godlike men,* lived apart. They had everything that was appropriate for their sustenance and training, they owned no private property and regarded d

everything as held in common by them all, and they did not
expect the rest of their fellow citizens to provide them with
more than an adequate supply of food. In fact, their way of
life was in all respects the same as that described yesterday
for our imaginary guardians.*

Then again, the old stories about our land are reliable and
true: above all, in those days its border was formed by the
Isthmus and, in relation to the rest of the mainland, our ter-
e ritory extended as far as the hills of Cithaeron and Parnes,
and went down to the coast, with Oropus on the right and
the Asopus forming the border on the left.* There was no
soil to compare with ours anywhere in the world, which is
why the territory was capable in those days of supporting a
large number of soldiers who were exempt from working the
land.* There is convincing proof of how good the soil was:
the remnant of it that still exists is a match for any soil in its
ability to produce a good yield of any crop, and in the rich
111a pasturage it provides for all sorts of animals. But in those
days the soil produced crops in vast quantities and of high
quality.

Why should we trust this picture? Why are we right to
call the soil of modern Attica a remnant of the soil of those
days? Attica is nothing but a headland, so to speak, jutting
far out into the sea from the rest of the mainland, surrounded by a seabed which drops off close to the shore to a
considerable depth. So although there have been many devastating floods in the course of the 9,000-year interval
b between then and now, the soil washed down from the highlands in all these years and during these disasters has not
formed any considerable pile of sediment, as it does elsewhere, but is constantly rolled down into the depths, where
it vanishes. Just as on the small islands,* what remains now
is, compared with those days, like the skeleton of a body
wasted by disease: the soil, or at any rate as much of it as is
rich and soft, has rolled away, and only the spare body of the
land remains.

In those days, however, the land was intact, our moun- c
tains were just high mounds, what we now call the Stony
Plains were filled with rich soil, and the highlands were covered with dense forests (of which there are traces even now).
Nowadays some of our mountains sustain only bees, but not
long ago trees from there were cut as roof-timbers for very
substantial buildings, and the roofs are still sound. Cultivated
trees grew tall and plentiful, and the soil bore limitless fod-
der for our flocks and herds. Moreover, the ground bene-
fited from the rain sent each year by Zeus and didn't lose it, d
as it does nowadays with the water flowing off the bare
ground and into the sea. Instead, because the ground had
plenty of soil to absorb moisture, it stored the rain on a layer
of impermeable clay, let the water flow down from the high
ground into the low ground of every district, and so provided abundant springs to feed streams and rivers. Even
now there are still shrines, left over from the old days, at the
sites of former springs, as tokens of the truth of this account
of the land.

So much for the characteristics of the land in general. It e
was ordered as well as you might expect, given that the
farmers were true farmers (that is, they were specialists at
their job, and were endowed with noble aims and natural
ability) and given that they had outstandingly good soil to
work with, plenty of water, and a perfectly tempered climate
from the skies above. As for the state of the town in those
days, in the first place the Acropolis was different from now,
since by now it has suffered from the effects of a single night 112a
of torrential rain which washed away the soil and left the
Acropolis bare; and this appalling deluge—the third
destruction by water before the one that took place in the
time of Deucalion*—was also accompanied by earthquakes.
Before then, the Acropolis extended from the Eridanus to
the Ilissus, included the Pnyx,* and ended, on the side opposite the Pnyx, with the Lycabettus; and the entire Acropolis
was covered in soil and was almost all level. Outside the b

Acropolis, under its flanks, were the dwellings of the craftsmen and those farmers who worked the nearby land.

The top of the Acropolis had been settled by the warriors,
who lived all by themselves around the temple of Athena and
Hephaestus, and had also enclosed the heights within a single
wall, like the garden of a single house. They lived in communal houses on the northern side of the Acropolis, they had
constructed messes to be shared by all in cold weather, and
they had provided themselves with everything that was in
c   keeping with their communal institutions—everything in the
way of buildings and temples, that is, not gold and silver, for
which they never had any use. In pursuit of the mean between
extravagance and dependence, they built moderate houses in
which they and their descendants could grow old and which
they could bequeath to others just like themselves. And when,
as you would expect in the summer, they left their gardens,
gymnasia, and messes, they used the southern side for these
functions. There was a single spring in the area of the present
d   Acropolis, but it has been clogged up by earthquakes, so that
now there's only a trickle of water near the present hill; but in
those days it supplied everyone with plenty of water and kept
a constant temperature throughout the year.

That was how they lived. As guardians of their own fellow
citizens and of all other Greeks, who were their willing subjects,* they did their best to ensure that at any given time there
were among them the same number of men and women—
around twenty thousand—who had reached the age of mili-
e   tary service or were not too old for it. This, then, was what the
Athenians were like in those days, and their way of life was
more or less as I've said. They equitably managed their own
affairs and those of Greece, and they were renowned throughout Europe and Asia for their physical beauty and for their
many outstanding mental qualities. Their fame surpassed that
of all their contemporaries.

Now let's turn to their opponents in the war. Friends hold
all things in common, so assuming I can remember it, I shall

now reveal to you what I was told in my childhood about what they were like and how their way of life evolved. But first, there's a small point I should explain before telling the tale, 113a otherwise you might be surprised at constantly hearing Greek names applied to non-Greek people. I'll tell you how this came about. Solon was planning to compose a poetic version of the tale, so he asked about the meanings of the names and found that the Egyptians who had first written the story down had translated them into their own language. So he did the same: he referred back to the sense of each name and adapted it to our language before committing it to b writing. And it is his written version which once belonged to my grandfather and is now in my possession. I studied the manuscript carefully when I was young. So if you hear Greek-sounding names, don't be surprised: you now know why.* Anyway, it's a long story and it began somewhat as follows.

As I said earlier, the gods parcelled out the entire world among themselves, allocated themselves larger or smaller territories, and established their own shrines and sacrificial c rituals. Poseidon gained the island of Atlantis as his province, and he settled there the children borne for him by a mortal woman in a certain part of the island. To be specific, halfway along the coastline there was a plain which is said to have been unsurpassable in its beauty, and good and fertile too. Close to the plain and halfway along its extent, about fifty stades* distant from the coast, there was a hill of no great prominence. There lived on this hill a man who was one of the original earth-born men of the land. He was called d Evenor and he lived with his wife, Leucippe. They had just the one child, a daughter called Cleito. When the girl reached the age for marriage, both her mother and her father died, but Poseidon, who had come to desire her, made her his concubine. He gave the hill where she lived secure defences by breaking it off from the surrounding land and creating increasingly large concentric rings, alternately of land and

water, around it. Two of the rings were of land, three of water, and he made them equidistant from the centre, as if he had taken the middle of the island as the pivot of a lathe.* And
e so the island became inaccessible to others, because in those days ships and sailing had not yet been invented.*

Poseidon, as a god, easily organized the central island. Once he had fetched up two underground springs—one warm, the other flowing cold from its source—and caused all kinds of food to grow in sufficient quantities from the soil, he fathered and reared five pairs of twin sons. Then he divided the island of Atlantis into ten parts. He gave the firstborn of
114a the eldest twins his mother's home and the plot of land around it, which was larger and more fertile than anywhere else, and made him king of all his brothers, while giving each of the others many subjects and plenty of land to rule over.

He named all his sons. To the eldest, the king, he gave the name from which the names of the whole island and of the ocean are derived—that is, the ocean was called the Atlantic
b because the name of the first king was Atlas. To his twin, the one who was born next, who was assigned the edge of the island which is closest to the Pillars of Heracles and faces the land which is now called the territory of Gadeira after him, he gave a name which in Greek would be Eumelus, though in the local language it was Gadeirus, and so this must be the origin of the name of Gadeira.* He called the next pair of twins Ampheres and Evaemon; he named the elder of the
c third pair Mneseus and the younger one Autochthon; of the fourth pair, the eldest was called Elasippus and the younger one Mestor; in the case of the fifth pair, he called the firstborn Azaes and the second-born Diaprepes. So all his sons and their descendants lived there for many generations, and in addition to ruling over numerous other islands in the ocean, they also, as I said before,* governed all the land this side of the Pillars of Heracles up to Egypt and Etruria.

d Atlas' family flourished in numbers and prestige. In each generation the eldest was king and passed the kingship on to the eldest of his offspring. In this way the dynasty survived for many generations and they grew enormously rich, with more wealth than anyone from any earlier royal line and more than anyone later would easily gain either; and they were supplied with everything they needed for the city and the rest of their territory too. Their empire brought them many goods from abroad, but the island by itself provided e them with most of the necessities of life. In the first place, they had everything, solid or fusible,* that could be mined from the ground, and in fact in many parts of the island there was dug up from the ground something which is now no more than a name, although in those days it was an actual fact and was second in value only to gold—orichalc.* Second, woodland produced plenty of every kind of timber that builders might need for their labours, and bore enough food for both wild and domesticated animals. In fact, there were even large numbers of elephants there, because there was ample grazing for all creatures—not just for those whose habitats were marshes and lakes and rivers, or again for those that lived in mountains or on the plains, but equally 115a for this creature too, the largest and most voracious in the world.

Third, everything aromatic the earth produces today in the way of roots or shoots or shrubs or gums exuded by flowers or fruits was produced and supported by the island then. Fourth, as for cultivated crops—both the dry sort (that is, our staple and all the others we use as foodstuffs, which we collectively call 'pulses') and the arboreal sort b (not only the sources of our drink and food and oil, but also the produce of fruit-bearing trees which, though hard to store, exists for the sake of our amusement and our pleasure, and also all those things we offer a man who is full up as an enjoyable dessert to relieve his satiety*)—all these things were in those days produced in vast quantities and of a remarkably high quality by that sacred, sun-drenched island.

Enriched by all these agricultural products, they set about
c building shrines, royal mansions, harbours, and shipyards,
and organized the whole of their territory along the following lines. The first thing they did was build bridges across
the rings of water surrounding the ancient mother-city, to
create a road to and from the palace. The palace was the very
first thing they had built in the place where Poseidon and
their ancestors had lived, and it was passed down from generation to generation, with each new king embellishing what
d was already embellished and trying as best he could to outdo
his predecessors, until they had created a building of aston-
ishing size and beauty.

What they did first was dig a canal from the sea to the
outermost ring. The canal was three plethra wide, a hundred
feet deep, and fifty stades long,* and with a mouth wide
enough for the largest ships it allowed vessels to sail from
the sea to the outermost ring and to use it as a harbour.
e Moreover, at the points where they had built the bridges,
they opened up gaps in the intermediate rings of land wide
enough to allow a single warship to sail through from one
ring of water to another, and they roofed these canals over
so as to create an underground sailing passage below,* for
the banks of the rings of land were high enough above the
level of the water to allow them to do this.

The largest ring of water—the one into which the sea
had been channelled—was three stades wide, and the next
ring of land was the same size. Of the second pair, the ring
of water was two stades wide, and the ring of land was again
the same size as the preceding ring of water. The ring of
water which immediately surrounded the central island was
116a a stade in width, while the island (where the palace was) had
a diameter of five stades.

They surrounded the central island and the rings of land
and the bridges (which were one plethron wide) on both sides
with a stone wall, and built towers and gates on the bridges
at each side, at the points where there were the passages for

the water. They quarried the stone (some white, some black, and some red) from underneath the perimeter of the central island and from under the outside and inside of the rings of land, so that at the same time they hollowed out internal, b double-sided docks, roofed over by bedrock. They made some of their buildings plain, but to avoid monotony they patterned others by combining stones, which gave the buildings a naturally pleasant appearance. They covered the entire circuit of the wall around the outermost ring with a paste, so to speak, of bronze; they smeared a layer of melted tin on the wall of the inner ring; and for the wall around the acropolis itself they used orichalc, which gleamed like fire. c

The palace inside the acropolis was laid out with, in its very centre, a sacrosanct shrine dedicated to Cleito and Poseidon, surrounded by a low wall of gold. This was the spot where they had originally conceived and fathered the ten kings. It was here too, in this shrine, that in an annual ritual each of the ten kings received first-fruits from all the ten regions. There was a temple of Poseidon there, which was a stade long and three plethra wide, and its height was aesthetically d proportionate with these base measurements. There was something non-Greek about the appearance of the temple.* Outside, it was entirely covered with silver, except for the acroteria,* which were gold. Inside, the entire surface of the ceiling was ivory decorated with gold, silver, and orichalc, and all the walls, pillars, and pavements were covered with orichalc. They set up a golden statue there of the god standing on a chariot with a team of six winged horses, tall enough to e touch the roof with his head. He was surrounded by a hundred further statues of Nereids on dolphins (in those days, people thought there were this many Nereids*), and the temple also held many other statues, which had been dedicated by private individuals.

Outside, the temple was surrounded by golden statues of all the ten kings and their wives, and there were numerous other substantial dedications, given by both the kings and

private individuals from the city itself and also from the for-
117a eign territories of their empire. The altar conformed to this
structure in size and workmanship, and the palace was equally
in keeping not just with the size of the empire, but also with
the beauty of the shrine.

They drew their water from the two springs (one of cold
and the other of warm water), each of which was fantastic-
ally well suited to its function in respect of the taste and the
quality of the water, which it produced in generous quantities. They surrounded the springs with buildings and with
b copses of suitable trees, and also with pools, some of which
they left open to the air, while they protected with roofs
those that were used in the winters as warm baths. There
were separate sets of pools—some for the royal families,
some for private citizens, others for women, and yet others
for horses and other working animals—and each pool was
organized in the appropriate fashion. Any water which over-
flowed was channelled to the grove of Poseidon, where all
the various species of trees grew to be beautiful and extraor-
dinarily tall thanks to the fertility of the soil, and was then
conducted to the rings beyond the island by pipes beside the
bridges.

c Numerous shrines, sacred to a large number of gods, had
been built on these outer rings, and there were plenty of gardens and gymnasia there too. There were separate exercise-
grounds for men and for horses on each of the two islands
formed by the rings and, above all, in the middle of the
larger of the two island-rings they had an area reserved as a
hippodrome. The hippodrome was a stade wide and ran all
the way around the ring, as a space dedicated to equestrian
contests. Most of the bodyguards* lived in guardhouses on
d either side of the hippodrome, but the more trusted ones were
assigned barracks on the smaller ring, closer to the acropolis,
and those who were exceptionally trustworthy were allowed
to live in close proximity to the kings themselves within the
acropolis. The shipyards were filled with warships and with

all the equipment they required, and everything was kept in a state of readiness.

So much for the way the royal household was fitted out. Past the three external harbours a wall ran all around, starting at the sea, at a constant distance of fifty stades from the largest ring and its harbour, and completed its circuit at the point where it began, at the mouth of the canal by the sea. This whole area was crowded with a great many houses, and the canal and the largest harbour teemed with merchant ships and traders arriving from all over the world, in such large numbers that all day and all night long the place resounded with shouts and with general uproar and noise.

I have now pretty well covered the original account of the town and the ancient palace, and I had better try to tell you what the character and the arrangement of the rest of the land was like. To begin with, the whole region was said to be very high, with sheer cliffs along the coastline, but near the city there was nothing but a plain, which surrounded the city and was itself surrounded by mountains which reached down to the sea. The plain was uniformly flat and basically oblong: it extended in one direction for 3,000 stades and inland across its centre for 2,000 stades from the sea. This part of the island as a whole faced south* and was sheltered from the north winds. The mountains that surrounded the plain were celebrated in those days for their number, size, and beauty; there are no mountains today which come close to them in these respects. There were in the mountains many wealthy villages with their rural populations; rivers, lakes, and meadows kept every species of tame and wild creature adequately supplied with food; and there was plenty of timber, of various types, which was more than sufficient for any kind of task and for every occasion.

As a result of its nature, and of many years of engineering by successive kings, the plain had taken on the following character. It was originally, as I said, largely rectangular, straight-sided, and oblong, but because it wasn't perfectly oblong they made it straight by surrounding it with a trench. The reported scale of this trench — its depth and width and length — was incredible: it's hard to believe that, on top of all their other labours, any work of human hands should be so huge. Still, I must tell you what I was told. It was excavated to a depth of a plethron, it was a stade wide all the way d around, and its length, once the whole perimeter of the plain had been excavated, was 10,000 stades. Streams descending from the mountains drained into it, and it made a complete circuit of the plain, so that it reached the city from both sides, and then the water was allowed to discharge into the sea.

Inland from the city straight canals with a width of about 100 feet had been cut across the plain and debouched into the trench on the coastal side; each canal was 100 stades away from its neighbours. They used them not only to bring e timber down to the city from the mountains, but also for the ships with which they transported all the rest of their produce in its season. They also cut cross-channels at right angles to the canals, linking the canals to one another and to the city. They harvested their crops twice a year; in winter they relied on rain sent by Zeus, but in summer they diverted water from the canals to all their crops.

As for the number of plain-dwelling men who were to be 119a available for military service, it had been decreed that each plot (there were 60,000 in all, each ten by ten stades in area) was to provide one officer. There were, apparently, enormous numbers of men from the mountains and the rest of the land, and they were all assigned, district by district and village by village, to these plots and their officers. Each officer was instructed to supply for military use a sixth part of a war chariot (making a total of 10,000 chariots); two horses with riders; a pair of team horses without a chariot b but with a light-armed soldier for dismounting, a charioteer for the pair of horses, and an on-board soldier; two hoplites; two archers and the same number of slingers; three unarmed men to throw stones and the same number to throw javelins; and four sailors towards the total of 1,200 ships. This was how the royal city was organized militarily; the other nine cities did things differently, but it would take too long to explain their systems too.

I shall now tell you what the original arrangements were c for the wielding of power and authority. In his own particular region and where his own city was concerned, each of the ten kings had authority over the citizens and was more powerful than most of the laws, in the sense that he could punish and kill at whim. But among themselves authority and interaction were governed by the regulations of Poseidon, as bequeathed to them by tradition and by a stele of orichalc inscribed by their first ancestors and set up in the middle of d the island in the shrine of Poseidon, where they used to meet, at intervals alternately of four and five years, so as to privilege neither odd nor even numbers. When they met, they would not only discuss matters of general interest, but also test one another, to see if any of them had infringed the regulations, and try any offender.

When the time of trial arrived, the first thing they did was give assurances to one another, as follows. In the shrine of Poseidon there were consecrated bulls, and once the ten were alone they asked the god in their prayers to allow them to capture a sacrificial victim that would please him. They e then took up sticks and nooses (not weapons of iron) and set about chasing the bulls, and once they had caught one they led it to the stele and cut its throat above the crown of the stele, so that its blood flowed over the inscription. In addition to the regulations the stele was inscribed with an oath which called down terrible curses on anyone who disobeyed the regulations.

So when they had sacrificed the bull in their traditional 120a manner and had burnt all its limbs, they prepared a mixing-bowl of wine and threw in one clot of blood for each of them. The rest of the blood they poured into the fire, after thoroughly cleaning the stele. Next, they used golden cups to scoop up some wine from the bowl, and while pouring a libation onto the fire they swore that they would adjudicate in conformity with the regulations inscribed on the stele, would punish any past infringements, would henceforth knowingly infringe none of the regulations, and would neither

b rule nor obey any ruler unless his injunctions accorded with their father's regulations. Once he had committed himself and his descendants with this vow, each of the kings drank and then dedicated his cup to the god's shrine, before occupying himself with the feast and whatever else he had to do. When darkness fell and the sacrificial fire had cooled down, they all put on gorgeous robes of dark blue, sat down in the dark on the ground by the charred remains of the sacrificial

c victim, and once they had extinguished every flame in the shrine, they turned to the trial. They gave and received judgements for any infringement of the regulations and then, the following day, they inscribed their decisions on a golden tablet, which they dedicated in the shrine, along with their robes, as a memorial.

There were many other rules and customs pertaining only to the prerogatives of each of the kings, but the most important points were that they should never take up arms against one another; that they should resist any attempt to overthrow the royal family in any city; that, as their prede-

d cessors had, they should collectively debate any decisions that were to be made about all matters such as warfare, while giving overall authority to the descendants of Atlas; and that no king should have the right to put any of his relatives to death, unless half of the ten agreed with his decision.

So much for a description of the mighty power that existed in Atlantis in those days. It was this force that the god* mustered and brought against these regions here, and the account gave the following reason for his doing so. For

e many generations, as long as Poseidon's nature was vigorous enough in them, they obeyed the laws and were on good terms with the gods, who were their kin. Because the principles they held were true and perfectly high-minded, and because they reacted with self-possession and practical intelligence to the vicissitudes of life and to one another, they looked down on everything except virtue, counted their prosperity as trivial, and easily bore the burden, so to speak, of the mass 121a of their gold and other possessions. They were not made drunk by the luxury their wealth afforded them; they remained in control of themselves and never stumbled. As sober men do, they saw clearly that even prosperity is enhanced by the combination of mutual friendship and virtue—and that wealth declines and friendship is destroyed by materialistic goals and ambitions.

As a result of this kind of reasoning and of the persistence of the divine nature within them, they thrived in all the ways I've described. But when the divine portion within them began to fade, as a result of constantly being diluted by large measures of mortality, and their mortal nature began to pre- b dominate, they became incapable of bearing their prosperity and grew corrupt. Anyone with the eyes to see could mark the vileness of their behaviour as they destroyed the best of their valuable possessions; but those who were blind to the life that truly leads to happiness regarded them as having finally attained the most desirable and enviable life possible, now that they were infected with immoral greed and power.

Zeus, god of gods, who reigns by law, did have the eyes to see such things. He recognized the degenerate state of their fair line and wished to punish them, as a way of introducing c more harmony into their lives. He summoned all the gods to a meeting in the most awesome of his dwellings, which is located in the centre of the entire universe and so sees all of creation. And when the gods had assembled, he said:*

EXPLANATORY NOTES

TIMAEUS

17a *where's the fourth of yesterday's guests?*: we do not know who this missing fourth person, who has fallen ill, might be, nor why Plato has Socrates refer to him.

17b *Only partly*: Timaeus, Critias, and Hermocrates have forgotten at least part of what Socrates spoke of yesterday, giving Socrates a cue to give a summary, which will set the background for the main speeches of Timaeus and Critias.

17c *the political one*: Socrates proceeds to give a summary of the previous day's conversation. It has strong affinities to material presented in books II to V of *Republic*, concerning the organization of the ideal state, but leaves many other aspects of *Republic* untouched. We must take into consideration that what we in the twenty-first century find of interest or importance in *Republic* may differ from what Plato believed to be interesting or important. Even given that, though, it is hard to see that any summary of *Republic* could be complete without the analysis of the tripartite soul, the analogy between soul and state, and the allegories of sun, line, and cave. If the memory of those present is correct, yesterday's conversation cannot have been the whole of *Republic*. That is not problematic, as there may well have been other occasions when Socrates spoke of these issues, or Plato may have invented a fictional occasion.

19a *yesterday's conversation*: the preceding material has resembled some of the political theory of *Republic*. As with *Republic*, there is to be a separate warrior class to defend the city, while all other men have a single specific trade; these guardians are to have a special education and will live communally without private possessions; and the state will discretely manage marriage, procreation, and the nurture of children (*Republic* 459a ff.).

19b *someone who had gazed on . . . living creatures)*: see *Republic* 472d ff. (cf. 498d ff., 592a ff.), where Socrates compares his description of the ideal city to a painter who has produced a good portrait, but cannot prove that the subject exists.

19c *as it goes to war*: Plato's politics and vision of an ideal state are quite militaristic. In this he may well have been influenced by Athens' defeat by Sparta and the subsequent political unrest and upheavals in the city, and also by Athens' victory over the Persian invaders at Marathon, which he regards as the city's finest hour.

19d *in these respects*: this is typical self-deprecation by Socrates. In Plato's works Socrates often claims to know nothing, but proves very adept at discovering flaws in what other people claim to know. Nor is Socrates a politician, in the sense of running for office, nor is he a writer (if Socrates himself wrote anything, nothing survives), nor is he an orator, in the sense of someone using rhetoric to generate a fine speech about Athens.

19e *As for the sophists*: Plato generally has a very low opinion of the Sophists, men, according to him, who took either side of an argument depending on circumstances, and were paid to do so, rather than being concerned with the truth.

19e *That leaves only people with your qualifications*: Timaeus, Critias, and Hermocrates have philosophical ability and experience as well as political ability; cf. *Republic* on the ideal ruler.

20c *Hermocrates*: This is Hermocrates' only speech in *Timaeus*. He does not speak again until a short speech at the beginning of *Critias*.

20d *a story which, for all its strangeness, is absolutely true*: Critias claims that his story is entirely true; Timaeus will claim that his account of the origins of the cosmos and the origins of man is a 'likely account'.

20e *Solon, the wisest of the seven sages*: Solon was a noted Athenian statesman, responsible for revising the constitution of Athens early in the sixth century BC. The seven sages were the traditional wise men of Greece, dating back to 800–500 BC.

20e *in his verses*: not in any of the surviving fragments, which focus almost exclusively on describing and justifying his political reforms.

20e *the destruction of human life*: Plato seems to have believed in periodic catastrophes which destroy most of human life, cf. *Statesman* 270c ff., *Critias* 111a ff., *Laws* 677a ff.

21a *her festival*: the Panathenaea, the most important festival in Athens for the city's patron, Athena. It was celebrated towards the end of July each year, and with special splendour every four years.

21b *the Koureotis of the Apatouria*: an Athenian festival in late autumn where, on the third day (named 'Koureotis' after a Greek word for 'youth'), new male children were presented to their father's phratry — literally 'brotherhood', a kinship organization with religious and social functions.

21d *Who told him it was true?*: if we are to accept the word of Solon and Critias that the tale is true, it is important to know who told Solon that it is true.

21e *King Amasis*: Herodotus also tells us that Solon travelled in Egypt at the time of King Amasis (see Herodotus 2. 172 ff., on Amasis). As Amasis came to the throne in 570 and Solon died in 560 this is possible, though Plato has Solon visiting Egypt prior to his constitutional reforms, which is less likely.

22b *he was talking about*: in Argive legend Phoroneus was an early, or even the first, ancestor; his daughter Niobe was the founding mother, by Zeus, of the Argive race. The Noah-like legend of Deucalion and his wife Pyrrha has them warned that Zeus was going to destroy the corrupt human race; they built a boat, stocked it with provisions, and rode out the deluge before restocking the earth with human beings. It sounds as though Solon attempted to systematize and rationalize the chaos of Greek legend in the way that several Greek proto-historians of the fifth century had done.

22d *a real event*: so myths can be disguised truth. This may be a model for how we are to think of the Atlantis story—as true, not in the sense that it describes hard historical facts, but in the sense that it communicates a general truth, in this case how the ideally good citizens of Plato's *Republic* would behave if they were to become actual.

22d *the deviation of the heavenly bodies*: Critias' tale contradicts what Timaeus will say about the cosmos. The cause of the periodic destruction of human beings is a shift in the bodies which orbit the earth. Not only is there no mention of this in Timaeus' account, but it runs against the general notions of cosmic stability, and in particular it is contrary to the notion of the predictable great year. The Greek word here for deviation, *paralattein*, can be found in the cosmological accounts of the *Republic* and the *Statesman*, but not in Timaeus' account.

22d *by being released*: the Egyptians had a complex system of floodable canals attached to the Nile for irrigation purposes. The old priest's suggestion seems to be that releasing the river-water into this network of canals keeps the land and its inhabitants from being scorched by the cosmic fire.

22e *rises up from below*: Egypt's lack of rain was notorious, and it had a largely flood-plain agriculture. The Nile would flood, inundating a wide flood basin, and would deposit fertile silt which was farmed when the Nile receded. Why the Nile flooded was a matter of speculation, as it was not related to rain. It is in fact due to melting snow much nearer the Nile's source.

23e *a thousand years later*: the antiquity and primacy of Egypt was almost universally acknowledged among the Greeks, and so this statement of the primacy of Athens is truly remarkable. In Athenian legend Erichthonius, their first ancestor, was the offspring of the deities Earth and Hephaestus (or the elements earth and fire), after Hephaestus' seed had spilled onto the earth during a bungled rape of Athena. How will that fit with Timaeus' account of the origins of humans? Cf. *Critias* 113c–d, where there again seems to be at least one man born from the earth.

24b *the example of the goddess*: the goddess Athena was traditionally armed with a spear and a shield.

24d *men of outstanding intelligence*: the idea that Athens had a climate conducive to producing intelligent men is common in Greek literature—cf.

Euripides, *Medea* 826–9; ps.-Hippocrates, *Airs, Waters, Places* 5; Aristotle, *Politics* 1327b.

24e *Pillars of Heracles*: the straits of Gibraltar.

25a *that genuine sea*: Greek geography recognized three continents (Europe, Asia, and Africa, in our terms) grouped around the Mediterranean, with a further sea surrounding all of them. Here Plato supposes a further continent surrounding the outer ocean.

25b *Etruria*: specifically the central part of Italy, but here meaning Italy as a whole.

25c *abandoned . . . brink of disaster*: this description sounds rather like the plight of Athens in the Persian invasion of 480–479 BC.

26c *for permanence*: the 'encaustic' method of painting involved applying coloured waxes to a surface and fixing the colours in place by means of a heated metal rod. It was used especially for painting difficult surfaces such as stone, or other objects that would stand outdoors.

26e *a true historical account*: Socrates is delighted with Critias' story, though he gives no grounds or criteria for his judgement that it is true.

27a *specialized in natural science*: we know nothing of any real Timaeus, but the fictional characteristics suit him well for the task of describing the origins of the cosmos and of man. 'Natural science' was a broad discipline, covering everything from cosmology and astronomy and the laws of nature, to biology and medicine.

27a *from you*: from Socrates, because Critias has already identified the citizens of bygone Athens with those of Socrates' imaginary community (26d).

27d *what is it that always is . . . never is?*: Timaeus begins his discourse with a distinction that will affect the nature of his whole account, between being and becoming. Some things (i.e. forms) always are, without ever changing, while others undergo change. The verb 'to become' in Ancient Greek has two different senses. It can mean to come into existence (or be created), or it can mean to come to be something.

28a *object of belief, supported by unreasoning sensation*: the things that do change are those of the world about us, which we perceive with our senses. Similar views are expressed in *Republic* (510 ff.), where Plato develops the analogy of the divided line, to explicate his views on knowledge. A line is divided into four sections (L1–L4), with types of belief/knowledge correlated to types of entity. The task of the philosopher is to ascend the line (cf. the cave analogy of *Republic*, which follows on from the divided line).

noêsis, understanding	L4	*epistême*, knowledge	Intelligible entities
dianoia, intelligence	L3		
pistis, belief	L2	*doxa*, opinion	Sensible entities
eikasia, illusion	L1		

So Timaeus will deny that we can have knowledge, in the strong Platonic sense, of the world about us and we have to settle for opinion.

28a *anything created is necessarily created by some cause*: a strong principle, which lays the foundations for the view that as the cosmos has come into being, it too must have a cause.

28b *did it always exist . . . in the first place?*: another key question for Timaeus' account. Has the world come into existence, or has it always existed? If it has come into existence, he will have to explain how and why it came into existence. And his answer is unequivocal—it has come into existence.

29a *two kinds of model*: it is not clear that Plato gives a real choice between the two models that the demiurge may base the cosmos on. What would the changing model be? The conclusion, that the demiurge bases his work on the eternal model, is no surprise, though it is not entirely clear what the eternal model is either. Timaeus' argumentation here is far from watertight; he is effectively presenting an overview in an introductory speech.

29b *are themselves stable and reliable*: our accounts of the stable, intelligible entities have to be stable themselves and entirely reliable, or in other terms, have to be secure knowledge, while (29c) our account of what are likenesses, on the other hand, can be no more than likely. Note the word-play (see p. xxxiv).

29c *to the plausibility of the other*: the analogy is again reminiscent of the divided line of *Republic*.

29c *impossible to give accounts that are . . . perfectly precise . . . as plausible as anyone else's*: the account that Timaeus will give will deal with the physical, sensible world and so can be no more than likely, but he will make sure that it is as good as or better than any other account of the world. There are certain affinities between Parmenides' poem and Timaeus' speech here. Both separate the objects of reason and sensation, reckoning these to be co-ordinate with what is knowable and what is opinable, and both require explanations to be similar in type to what they explain (see especially Parmenides, Fr. 1 28 ff.). We might also compare Timaeus' repeated use of *eikos* to describe the status of any account of the physical with Parmenides' similar usage at Fr. 8 60–1, 'I tell you this way of composing things in all its plausibility, so that never shall any mortal man outstrip you in judgement.'

29d *You're absolutely right*: unlike the Socrates of Plato's earlier works, here Socrates is remarkably compliant, as he was with Critias too.

29e *being free of jealousy*: this establishes a theme for the whole of *Timaeus*. Whoever constructed the cosmos is good, and has no jealousy: he desires that everything should be as good as possible; he creates maximum order, as order is always better than disorder. This passage marks the culmination of a move away from the gods of Greek myth. Contrary to those gods, the generator of the universe is entirely good and entirely free from jealousy (see also pp. xxxii–xxxiv). For the first time, an independent creator is focused solely on the good.

30a *moving in a discordant and chaotic manner*: prior to the intervention of the demiurge, there is chaos. The demiurge will not only establish order, but will also generate harmony in the cosmos.

30a *in all ways better*: a basic assumption throughout *Timaeus* is that order is better than chaos.

30c *endowed . . . with soul and intelligence*: see pp. xxiv–xxvi for why the cosmos needs to be intelligent.

30c *living being the maker made the universe in the likeness of*: quite what Plato has in mind here is unclear. Is the universe modelled on some type of living creature, or on the form of living creatures?

31a *an infinite plurality*: the early atomists Leucippus and Democritus had supposed there to be an infinite plurality of worlds, all occurring due to chance and necessity rather than by any design, but for Plato there is one and only one universe, and it is designed.

31b *is and always will be a unique creation*: Plato has emphasized that there is only one world at any one time, and here he emphasizes that there is only one world through time as well. Prior to Plato, Empedocles had held that, although there was only one world at any one time, it would eventually be destroyed and replaced by another world in an unending cycle.

32a *three solids or three powers*: the reference here may be to cubic and square numbers. See F. M. Cornford, *Plato's Cosmology* (London: Routledge & Kegan Paul, 1937), 44.

32c *can be taken apart only by him who bound it together*: so apart from earth and fire, two more constituents are required for the cosmos, water and air. However we interpret Plato's somewhat obscure remarks about proportion here, the consequence is clear enough. When the cosmos is put together in this way, it becomes a unity, dissoluble only by the creature who bound it together. In what follows, the cosmos will be presumed to be exhaustive of the constituents, so it cannot be attacked from the outside; here we find that, thanks to its internal cohesion through proportion, it will also not deteriorate of itself.

33a *unageing, and untroubled by disease*: the assumption being that it will not become ill or age of itself without external interference.

33b *so he made it perfectly spherical*: the idea that one shape is better than another is a strange one to the modern mind, but came quite easily to the ancients, especially those with a strong teleology.

33b *vastly superior to dissimilarity*: another basic supposition of *Timaeus*, like the earlier idea that order is in all ways better than chaos; we will shortly meet another such axiom, that self-sufficiency is better than dependency.

33d *equip it with hands*: Plato may describe the cosmos as a living entity, but this is no simple anthropomorphism or animism, as we can see here from the description of the cosmos. There may well be assorted criticisms of some presocratics implicit here too, notably perhaps the Pythagoreans. Quoting Aristotle's lost *On the Pythagoreans*, Stobaeus tells us that: 'The universe [according to the Pythagoreans] is unique, and from the infinite it draws in time, breath and void, which distinguishes the places of separate things' (Stobaeus 1.18.1, Wright's translation and brackets (1995), 62). So too the idea of a unique, self-sufficient, and exhaustive cosmos tells against the views of the atomists. One might also compare Parmenides' 'well-rounded sphere' from his *Way of Truth*, though the differences from Parmenides are perhaps more important than any such similarities. Plato's cosmos is alive and in motion, has a beginning, is not homogenous, and is designed to support life.

34a *the other six kinds of motion*: the cosmos has perfect regular circular motion. It has no part in any of the other six motions (up, down, left, right, forward, back), so there can be no metaphysical reason, relating to the imperfection of the sensible world, why there cannot be entirely regular circular motion.

34a *he created it without legs and feet*: the apparently trivial fact that the cosmos has no feet is significant for two reasons. It is the culmination of a line of thought beginning with Thales—why does the earth not fall? This is now treated with full generality—why does the cosmos, the totality of everything, not fall? Secondly, in previous works (notably *Republic* and *Statesman*; see pp. xxii–xxiv) Plato has the cosmos turning on a pivot. Now it does not need any such support, nor is motion going to be affected by any friction from a pivot. The cosmos will not wind down and be in need of the intervention of deities as it is in *Republic* and *Statesman*.

34b *the god who exists for ever took thought for the god that was to be*: rephrased, the demiurge (the god who always exists) took thought for the world-soul (the god who is generated).

34c *the coincidence and contingency that characterize our lives*: this may be one reason why we can have only a likely account of the cosmos, though 37b–c and 44b–c suggest that it may be something we can at least attempt to control or ameliorate.

35a *third kind of substance*: the reason for this mixing will become clearer. Essentially, perception takes place by the principle of like to like, so soul must have a part in the unchanging to have some cognition of forms and so on, and some part in the changing to perceive bodies. So the third substance is a blend of indivisible and never-changing substance, so it will be able to apprehend and make judgements about the intelligible, and of divisible and changing substance, so that it will be able to perceive and make judgements about the sensible.

35a *difference does not readily form mixtures*: so this process could not occur accidentally and the action of the demiurge is required. Just as the physical cosmos could not have come together accidentally, but needs a provident designer, so the world-soul does too.

36a *twenty-seven times the quantity of the first*: this gives us the sequence: 1–2–3–4–9–8–27.

36a *exceeded by the other extreme*: Timaeus treats 1–2–3–4–9–8–27 as two sequences, 1–2–4–8 and 1–3–9–27, and goes on to fill these intervals with the harmonic means (2ab/a+b) and the arithmetic means (a+b/2), giving a sequence of: 1–4/3–3/2–2–8/3–3–4–9/2–16/3–6–8–9–27/ 2–18–27.

36b *were 256:243*: there is then some further filling of intervals where multiplying one of the numbers in this sequence by 9/8 does not exceed the next number in the sequence. So the first part of the sequence will run: 1–9/8–81/64–4/3–3/2–27/16–243/128–2. These divisions have a musical significance, as 3/2 represents a musical fifth, 4/3 a fourth, 9/8 a tone. The remainder between the 9/8 multiplications and the next number is 256/243, close to a semitone. In musical notation, beginning with C for the sake of simplicity, we can represent this sequence as follows:

This represents the notes C, D, E, F, G, A, B, C. Further notes above these will be generated by the division of the sequence from 2 to 27, covering three-and-a-half octaves. Plato stops with the seventh term, 27, as there are only five planets in addition to the sun and moon. There is a need to go as far as the seventh term to generate the harmony of the heavens, but no need to go any further. In *Timaeus* and subsequent works there is no mention of any audible harmony of the heavenly bodies. There is a harmony to the structure of the world-soul, but no sound. This differs from the Pythagoreans, and also differs from the Myth of Er at 617b–c of *Republic*.

36b *was all used up*: the soul-stuff is entirely used up, as the physical stuff of the cosmos was.

36c *a point opposite their original junction*: the demiurge splits the soul-stuff lengthwise and joins the two resulting lengths together, initially as a

Greek letter *chi*, X, and then joins the limbs of the *chi* together. This can be represented like this:

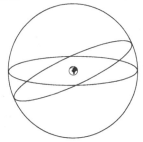

The horizontal arm of the *chi* will move the whole cosmos in a once-a-day rotation. The other arm of the *chi* will move the sun, moon, and five planets relative to the fixed stars.

36d *seven unequal rings*: this gives the orbits for the sun, moon, Mercury, Venus, Mars, Jupiter, and Saturn.

36d *three of them being similar in speed*: the sun, Mercury, and Venus, with the 'other four' being the moon, Mars, Jupiter, and Saturn.

37b *the same or different*: the world-soul, *qua* compounded from being, sameness, and difference, is able to make judgements concerning being, sameness, and difference in whatever it encounters. Note that 'identity' has occasionally been used in the translation instead of 'sameness', in order to cover not just judgements of the form 'This is the same as that', but also 'This is the same as itself'.

37b *that which is eternally consistent*: so the soul can not only compare material objects to one another (as identical or different), but can also compare material objects to immaterial objects (e.g. 'this apple both resembles and is dissimilar from the Ideal Apple'). This latter kind of judgement gives us, as possessors of soul, access to the world of Platonic forms: see *Phaedo* 74c.

37b *beliefs and opinions . . . are the result*: even for the world-soul there is a difference between judgements about intelligible entities and those concerned with perceptible entities. As at *Timaeus* 27c–28d, we can have knowledge of the intelligible but only opinion of the sensible. The world-soul may have true opinion, but for Plato there is a considerable difference between true opinion and knowledge.

37c *the place where belief and knowledge arise*: it is a typically Platonic belief that knowledge is generated by the soul, not by the brain, the blood (some presocratics believed that we think with the blood), or the senses.

37d *while eternity abides in oneness*: this contrast is important for *Timaeus*. The physical cosmos is less perfect than what it is a model of. Does this mean that it moves in an irregular manner? No, because the contrast is framed as one of movement according to number, as opposed to stability.

37d *'time'*: if the motions are time, and time is regular (and nowhere does Plato suggest otherwise), then the motions must be regular too.

37e *before the creation of the universe*: measured and orderly time only comes into being with the ordering of the cosmos. Prior to that there are no days, nights, months, or years.

37e *mistakenly apply to that which is eternal*: 'was' and 'will be' are tenses which apply to things which change. Only 'is' is appropriate in the description of things which do not change.

38b *now is not the appropriate moment*: Plato shies away from a full metaphysical discussion of time and tenses. The second part of *Parmenides* contains several arguments about time.

38c *the model exists for all eternity, while the universe was and is and always will be for all time*: this is all that Plato needs to get out of this discussion of time here—a reasonable contrast between eternity and time, and how the cosmos can be said to be in time.

38c *were created to determine and preserve the numbers of time*: this is the purpose the demiurge has in creating the sun, moon, and planets. They must move in a regular fashion if they are to distinguish and preserve time.

38d *sun into the circle second closest to the earth*: this is typical of the order of the heavenly bodies in early, geocentric astronomy.

38d *assigned them tendencies that oppose it*: as Mercury (Hermes) and Venus (the Morning Star) change their position relative to the sun (see next note), they cannot have exactly the same speed as the sun but must have some other motion as well. Does the 'opposing tendency' invoked here for Mercury and Venus entail a breach of the principle of regular circular motion? It is possible that Plato does not give us the full details in this compressed account, and the opposing tendency involves further regular circular motions, or that Plato knew there was a problem here which he as yet had no solution for, but hoped would be solved by further regular circular motions; see pp. xli–xlii.

38d *constantly overtake and are overtaken by one another*: it is important to be aware of which phenomenon is being referred to here. In modern terms, Mercury and Venus are inferior planets, that is, the radius of their orbit around the sun is less than that of the earth, while Mars, Jupiter, and Saturn are superior planets, having larger orbits than the earth. This is significant because of the limitations of where inferior planets can be seen in relation to the sun: Mercury and Venus are always seen relatively close to the sun. In the following diagram, the inferior planet is at its maximum angular distance from the sun relative to the earth. Move the earth anywhere else in the diagram, and the angle will be less:

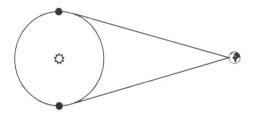

Mercury and Venus will sometimes appear to precede the sun, and sometimes to follow it. In practical terms, Mercury and Venus are seen fairly low on the horizon either just before sunrise (when they precede the sun) or just after sunset (when they follow the sun). So at one extreme of their orbits of the sun, Mercury and Venus are seen at their maximum elongation from the sun while preceding it. As they go round their orbits, they precede the sun less and are eventually 'overtaken' by it. They then gradually go to the other extreme of following the sun, and then begin to catch the sun up again and eventually overtake it again. As Mercury and Venus have different speeds of orbit, they will overtake and be overtaken by each other as well; that is, sometimes Mercury will precede Venus, and sometimes Venus will precede Mercury.

39a *though in fact they were overtaking them*: there may be a critique of Democritus here. According to Democritus, the nearer celestial objects are to the earth, the less they are carried around by the vortex (Democritus' views are reported by Lucretius at *De Rerum Natura* 5. 621 ff.). So the moon, the nearest body to the earth, moves most slowly and is left behind most. This creates the greatest difference in motion relative to the fixed stars, so the moon (on this theory) appears to move swiftly relative to the fixed stars, completing a circuit in a month, when actually (on this theory) its absolute motion is the slowest. Plato changes this. The fixed stars still move the most rapidly, but the sun, moon, and planets now have their own motions (so they are no longer 'left behind' in a vortex), and the most rapid of them completes its motion relative to the fixed stars in the shortest time, so now the moon has the most rapid motion. There is another interesting consequence of Plato's combinations of regular circular motions. If there is a single vortex, one can see how the fixed stars will be swept around by it. One can also see how there will be some relative motion between sun, moon, and planets and the fixed stars, if the former are to some extent 'left behind' by the vortex. But if sun, moon, and planets are thought to have a combination of two circular motions, these motions having different axes, how can that be accounted for in one vortex with one axis of rotation?

39d *constitute time*: if the motions of the planets constitute time, and these motions are irregular, then time will be irregular. So, however complex the motions of the heavens, they must be regular.

39d *perfect year*: if there is a specific amount of time between grand conjunctions, then celestial motion must be regular, or we are left with the highly improbable alternative that the irregular motions somehow cancel each other out. In that case, the great year would lose its significance as a sign of the rational ordering of the universe. If the great year recurs—and there is no suggestion in *Timaeus* that it does not—then celestial motion must be regular and the solar system stable and free from any degeneration. The predictable recurrence of the great year is a sign of cosmological stability.

40a *mostly out of fire*: the stars are rounded, made of fire for the most part, and each has intelligence set in it. Plato does not have a spherical shell in which the stars are embedded, as with some later cosmologies. The stars keep formation due to each having an intelligence.

40b *winding around*: the earth is generally taken to be central and immobile in Plato, as in all Greek thinking prior to Plato with the exception of the Pythagoreans. What winding or turning motion might the earth have? Two older ideas, that the earth orbits the centre of the cosmos, or moves up and down on the central axis of the cosmos, have now generally been rejected, as the objections to them are, to say the least, considerable. As we saw earlier, there is a careful division of the same in order to produce orbits for the sun, moon, and five planets. If the earth orbits the centre of the cosmos, why is there not a division of the different for it? If the earth is not at the centre of the cosmos, what is at the centre of the cosmos? There is no reason here to suppose that Plato is thinking of any sort of Pythagorean system with a central fire, as no central fire and no counter-earth are mentioned. The earth is supposed to define and guard time, which it would have trouble doing if it has either of these motions. It is very hard to see what would motivate Plato to have the earth in motion around the centre of the cosmos. It would not help the astronomy of *Timaeus*, there is no physical necessity for the earth to move in such a manner, and it would not help to explain any physical phenomena.

Cornford (*Plato's Cosmology*, 130 ff.) suggested that there is a sense in which the earth might be said to have motion, while in fact it stands still. If the entire cosmos is rotating, then, in the absence of any other consideration, the earth would rotate with it, especially as the world-soul permeates the cosmos from the centre to the extremes, including the earth (36e). But this fails to allow for the existence of night and day, as the earth would be rotating at the same rate as the cosmos. The earth, in the absence of any other consideration, may rotate on its own, like the stars and the planets. If the earth's own rotation is equal and opposite to that of the cosmos, then the earth would stand still. There are other possibilities here. The cosmos might have an absolute rotation of less than once a day, with the earth rotating in the opposite sense, giving a relative rotation of once a day between them. Similarly, the cosmos might have an absolute rotation of more than once a day and the earth a smaller rate of rotation in the same sense, again giving a relative rotation of once a day between them. Cornford's proposal is attractive as it is simple, and allows the earth to be stationary and the cosmos to have an absolute rotation of once a day. The objection that this proposal ignores the different does not carry great weight. While everything is subject to the motion of the same—or, put another way, all the components of the intelligent whole of the cosmos rotate with the cosmos—only certain components of the whole (moon, sun, five planets) are subject to the motion of the different. The stars are not subject to it, and even though its motion is centred on the earth, the earth need not be subject to it.

A different solution here is to argue that we should read *eillomenēn*, 'packed around' rather than *illomenēn*, 'winding around'. If the earth is simply 'packed around' the central axis, then there need be no question of its motion.

40c *turn back on themselves and go forward again*: Plato appears to be aware of the retrograde motion of the planets. This is certainly the most natural reading of *epanakuklēseis*, literally a 'circling back', in this context. The planets move relative to the fixed stars, but will occasionally stop relative to the stars, move backwards, stop again, and move forwards again: see p. xli.

40c *conjunction and opposition with one another*: Plato may also have good knowledge of what happens when planets pass each other, depending on whether he uses different words to refer to one or several phenomena here. When planets pass each other, there are three things which may happen: they may pass each other with sufficient distance between them that they remain two distinct objects; they may 'touch' each other, such that they appear to be one brighter object; or one may pass in front of the other and occlude it.

40d *veiled from our sight and then reappear*: Plato was aware of Mercury and Venus 'overtaking and being overtaken by' the sun (see 38d). He may well also be aware of another phenomenon, which is that Mercury and Venus are not visible when they are close to the sun. They disappear from view as they approach the sun and reappear on the far side. This was a phenomenon much studied by Babylonian astronomers.

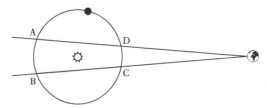

A–B and C–D are sections of the planet's orbit where it
would be invisible due to its proximity to the sun.

40d *without visible models*: Plato may have had some form of rudimentary armillary sphere to help him envisage the motions of the heavens.

40e *implausible and illogical*: Timaeus seems to have his tongue in his cheek.

41a *gave birth to further offspring*: genealogies of the gods were typical in Greek mythology; see e.g. Hesiod's *Theogony*.

41a *anything created by me is imperishable unless I will it*: Timaeus here expresses the view that the cosmos is dissoluble, but will not in fact be dissolved because of the goodness of the demiurge. This is significant as a statement of the long-term stability of the cosmos. *Timaeus* differs from *Statesman* in this respect.

41b *a mark of evil*: this passage seems to have provoked Aristotle, who attempts to demonstrate that whatever is generated can also undergo destruction, and whatever is not generated cannot undergo destruction, and that there is nothing which is generated which is everlasting (*On the Heavens* I. 12).

41b *remain yet uncreated*: the three kinds are creatures of the air, water, and earth (39e–40a), but since they all develop by reincarnation from human beings (42b–c, 91d–92c), Timaeus focuses in what follows on the creation of human beings.

41c *imitate the power that I used*: human beings and all other earthly living things are to be made by the demigods that the demiurge has created, not by the demiurge himself, though the highest part of the human soul will be generated by the demiurge, and it will then be the job of the demigods to house this soul.

41d *lower in the scale of purity*: the demiurge generates human souls in a manner analogous to that in which he generated the soul of the cosmos, but the mix of sameness, being, and difference is not quite as good. It seems that the same harmonic proportions are employed. This is not made clear here, but at 43d we find that these proportions are disrupted by sensation when the soul is first given a body.

41e *planted each of them in the appropriate instrument of time*: one human soul is paired with one star. The human soul will come to earth to be embodied, and may, if it lives a good life, return to its star. Although each human soul is assigned a star, the stars themselves are ensouled by the heavenly gods. The cosmos as a whole has a soul and spins on one spot. The stars (including sun, moon, five planets, and probably, in a slightly odd sense relating to 40b, the earth as well) all spin and have other motions as appropriate. If they did not have these divine souls, they would not spin in a regular manner nor have other motions in a regular manner.

42a *come to be called 'male'*: it was usual in ancient Greece for the male to be considered superior.

42a *powerful properties*: that is, properties that are powerful enough to penetrate the insensitive body and be registered by the soul: see *Philebus* 33d–34a.

42b *in control of these things or were controlled by them*: an important theme in the *Timaeus*' psychology is that humans should be in control of their sensations and emotions rather than be controlled by them. If they control them, they will lead a good life.

42c *become a woman instead of a man*: compare this cycle of incarnation with *Phaedrus* 248c–e and with the Myth of Er at the end of *Republic*. It is notable again that any woes that befall a soul are its own fault and the downward cycle of man to woman to animal can be reversed by that soul. Timaeus says more about this degeneration at 90e. Not surprisingly, 42d tells us that the first condition is the best condition for humans, and adds the important principle that the demiurge is not responsible for any wrongdoing by humankind. The demiurge is wholly good and free from jealousy, and so wants only the best for human beings. He sets everything up so that they can achieve good things in life, but if humans fail to do so it is not his fault.

42d *its original, best state*: our minds are at their best before they are bound into our bodies and subject to sensations and emotions. It is this sort of state we can seek to achieve by controlling our sensations and emotions.

42e *govern and steer*: see also 90a, and the Myth of Er in *Republic* on each person having his own personal deity in life.

42e *he resumed his life in his proper abode*: it would be wrong to impose onto Plato here the terms of the seventeenth-century debate between Newton and Leibniz. Leibniz argued that an omnipotent god would produce a universe which had no need of his subsequent interference; the belief that god 'needed to wind his watch' detracted from the notion of god and led to atheism. Newton, through his intermediary Samuel Clarke, replied that god could hardly be an 'absent landlord' and must care for his creation, and so must interfere with it; any other view would lead to atheism. But Plato lacks the notion of omnipotence. The demiurge still cares for the cosmos (it will not be dissolved except through his will), even if he returns to his proper place. He has delegated to the lesser gods much of the running of the cosmos, and not least the way that the heavens move. Later in antiquity thinkers concerned themselves with questions such as why, if the cosmos is generated, does god choose this specific moment to generate the cosmos rather than any other? What was god doing prior to the generation of the cosmos? More subtly, did the generation of the cosmos entail any change of mind on god's part? Does generating the cosmos change god? Christian theologians took up many of these issues, with St Augustine's work probably being the pinnacle of this tradition.

43a *together with countless rivets*: the lesser gods begin the process of making humans by placing the 'immortal principle' in a body made from earth, water, air, and fire, and by unifying the body with many rivets. So the 'revolutions' of the human mind will now become prone to the problems affecting the body.

43c *'sensations'*: as elsewhere in the dialogues, Plato is trying out an etymology—but here it is completely unclear what etymology of *aisthēseis*, sensations, he is getting at.

44b *things increasingly return to normal*: when the stream of nutrition lessens a little, the revolutions can stabilize and pursue their natural path. When they do this, they can make correct attributions of sameness and difference. This makes the soul intelligent. There does not seem to be a limit on what humans can achieve here if they have proper nurture and education. Indeed, this should be the goal of life, rather than limping through life and returning to Hades unfulfilled.

44d *In imitation of the rounded shape of the universe*: this keeps up the macrocosm–microcosm analogy between man and the universe.

44d *vehicle and means of transport*: see p. xviii for this as possibly criticism of Empedocles.

45b *to enable the soul to be fully aware*: this too may be aimed at Empedocles: see Fr. 61 quoted on pp. xvi–xvii. According to Plato, the gods organize the human body with the face and body pointing forwards. If human parts meet by chance, as Empedocles had argued, how plausible is it that all the parts fit in exactly the right way? Empedocles' reply might have been that though there are mismatches, it is only when beings capable of reproduction are formed that species are generated.

45b *flow through the eyes*: Plato believes that vision is the result of the interaction of light flowing out through the eyes and light in the external world.

46a *mirrors or any other reflective surface*: a consequence of the theory of vision is being able to explain why, in mirror images, left appears right and right appears to be left. There is also a discussion of this topic at *Sophist* 266c.

46c *contributory causes*: this could have come straight from the 'autobiographical' passage of *Phaedo* 96a ff. There are contributory causes, but most people wrongly take them to be the sole causes, when they should be considering teleology.

46d *cooling things down and heating them, or thickening and thinning them*: cooling and heating is possibly a reference to Anaximander (see ps.-Plutarch, *Stromateis* 2), while thickening and thinning is possibly a reference to Anaximenes (ibid. 3). But the attack is quite general: none of these processes are capable of acting with intelligence, nor are any of the traditional four elements. This is an important critique of a good deal of presocratic cosmogony. One might try to explain how a cosmos is formed by attributing to a fundamental substance or process the capacity to direct things. Anaximander believed that his Unlimited 'steers', while Anaximenes may have held a similar view about air (his follower, Diogenes of Apollonia, certainly did). If one rules out this kind of possibility, as Plato seems to do here, one is left with an external god imposing order, or with supposing the cosmos to have come into being through chance. The final comment in this passage is also critical for Plato's notion of cosmogony. There are causes which will produce only disorderly and chance effects, but without intelligence causes will produce nothing of any worth; this rules out the possibility of chance generating a cosmos.

47b *the rational revolutions of the heavens*: it is from our observation of the heavens that we have derived number and all philosophy, so it is no great surprise that this is the greatest gift from gods to men. On some readings of *Republic* VII, though, this passage comes as a considerable surprise. If Plato bans or denigrates observational astronomy in *Republic*, what of this passage? Is this a change of mind? As argued in the Introduction, Plato does not ban observational astronomy in *Republic* VII, but rather draws a distinction between how astronomy is done now and how the guardians ought to use astronomy in their education.

47c *the perfect evenness of the god's*: there is a contrast between the entirely unwandering motions of the mind of god and the wandering motions in our own heads. Here is very strong evidence that stars, sun, moon, and planets move in a perfectly orderly manner.

47c *sound and hearing too*: sound, here meaning speech and music, is another gift from the gods for the same general purposes as eyesight. It allows us to bring the disorderly motions within our own heads into order. It is interesting and perhaps significant that here we have the same order (sight, hearing, music) as we do at *Republic* 530d. If the previous section on sight gives us at least a different emphasis on the benefits of eyesight, and another role for astronomy, here we have similar moves for hearing and harmony.

47e *digression*: 45b–46a.

47e *an account of the creations of necessity*: Timaeus signals very clearly a shift from talking about the products of intelligence to the products of necessity. There will be a similar clear shift to talking about the products of a combination of reason and necessity at 69a.

48a *towards perfection*: see pp. xlvii–xlix on the relation of intelligence and necessity.

48a *wandering cause as well*: 'Matter, having no inherent tendency toward good ends, acts in a purposeless way unless it is directed, or in Timaeus's preferred idiom, "persuaded", by intelligence' (Sedley, *Creationism and Its Critics*, 114–15).'

48b *how they were created*: or at least it has not been explained to Plato's satisfaction. Some thinkers (e.g. Thales, Anaximenes, Heraclitus) took one 'element' (respectively, water, air, fire) as basic and outlined how it might be changed into the others, but they left unexplained the origin of the basic element.

48b *compared to syllables*: *Timaeus* will give us a version of the letters-and-syllables analogy which is common in later Plato (*Theaetetus* 201d ff., *Statesman* 277d ff., *Sophist* 253a ff., *Philebus* 18b ff.). Plato employs the analogy to illustrate not only something about the nature of language, but also, arguably in some or all of these cases, about the nature of the world. Plato is often interested in which letters do or do not combine to make syllables, and is concerned with the bonds between letters (see *Sophist* 253a, *Philebus* 18c). Why do earth, water, air, and fire not even constitute syllables? If we glance ahead for a moment to geometrical atomism, the 'letters' are taken to be the two basic triangles. These form either squares or other triangles, which figures in turn then form a cube of earth, a tetrahedron of fire, an octahedron of air, or an icosahedron of water. Any perceptible amount of earth, water, air, or fire will contain a considerable number of these three-dimensional figures. No one of any sense, then, would call earth, water, air and fire even syllables, let alone consider them to be letters.

48c *such a conception*: several presocratic philosophers did identify one element as fundamental and basic: see the first note to 48b.

48e *start again from the beginning*: Timaeus calls upon the gods as he did at the outset of his discourse, reaffirms the likely nature of the account, and begins a new line of thought.

49a *this difficult and obscure kind of thing*: from the outset Plato recognizes that the receptacle is difficult to describe.

49a *the receptacle (or nurse, if you like) of all creation*: it is never made clear in what sense the receptacle is a 'nurse'. It is possible to take it as a material metaphor, whereby the 'nurse' is a wet-nurse, giving material sustenance to what comes to be in the receptacle, but there is nothing that compels us to take the metaphor this way. Another possibility is that the receptacle is a nurse in the sense of rocking its charges: the use of the word at 52d leads up to the description of the receptacle shaking the things that are in it, and 88d has the 'nurse and the nurturer of the universe' always moving and agitating the cosmos.

49b *by all four names, one after another*: if earth, water, air, and fire all change into one another, as was perfectly possible in most ancient theories of the elements, and indeed was a common view, which of them is more basic than any other?

49c *water in turn gives rise to earth and stones*: one can find explanations of this type in many presocratic thinkers. They originate in Egyptian and Babylonian cosmogonies, which were impressed by the observation of the annual flood receding and revealing new land.

49d *'something of this sort'*: the translation and interpretation of this passage have been much disputed. Debate centres on the phrase, *mē touto alla to toiouton hekastote prosagoreuein pur*.

The traditional reading is that *touto* ('this') and *to toiouton* ('suchlike') are competing predicates for the subject *pur*, fire. The phrase then concerns ways in which we may talk of fire, one proper and one improper: we ought not to call phenomenal fire 'this', but we can call it 'suchlike'.

The alternative reading takes *touto* and *toiouton* to be competing subjects for the predicate *pur*. This then reads, 'do not call this (phenomenal fire) fire, but do call what is each time "the suchlike" fire'. On this reading the sense is that words such as fire, which we now apply to transient phenomena, are better applied to more stable entities. So if we are to use 'fire' properly, we should only use it to refer to entities which are 'this', and not those which are 'suchlike'.

On the traditional version we can call phenomenal fire 'suchlike', so it is permissible to call this phenomenon 'fiery' or 'fire-like'. Forms and the receptacle, however, as they are unchanging, can have normal names and can each be regarded as a 'this'. On the alternative reading, we are not told how we can refer to phenomenal fire, only that it cannot be called 'fire'. We can call 'what is each time suchlike' fire, though it is not clear what 'what is each time suchlike' might be. Both of these interpretations are acceptable renderings of the Greek. Which we choose to accept, however tentatively, will depend on more general considerations. Here are two:

(1) A major concern over the traditional reading was the apparent discord between *Timaeus* and *Theaetetus*. It has been argued that *Theaetetus* postdates and corrects *Timaeus*' view on the relation of flux and language (G. E. L. Owen, 'The Place of the *Timaeus* in Plato's Later Dialogues' (1953), repr. in R. E. Allen (ed.), *Studies in Plato's Metaphysics* (London: Routledge & Kegan Paul, 1965), 322 ff.). It is surely true, so Owen argued, that if everything is in radical flux, we cannot successfully refer

to anything at all, and this is a better position than the 'lame plea' of *Timaeus* 49d ff. that we can refer to the four elements as 'the suchlike'. The alternative view was pioneered by H. F. Cherniss, 'A Much Misread Passage in the Timaeus (49c7–50b5)' (1954), repr. in Cherniss, *Selected Papers* (Leiden: Brill, 1977), 346–63). The key passages in *Theaetetus* are 182c ff. and 183a ff. The flux described there is very radical. If something is always in motion and always changing all of its characteristics all the time, then we cannot refer to it at all (cf. *Cratylus* 439d). However, it is not clear that *Timaeus* envisages the world being in so radical a flux. Some passages can be interpreted in that way, but it is not necessary to do so. Nor is it clear that Plato is committed to a radical flux in *Theaetetus*.

(2) A major concern with the alternative reading is what things are 'each time suchlike' that we can call, for example, fire? Clearly not the phenomena, nor the receptacle, nor, it would seem, forms. The 'suchlike' entities are explicitly said to enter and leave the receptacle (49e ff.), which forms explicitly (52a) do not do. This leaves the alternative reading supposing some fourth kind of thing, beyond forms, receptacle, and phenomena, where *Timaeus* is explicit that there are three. As Plato never explicitly says anything of this fourth kind, the alternative reading seems somewhat unnatural.

49e *refer to fire as 'something that is regularly of this sort'*: when we see what we had previously called 'fire', we should call it 'fiery' instead; we should not identify it as 'fire', as it will change to something that is not fire, but we can say that currently it is 'fiery'.

50a *and from which it subsequently passes away*: we can refer to the receptacle in this manner, as it is stable, but not to what occurs in it, which is liable to change. The 'from which it comes and into which it is destroyed' formula that Plato uses here was applied by some presocratics to the element which they considered to be basic.

50b *in fact they're changing even while they're being identified*: to be safe, we must call what we have here 'gold', rather than name any shape the gold may be in. Analogously, the safest thing to do is call anything 'receptacle' (i.e. that which does not change which underlies the changes), rather than call it by any name we currently give to transient phenomena.

50c *appears different at different times*: the receptacle can only *appear* to be different at different times. If it were to change in its own nature, we would need to look for something unchanging which underlies that change in the receptacle.

50c *later*: this promise is never fulfilled.

50e *altogether characterless*: that the receptacle is entirely characterless is required by this line of argument, but gives rise to a problem. How can one either grasp or talk about something that is entirely characterless? See 52a–b.

51b *It's almost incomprehensible*: throughout this passage Timaeus is aware of the difficulties of giving an account of the receptacle.

51b *Is there such a thing as fire which is just itself?*: this question cannot be ignored, but cannot be treated at length either in this context, so we get a brief argument only. It is remarkable that forms have not been mentioned or argued for until now. We might take them to be implicit in the distinction made at the outset of Timaeus' discourse (between what is, is stable, and is apprehended by intellect and what becomes, changes, and is perceived), but this is their first explicit mention.

51d *if knowledge and true belief are two distinct kinds of thing*: it is an important tenet of Platonism that knowledge and true opinion are very different, and Timaeus goes on to summarize why. Compare 27d ff. on the differences between what is and what becomes.

52a *there is space*: this is the first time that the receptacle has been referred to specifically as space.

52b *hardly credible*: it is difficult to talk about something as characterless as the receptacle. If the receptacle is neither intelligible, nor perceptible, it is also difficult to apprehend. This gives it a rather odd epistemological status.

53a *those that were most similar were pushed the closest together*: the shaking of the receptacle produces a like-to-like sorting. There were hand-held baskets which were used in agriculture for sorting grain, oats, barley, and the like. When shaken, they sorted seeds of similar density together. Cornford, *Plato's Cosmology*, 201, has a good illustration.

53b *with no god present*: the pre-cosmic chaos is non-progressive. Although there is a like-to-like sorting, this is not enough to produce a cosmos. See pp. xvii–xviii.

53b *use shapes and numbers to assign them definite forms*: an important theme in *Timaeus*, both in the cosmology, where the orbits of the heavenly bodies are given shape and number, and here in the theory of matter as well. Hence the demiurge may be called a geometer god.

53b *as beautiful and as perfect as they could possibly be*: Timaeus restates another important theme, familiar from 30a.

53c *consists of triangles*: the restriction to *rectilinear* plane figures has no logical basis and is designed purely to lead into what follows.

53d *half of a right angle which has been divided by equal sides*: the first of Timaeus' two basic triangles, then, is like this:

53d *two parts by unequal sides*: the other type of basic triangle is to be a scalene triangle, but we are not yet told which of many scalene triangles is going to be used.

53e *more perfect visible bodies than these four*: the four that will be chosen are the cube, the tetrahedron, the octahedron, and the icosahedron. All these are known as Platonic solids, and are constructed from identical faces (the cube from six identical squares, the tetrahedron from four identical triangles, etc.). There are very few solids with these properties.

54b *triple the square of the shorter side*: there are an unlimited number of scalene triangles, so Timaeus chooses the best, which he takes to be the scalene which is half of an equilateral triangle. This is one advantage of Plato's teleology, that when faced with a choice from an unlimited field, the best can be chosen. The drawback here is in defining criteria for what is the best, and Timaeus has little to say on this, other than some cryptic remarks about the construction of the four best solid bodies for earth, water, air, and fire.

54c *Only the three can do that*: Timaeus now clarifies whether all the bodies can transform into each other. Going back to 49b ff., it appeared that earth, water, air, and fire could all transform into each other, but this is illusory. Three of the four types (water, air, and fire, though they are not mentioned specifically here) can transform into each other, being constructed from one type of triangle; the fourth type (earth) cannot, being constructed from the other type of triangle.

54e *a single equilateral triangle made up of six triangles*: Timaeus now begins to construct complex triangles, with the intention of generating the simplest solid. The first is an equilateral, made up of six basic scalene triangles.

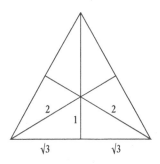

55a *Four of these solid angles form the first solid figure*: out of these complex equilateral triangles, certain solid bodies can be made—first the tetrahedron, and then in what immediately follows the octahedron and the icosahedron. 'The angle that comes straight after the most obtuse possible plane angle' is an overly precise way of saying '180° angle'.

55c *The resulting construct had the shape of a cube*: first, the second type of triangle forms up in fours in squares:

Then these squares form cubes:

55c *used it for the whole*: so far, Timaeus has used four bodies of a certain type, all constructed from faces of the same size and shape. There is another figure of this type, the dodecahedron. This cannot be constructed from either of the two basic types of triangle and is not required for the theory of the elements. It is unclear what Timaeus means when he says that god 'used it for the whole'. It is possible that it is used for the earth, with reference here to *Phaedo* 110b and the comment that the earth is like a ball made of twelve pieces. I find this unlikely, especially as it makes little sense of the phrase about decoration, which can also be rendered as 'covering with animals', which might well be a reference to constellations. So perhaps the dodecahedron is used either for the zodiac or the cosmos as a whole, though it is hard to see the connection with either, especially as the cosmos is specifically described as spherical.

55d *a boundless plurality*: there were ancient thinkers who did believe in a boundless plurality of worlds, most notably, prior to Plato, Leucippus and Democritus.

55d *five worlds*: five worlds corresponding to the five Platonic solids.

55e *a square is more stable than a triangle*: the most stable of the solids we have generated is assigned to earth, which is perceived to be the most stable of the four elements. Timaeus uses similar principles to assign the three remaining figures to the three remaining elements.

56c *lumps made up of a lot of them all at once*: it is no great surprise that individual elemental bodies are too small for us to perceive, but is also quite significant. While what we perceive may change, what is below our threshold of perception may have greater stability.

56e *into a single complete water-figure*: Timaeus begins his account of the transformation of the elements. Earth cannot transform into the others, as we have seen, but it can be affected by the others. This passage is significant in that it seems to imply that cubes of earth can be broken up, and then recombine at some later stage. This would imply that there can be 'loose' faces and perhaps even 'loose' triangles for some considerable time, not just in the transformation of, say, water and air.

57b *fire turns into air, or air into water*: where we have two unlike substances, the weaker will be assimilated by these transformations into the stronger.

57c *by the movement of the receptacle*: the shaking of the receptacle mentioned at 52e ff., which produces a like-to-like sorting.

57d *engendered a triangle of just a single size*: the basic triangles come together to form either squares or equilateral triangles. The squares and equilateral triangles can have different sizes, depending on how they are made up. So we can put four squares together to get a bigger square or, four equilateral triangles together to get a larger equilateral triangle. Other combinations of this type, resulting in other sizes of square or equilateral triangle, are possible. The larger sizes join up to form solids of a larger size.

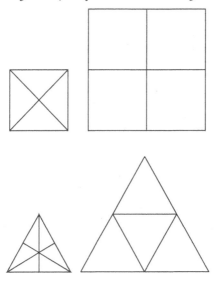

58a *already discussed*: presumably Plato is thinking of the 'inequality' between all the different elementary triangles.

58a *every last bit of void*: circular motion does not produce this compressive effect, but ancient scientists inferred that it did from observation of how a whirlpool moves objects to its centre (Aristotle, *On the Heavens* 295a ff.).

58b *gaps within the large bodies*: the solids that Plato supposes for the elements cannot fit together to fill space completely. The compressive effect of the revolution of the whole, though, will push them together so that the smaller particles fill the spaces as best as possible. It is hard to believe that Plato was not aware that his theory of atoms and how they move and change implied that there must be gaps between atoms and spaces when they change. Certainly Aristotle is aware of this sort of problem (*On the Heavens* 306b3 ff.).

59a *'cooling'* . . . *'solidification'*: the idea that fire is a substance, and that its presence brings heat and its leaving produces coolness, had a long history. Even when eighteenth- and nineteenth-century scientists broke with the ancient idea of fire as an element, they substituted first phlogiston, a substance with weight that carried heat, then caloric, a substance without weight that carried heat. The modern idea of heat as the rapid motion of particles dates from the mid-nineteenth century.

59c *its constituent earth and water*: the ancient elements of earth, water, and air can be thought of as principles of solidity, fluidity, and gaseousness. This is important for understanding the supposed composition of some materials. Materials that did not melt when heated (e.g. stones) were thought to be composed almost entirely of earth. Materials that did melt, such as metals, were thought to be composed of earth and water, water explaining the fluidity of the heated metal.

60b *their normal, loose-textured state*: this fits with one of the general ideas of this section of *Timaeus*, that pleasure is associated with the return to a normal state.

60c *the new air pushes at the adjacent air*: should air be able to push air, according to the principles laid down at 57d ff.? Plato explains at 61a that if air is compressed, nothing dissolves it.

60c *the more beautiful kind*: crystals.

60d *dark-coloured millstone*: millstones were often made out of lava.

62a *its name*: Plato seems to want to link 'heat' (*therm-* words) with 'cutting' (*kerm-* words).

62d *altogether incorrect*: this passage is significant for its rejection of a type of cosmology. Much early Greek cosmology was of the 'parallel' type (on this see D. Furley, *The Greek Cosmologists*, vol. 1: *The Formation of the Atomic Theory and its Earliest Critics* (Cambridge: Cambridge University

Press, 1987)), in which heavy objects drop from the 'top' of the cosmos to the 'bottom'. Hence the problem Thales has with the question of why the earth does not drop, and what supports the earth. Gradually a new type of cosmology took over, the 'centrifocal' type, most clearly typified by Aristotle, where there is a central point of the cosmos to which heavy objects move. Plato played a significant part in the transition.

62d *it's just in the centre*: so in Timaeus' cosmos there can be no up and down. The cosmos is spherical and the opposite of a point on the extremity is the point in the centre. Note, however, the careless use of 'up' at the beginning of 60c.

63d *we use 'heavy' and 'down' for the opposite property and place*: the basic principle here is that of like to like. If we forcibly shift earth away from the mass of earth, it will attempt to return and so feel heavy. Plato's account here, though centrifocal, is different from Aristotle's. For Aristotle, earth moves naturally to the centre of the cosmos, not to its own kind. If the earth in the cosmos were gathered elsewhere for Plato, earth would move to this other place. Aristotle's distinction between heavy and light is also more absolute, based on whether elements move naturally towards or away from the centre of the cosmos. For Plato this is relative, depending on the situation of the gathered mass of an element. While this may all seem a little odd and archaic, universal gravitation is not the easiest of ideas to develop. Certainly no one in the ancient world came close to it, and it required the work of many hands to develop it into a coherent theory in the seventeenth century. The Newtonian account involving attraction at a distance only won out over the Cartesian account involving vortices in the mid-eighteenth century.

64c *bones and hair*: those parts of the body that are composed mainly of earth do not pass on motion to the soul, and so perception does not occur.

65b *observed when the body is burnt and cut*: where the normal state is disrupted slowly or restored slowly, no pain or pleasure is felt. It is possible for the normal state to be disrupted slowly, with no pain, and restored rapidly, with pleasure; and for the normal state to be disrupted violently and with pain and restored slowly without pleasure, as in the case of burns. Compare *Philebus* 31d ff. on the nature of pleasure.

66d *too broad for fire and air*: the account of smell is unsatisfactory. The passages with which we smell are said to be too fine for earth and water, too large for air and fire, so these elements cannot be smelled in their pure form. That seems odd for air and fire, which could easily collide with the walls of the passages rather than pass straight through. It is also odd in that there may be larger sizes of the elements (e.g. cubes of earth with sixteen rather than four triangles per face), which should then either be smellable or even too large for the passages.

67c *great and small movements*: a stroke is transmitted from the air through the ears to the blood and brain, and is then passed on to the soul. The motion this causes, from head to liver, is hearing. The eardrum appears to play no part in this account. Pitch is related to speed, 'smoothness' (as opposed to 'harshness') is related to uniformity, volume is related to magnitude.

67c *later stage of the discussion*: 80a–b.

67c *fourth and final*: of our canonical five senses Plato omits touch, though he discussed tactile qualities in 61d–64a.

67c *how sight occurs*: see 45b–46a.

67e *'white' is what expands the visual ray, and 'black' is the opposite*: Plato refers back to his theory of vision as the interaction of two streams, one from the eye and one from the outside world; see 45b ff.

68a *'bright' and 'shiny'*: we would not describe 'bright' and 'shiny' as colours, but as qualities or intensities of light. Plato treats them like colours, though, as he describes the mixing of colours with 'bright'.

68b *the result is orange-yellow*: there are two difficulties in trying to understand Plato's theory here. First, Greek colour terms do not match up in any simple way with our own. Quite often the Greeks would emphasize hue rather than colour, so the description 'wine-dark' might be used of the sea or of sheep, and the word for 'black' also means 'dark-hued'. Secondly, it is not always clear in this section whether Plato is talking of the effects of fire particles on one another or the effects of mixing pigments together. If Plato is talking about pigments, we don't know specifically which pigments (that is, what the pigments consisted of) or how they would interact with each other when mixed. So some of his results seem strange to us.

68e *fathering the self-sufficient, perfect god*: i.e. the universe. Timaeus is moving towards a conclusion for this part of his discourse, and so recapitulates what the demiurge has done with the chaos he began with at 53b. The demiurge is responsible for everything good that has come out of the primordial chaos.

69a *apart from necessary ones*: compare 46e on divine and contributory causes, and *Phaedo* 99a on the relative importance of contributory and divine causes.

69a *the rest of our account*: while so far we have had a section on the works of intelligence and on what happens by necessity, in the third and final section we have an account of intelligence combined with necessity.

69b *proportionate and compatible*: as at 53b, where the demiurge imposes shape and number on the primordial chaos.

69b *except by chance*: Plato sees chaos as non-progressive. A body may, by chance, attain the characteristics of an element, but will lose those characteristics just as easily.

69d *pleasure, evil's most potent lure*: compare *Philebus* on the relation between pleasure, hedonism, and the properly good life.

69d *constrained by necessity*: if the soul is to be placed in a body, there are some unavoidable consequences, and inevitably the soul will be racked by assorted emotions and passions. This is a necessary constraint on how we are constructed.

70a *the diaphragm as a barrier between them*: the diaphragm separates the chest from the abdomen. It helps us breathe, and is continuous, except where it allows the spine, intestines, and blood vessels through.

70a *the dictates of reason issuing from the acropolis*: here we have an example of intelligence and necessity, seemingly of the logical kind. The mortal and immortal soul must be housed in the same body but it is best to keep them as far apart as possible, so they are housed in different parts of the body. Thus 'reason persuades necessity' as far as possible, though having mortal and immortal soul in the same body is necessary. The language of 'parts' of the soul is taken from *Republic* 436a ff., as is the theory that the soul consists of three predominant parts—a reasoning part, a passionate, defensive part, and an appetitive part.

70b *the blood that circulates vigorously throughout the body*: Plato did not believe in the circulation of the blood in the same way that we do, in the sense of a flow from the heart, through the arteries, through the capillaries, through the veins, and back to the heart. He did believe, however, that blood was transported around the body, and that the heart is in some sense the 'source' of blood.

70d *relief and comfort from the heat*: Plato is, of course, completely wrong here on the function of the lungs. However, ancient anatomists, while they knew the disposition of the organs, struggled to understand their function, and often believed that major organs (lungs, even the brain) existed mainly as a means of regulating heat and cold within the body. In Plato's time the lungs were thought of as a single organ, with right and left chambers.

71a *collectively and individually*: Plato uses a macrocosm–microcosm analogy between the cosmos and humans, but there is also a secondary theme, relating both the cosmos and the human body to a city. How is a city to be best governed? Like the body, it should be governed by the most intelligent and knowledgeable.

71a *bewitched by images and phantasms*: the lower the level of intelligence for Plato, the more easily will we be taken in by visual images. Compare here the cave analogy of *Republic* 514a ff., and the way that the prisoners in the cave are also prisoners of the images they see.

71b *images to look at*: in some way our thoughts are reflected on or form an image on the liver, and so will communicate themselves to our lowest parts. Since dissection of humans was not practised, it was hepatoscopy, the dissection and investigation of animal livers for divinatory purposes, that had enabled the Greeks to know something about the liver—for instance, that it presents a considerable diversity of appearances when dissected, and that its appearance is altered by various diseases, as Plato says in what follows.

71e *some kind of contact with truth*: for humans to be as good as possible, the baser instincts are kept as far away as possible from the higher intellectual functions, but some thought is taken by the designers even for the improvement of the baser part of the soul.

72a *present trouble or benefit*: it is important that we can make rational judgements about what is presented to us in dreams, etc. Compare 42b, where the injunction is that we should control our sensations and emotions and should not be controlled by them.

72a *to know himself*: 'know yourself' is a famous dictum of Socrates, stemming from advice inscribed in Apollo's sanctuary at Delphi.

72c *clear indications of meaning*: it is not clear how Plato would support the idea that the liver in life is so different in these respects from the liver in death. At any rate, he here casts doubt on hepatoscopy, since the animal victims were first killed before having their livers examined.

72d *cleans them all up*: the function of the spleen is simply to keep the liver clean, to help even the most base type of soul see the images clearly. Actually the functions of the spleen are to produce lymphocytes which help recycle red blood cells and play an important part in fighting infections in combination with white blood cells.

72e *formation of the rest of the body*: Plato refers back to his promise at 61d to cover this topic.

73b *in the marrow*: the marrow is the starting point for the construction of the body. The soul is in some way bound into the marrow for the extent of a human's life: see 81d, where death occurs when the soul eventually is released by the marrow.

73d *the 'head'*: the Greek word for 'brain' means literally 'the organ in the head'. Plato seems to be aware that the brain is bathed in cerebrospinal fluid, and the idea that the brain is marrow works well with the idea that the soul is bound into the marrow and that the flight of the soul from the marrow is death. The marrow is also supposed to be an individual's sperm bank, just as (73b–c) the original marrow-stuff contains the seeds of all life on earth.

73d *made out of bone*: the human body is constructed in layers. First the marrow, then the bones around the marrow (the skull and spine, in the first instance), then the sinews, etc., and finally the flesh.

74a *like hinges*: there may be a specific attack on Empedocles here, in the notion that the spine is designed to be flexible. According to Empedocles, the spine is broken into pieces by chance (cf. Aristotle, *Parts of Animals* 640a). The entire section, of course, runs contrary to Empedocles' thinking: Plato explains by design, Empedocles by a multiplicity of accidents.

75c *more sensitive and intelligent*: a good example of the relation between necessity and intelligence. Of necessity, humans must have bodies, and their minds must be housed, but intelligent design guides the construction to ensure that our heads are sensitive and intelligent rather than swathed in deep layers of bone and flesh, which might give us a longer life but not a more intelligent one.

76d *to think about the future*: the creators of human beings believed that at least some humans will fail in their lives (on the criteria laid out by Timaeus), and so they gave humans rudimentary nails that will be useful when they turn into animals in future incarnations (see 90a ff.).

77c *to move itself*: Plato follows a typical ancient distinction between plants, animals, and humans. Plants have a vegetative soul, that is, they can grow but not move from place to place or think. Animals have motion as well as growth, humans have intelligence as well as motion and growth.

77d *other parts of the body*: Plato does not know the difference between arteries and veins, and has no knowledge of the capillaries that link them. Nor does he give the heart any role in the movement of blood.

78a *permeable by smaller particles*: the principle here is important for what is to come. Bodies composed of small particles are impervious to larger particles, but those composed of larger particles are not impervious to smaller particles. One might take this to mean that there are small-scale voids. If there are interstices in the formation of larger bodies that small ones can pass through, what is in these interstices? One answer might be a constant stream of smaller particles, but as those particles neither tessellate with the larger ones nor with themselves, that still has to leave some void.

78b *like a fish-trap*: a simple but effective means of catching fish or crustaceans (there is a similar design for lobster pots). The overall shape is like a vase, with a funnel-like mouth leading into a broad body which tapers to an end. They can be made of reeds, flexible branches, or even netting strung around a skeleton of reed or branch. The fish find it easy to swim into them (and the traps were often baited), but very difficult to swim out. In relation to the body, the gods make a fish-trap with two funnels, one of which is branched into two again. This is generally understood to be a funnel each for the mouth and nose, with the nose forked into two again.

78c *into the abdomen*: the two tubes are the oesophagus and the trachea.

79c *through our porous flesh*: Plato needs to explain the sensation of breathing in and breathing out without recourse to a void. We cannot simply expel air and leave a void; air is simultaneously being drawn in through the pores of the body, and this is what makes the chest swell again and triggers an in-breath. Plato believes that the primary function of the diaphragm, the muscle wall which separates the chest and the abdomen, is to separate different parts of the soul, rather than to be a major cause of the deflation/inflation of the lungs.

80a *cupping-glasses that doctors use*: another phenomenon that can be explained by the no-void theory is the action of medical cups (to raise skin, now used only in alternative therapies). Next we see that objects which keep in motion after the mover has let them go can also be explained by the same principle. The ancients, lacking modern ideas such as momentum, struggled to explain why objects kept moving when the mover had released them. Here the idea is that air displaced by the motion of an object rushes in to fill any potential void behind a moving object, thus imparting some force and keeping the object in motion.

80b *blend of high and low pitch*: quite how the theory explains how music may be harmonious or dissonant is obscure.

80c *there's no attraction . . . and there's no void involved either*: Timaeus also wants to reject what we would call action at a distance, or attraction and repulsion. Two difficult cases here are the apparent electrostatic attraction generated when amber is rubbed, or magnetic attraction from permanent magnets. Timaeus wants to account for these by the contact action of particles. So instead of attraction across empty space, there is a close press of particles whose motion results in the appropriate bodies moving towards each other. Descartes came up with a very similar theory in the seventeenth century. The usual analogue here is a whirlpool. While an object on the surface (say a piece of wood) moves to the centre of a whirlpool, this is not due to any attraction from the centre of the whirlpool, but is rather due to the motion of the water particles.

80e *explained earlier*: 68b.

81b *universal movement*: the macrocosm–microcosm relation is being stressed again in this paragraph.

81b *at that time*: the like-to-like principle is being stressed again as well. While modern scientists tend to think in terms of fluids and nutrients being forced around the body (e.g. by the action of the heart, the heart acting as a pump), the ancients often took the view that parts of the body attracted what they needed. This sort of thinking was dominant until the seventeenth century and the discovery of the circulation of the blood by William Harvey.

81e *flies joyfully away*: the marrow includes the brain, so the higher intelligence located in the head can escape its mortal bonds.

82a *abnormal predominance and deficiency among them*: this sort of theory, that disease is due to an imbalance of crucial elements or fluids in the body, was typical of the ancient Greek world. But it turns out that Plato has three theories of disease: it may be caused by imbalance (82a–b, 86a), by decomposition (82b–84c), or by air, bile, or phlegm (84c–86a). Of these, the decomposition theory appears to be original to Plato.

83c *depending on its colour*: bile played a significant role in early theories of the constitution of the body and the nature of disease. The theory of the four humours held that there were four critical substances for the body: black bile, yellow bile, blood, and phlegm. When these four humours were in balance, the body was healthy; all diseases were due to an imbalance of the humours. For Plato, however, bile and phlegm were the unhealthy products of decomposition (83e).

84c *reverse the direction of their flows*: diseases involving putrefaction of the flesh, such as gangrene, were much more common in the ancient world.

84e *'tetanus' and 'opisthotonos'*: tetanus is actually caused by wound infection, and is an involuntary and prolonged contraction of the muscles. Typically, the contractions begin around the mouth, giving tetanus its other name of 'lockjaw'. Opisthotonos, literally a 'backward arching', involves the patient involuntarily arching his head, neck, and spine backwards. It is a symptom of tetanus, and also of meningitis. Before the advent of modern vaccines and antibiotics, tetanus was much more widespread and dangerous.

85a *air in its bubbles*: see 83c–d.

85b *the 'sacred disease'*: it is notable here that Timaeus believes the 'sacred disease' (epilepsy) to be well named, whereas the Hippocratic treatise *On the Sacred Disease* had attacked the idea that it was caused by the god, and argued for a natural explanation. Timaeus seems to agree that the disease has a natural cause, but as it attacks what he considers the highest part of a human, he allows it the name of the 'sacred disease'.

85d *combined action of the fibres and a cool environment soon causes the blood to clot*: there is a clotting agent in the blood called fibrin. It is a protein with fibre-like molecules which join together in appropriate circumstances to help generate a blood-clot. Plato would not have known this, but his ingenious theory involving blood fibres does give him a way of explaining the thickness of the blood and blood-clotting.

85e *sets the soul free*: in other words, the result is death.

86a *quotidian fevers*: quotidian fevers have daily crises. Fevers were carefully observed by the Hippocratics, who took care to note when a medical crisis occurred. Even if they could not cure the fever, they could at least give a good prognosis, important in a situation where they had to struggle against other practitioners (herbalists, faith-healers, etc.). Tertian fevers have a crisis every three days; quartan fevers have a crisis every four days.

86c *loses the ability to think rationally*: compare 43b ff.

86e *no one is bad of his own choice*: it was standard Platonic/Socratic doctrine that no one is willingly bad.

87a *soul's three locations*: see 69c–70a.

88c *at once*: the phrase 'the beautiful and the good' started life as a single compound epithet (kalokagathos) aristocrats applied to themselves in the fifth century. Plato's paradigms, by contrast, are 'beautiful' because of their physical fitness, and 'good' because of their philosophy.

88e *what I was saying before about the universe*: just as the 'nurse' of the universe (cf. 53a), that is, the receptacle, keeps in motion and shakes what is within it (cf. 49a, 52d), so we should keep our bodies in motion and shake what is within them. This helps to ward off external attacks and internal imbalances. Notice the macrocosm–microcosm relation again.

89b *medical use of drugs to purge the body*: Plato sides with the medical theorists who opposed radical purges of the body. Ancient medicine emphasized diet and exercise as preventatives, and had little in the way of effective cures for diseases. What they did have were emetics, laxatives, and diuretics to purge the body. Whether these procedures cured or exacerbated medical conditions was a matter of debate. Here Plato considers them to be a last resort only.

89d *the application of drugs*: in some ways this passage reads rather strangely to the modern eye, but one might well ask: the gym or liposuction? Jogging or anti-depressants? Fruit, vegetables, and fish to help the immune system, or antibiotics? The issue of the efficacy (or perceived efficacy) of available drugs is still an issue.

89d *controlling and being controlled by himself*: this looks back to 42b, where if we master our sensations and emotions, we will live just lives.

90a *in proportion with one another*: compare the proportions required in the cosmos to make it the best possible (see 35b ff.), and the proportions required in the human body (see 87c ff.).

90a *suspended our heads*: human beings have a greater natural kinship with the heavens, and should make astronomy an object of special study.

90c *giving it food and exercise that is congenial to it*: this, of course, is not physical food and exercise, but the intellectual kind best exemplified by astronomy. The idea that impressions are a kind of food was implied by 43b, and is argued for at *Republic* 401b–d.

90d *to its original condition*: the best condition for humans is the one that obtained before they were bound into their bodies, when the revolutions in their heads were not disrupted (42e–44c).

90d *within human reach*: a good life is attainable, if we work for it. As ever in *Timaeus*, jealousy is not a feature of the relation between gods and humans. The demiurge wants us to have good lives, and has given us the means to attain such a life.

91a *sexual desire*: this confirms that the original population were male, as sexual desire (or at least, heterosexual desire) is generated only with the advent of women.

91d *studied the heavens*: astronomy has figured significantly in *Timaeus*. It is the means by which we can bring the imperfect revolutions in our heads in tune with the perfect revolutions of the world-soul. It is no surprise, then, to be told that those who ignore philosophy and astronomy become brutish. But practising astronomy superficially is not good enough. We must not only observe, but must think about the heavens in a serious fashion.

92a *the most mindless of them*: there is a hierarchy among brutes, and the most mindless humans are reincarnated as snakes. It is apt that those who have reached the lowest levels of intelligence should be assigned to the lowest places on earth.

92c *their losing or gaining intelligence*: although this sequence has been given as a descent, there is also the possibility of ascent. If someone should live a life of one of the lower creatures in a virtuous manner, attempting as far as possible to gain knowledge and intelligence, she will be reincarnated further up the scale.

CRITIAS

106b *medicine*: this picks up the theme of some of the last pages of *Timaeus*.

107d *imprecise and deceptive outline*: Critias' mistake: to say that we are content with a discussion of heavenly bodies that bears only a faint resemblance to them is to assume that we know what they are like, because otherwise we would not know that it was no more than a faint resemblance.

108b *competent successor*: Socrates is comparing the speeches to a dramatic competition in Athens, where one after another three tragic playwrights displayed their work, and were explicitly awarded first, second, and third places. Hermocrates changes this to a military metaphor, which Critias extends.

108c *Apollo Paean*: soldiers chanted a paean, an invocation of Apollo, before advancing into battle.

108e *9,000 years*: actually, at *Timaeus* 23e the Egyptian priest said that Saïs and Egypt were involved in the war, and that Saïs (modern Sa-el Hagar) was not founded until 8,000 years previously. Moreover, in *Timaeus* the Atlanteans conscripted troops from this side of the strait, and so the war should not simply be characterized as between those on one side of the strait and those on the other. It is worth bearing in mind from the start that Plato never finished *Critias*, and that there are several indications that what we have of the book remained unrevised.

109a *into the ocean*: the mud and shallow water just beyond the Pillars of Heracles were apparently familiar: Aristotle mentions them at *Meteorologica* 354a.

109b *no disputes involved*: in keeping with the argument of *Republic* that the gods should not be portrayed in immoral terms, Plato denies traditional tales such as that Poseidon and Athena competed to gain patronage of Athens.

109d *for courage and intelligence*: see note on *Timaeus* 24c.

109d *born from the ground*: see note on *Timaeus* 23e.

110b *predecessors of Theseus*: the legendary first kings of Athens.

110c *godlike men*: the supposed founders of the city.

110d *for our imaginary guardians*: that is, the guardians of the ideal state imagined by Plato in *Republic*, or in the conversation that took place the day before that of *Timaeus*.

110e *on the left*: the idea that Attica once extended west as far as the Isthmus of Corinth was irredentist wishful thinking, but Oropus was the site of frequent border disputes between Athens and Boeotia.

110e *exempt from working the land*: as opposed to the norm in historical Athens, where citizens had a duty to double up as soldiers and where 90 per cent of them worked the land.

111b *the small islands*: quite a few of the smaller islands of the Aegean have little topsoil.

112a *in the time of Deucalion*: see *Timaeus* 22b, with note. The 'single night' of earthquakes and deluge is presumably the one mentioned at *Timaeus* 25d.

112a *opposite the Pnyx*: see Map of Athens (opposite).

112d *willing subjects*: the pattern of their leadership was not the more oppressive Athenian empire of the fifth century, but the ideal of the renewed empire of the fourth century, at the time Plato was writing. For further connections between the Atlantis myth and fourth-century Athens, see K. A. Morgan, 'Designer History: Plato's Atlantis Story and Fourth-century Ideology', *Journal of Hellenic Studies*, 118 (1998), 101–18. For the general thesis that the Atlantis myth was made up by Plato partly as a 'political parable' with messages for his contemporaries, partly to reflect the constitution of *Republic*, and partly as a piece of fiction, see C. Gill, 'The Genre of the Atlantis Story', *Classical Philology*, 72 (1977), 287–304, and the other papers by Gill listed in the Select Bibliography.

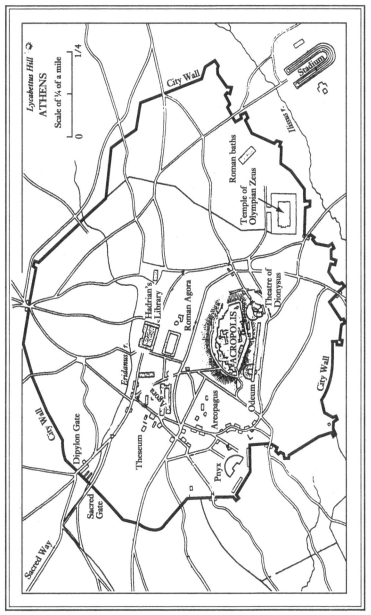

MAP OF ANCIENT ATHENS

113b *you now know why*: since Plato himself invites us to find the names of the inhabitants of Atlantis meaningful, here is a list of their meanings: Ampheres, 'well made'; Atlas, 'enduring'; Autochthon, 'born from the ground'; Azaes, 'enviable'; Cleito, 'bright fame'; Diaprepes, 'glorious'; Elasippus, 'horse-rider'; Eumelus, 'rich in sheep'; Evaemon, 'of good blood'; Evenor, 'man of courage'; Leucippe, 'white horse'; Mestor, 'adviser'; Mneseus, 'rememberer'.

113c *fifty stades*: on the Athenian scale a foot is 29.6 cm, a plethron is 29.6 m, and a stade is 177.6 m.

113d *pivot of a lathe*: more precise measurements are given at 115e–116a. For the general features of the city area, see Figure 1.

113e *been invented*: Plato leaves it ambiguous whether Poseidon is creating a utopian paradise, which was corrupted by later generations of Atlanteans, or the kind of place that would inevitably encourage the greed that would lead to the island's downfall. Poseidon is quite the opposite of the gods of Timaeus' speech (and the ideal gods of *Republic*): so far from being 'free of jealousy' (*Timaeus* 29e), Poseidon guards or imprisons his beloved away from everyone else.

114b *Gadeira*: modern Cadiz.

114c *as I said before*: *Timaeus* 25a–b.

114e *solid or fusible*: solid products are presumably minerals and stones, while fusible ones are all the metals. The simplicity of primeval Athens is contrasted with the profusion of ancient Atlantis, with its multiplicity of shrines, territories, types of building, and so on.

114e *orichalc*: 'orichalc' was a perfectly acceptable word (meaning literally 'mountain metal') in ancient Greek for copper alloys, or for the yellow copper ore used in such alloys. As such it was certainly 'more than just a name' in Plato's time, so he is using the term to refer to some more precious (and more fabulous) metal.

115b *his satiety*: we do not know what fruit was offered diners to relieve satiety—perhaps a lemon.

115d *fifty stades long*: see note on 113c.

115e *underground sailing passage below*: it is hard to see how the struts support-ing the bridges could coincide with the mouths of these underground canals, especially since in at least one instance the canal is wider than the bridge: the bridges are 1 plethron wide (116a) and the outermost canal is 3 plethra wide.

116d *the appearance of the temple*: it is non-Greek in its over-lavish use of pre-cious metals and in its enormous size (three times larger than the Parthenon), but its basic design is Greek, and many Greek temples were gaudy themselves.

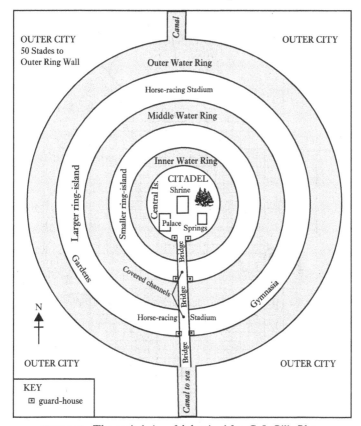

FIGURE 1. The capital city of Atlantis. After C. J. Gill, *Plato:
The Atlantis Story* (Bristol Classical Press, 1980)

116d *acroteria*: ornamental devices crowning the top or side angles of the triangular pediment of an ancient Greek temple.

116e *this many Nereids*: in classical times there were usually thought to be fifty
of them. Nereids were sea-nymphs, and as such they often accompanied
Poseidon.

117c *bodyguards*: perhaps for the first time a sour note is struck, since to Greek
thinking bodyguards indicated tyranny rather than fair and tolerant
leadership.

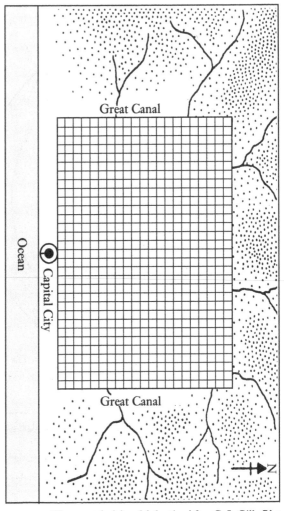

FIGURE 2. The coastal plain of Atlantis. After C. J. Gill, *Plato: The Atlantis Story* (Bristol Classical Press, 1980)

118b *faced south*: because there were mountains to the north, west, and east: see Figure 2.

120d *the god*: it was Zeus, as we discover at 121b, who sent the Atlanteans against primeval Athens, as a roundabout way of punishing the Atlanteans.

121c *he said*: the work breaks off here, and Plato never completed it. He would have continued at least with an account of how the punishment Zeus ordained for Atlantis was that it was to be defeated by the paradigm of virtue, primeval Athens, and a description of the war.

TEXTUAL NOTES

Variations from the Oxford Classical Text

TIMAEUS

25d5: Reading κατὰ βραχέος (Y, Cornford).

28a1: Omitting ἀεὶ with some MSS and ancient commentators.

35a4–5: Retaining αὖ πέρι (MSS and most ancient citations) and reading κατὰ ταῦτα (A, P, W, Y, John of Stobi). Literally: 'Next, in the case of identity and difference, in their case too he introduced [it] as intermediate . . .'.

36c3: Reading ἔβαλεν (Waterfield), πέριξ . . . ἔβαλεν being equivalent by tmesis to περιέβαλεν.

39a1–2: Reading ἰοῦσαν τε καὶ κρατουμένην (Y² and recent editors).

39a4: Reading δὲ δὴ (Waterfield).

39b3: Reading καθ' ἅ (Archer-Hind).

40a5: Reading φόρησιν (Waterfield).

40c1: Omitting τὴν (F, Y, Plutarch).

40d1: Omitting οὐ, which has little MS support and is clearly an 'ideological emendation' (John Dillon's phrase, *American Journal of Philology*, 110 (1989), 50–72). For Plato's commitment to astrology, see my article in *Culture and Cosmos*, 3: 2 (1999), 3–15.

41a7: Reading θεοί, θείων ὤν . . ., τὰ δι' ἐμοῦ (Robinson, Zeyl).

42e2: Omitting the comma after ἄρχειν (Cornford).

47d1: Reading φωνῆς (Cornford).

48b8: Adding καὶ before στοιχεῖα (West).

48d3: Reading μᾶλλον δ' ἢ καὶ ἔμπροσθεν (Hackforth).

49e3: Reading καὶ τὴν τοῦ ὧδε (Cook Wilson).

51a1: Adding νοητῶν before or after πάντων (Cook Wilson).

54a6: Reading ὑπερβάν τε (Waterfield).

54b2: Reading μὴ instead of δὴ (Hermann).

57b4: Reading ταῦτα ἢ (Y) . . . συνιόντα (Bury).

59d4: Reading πυρί τε καὶ ἀέρι (Waterfield).

60d4: Reading ἐπιμύλιον instead of λίθος (Waterfield, taking λίθος as a gloss), or ἔχων λίθος <μυλίας> (Cornford, referring to Plato, *Hippias Major* 292d5, and comparing this passage with Aristotle, *Meteorologica* 383b10 ff.).

60e1–2: Reading τὸ λεγόμενον (Waterfield).

61b5: Reading πῦρ ὕδωρ (Cook Wilson).

66a2: Retaining τῶν δὲ αὐτῶν with all the MSS (see, roughly, G. M. A. Grube, 'The Sense of Taste in *Timaeus* 65b–66c', *Classical Philology*, 25 (1930), 72–5).

67a1: Reading δι' οὖν ταῦτα (John of Stobi).

71c7: Reading πρὸς ἑαυτὸ (A, P).

74c2: Reading ἀνιδροῦσαν (F, W, Y, Galen).

84a2: Reading (with Zeyl) καὶ μηκέτι αὖ τὸ (A, W) ἐξ ἐκείνων (W, Y) ἅμα (Stallbaum) καὶ νεύρων.

85e9: Transposing the clause οἷον . . . ἐκπίπτουσα from a couple of lines later (Waterfield).

86e6: Adding ἢ before καὶ ὅσοι (Waterfield).

88a4: Deleting δι' (Madvig).

89c3: Deleting δυνατὰ (Lindau).

The Oxford World's Classics Website

www.worldsclassics.co.uk

- Browse the full range of Oxford World's Classics online

- Sign up for our monthly e-alert to receive information on new titles

- Read extracts from the Introductions

- Listen to our editors and translators talk about the world's greatest literature with our Oxford World's Classics audio guides

- Join the conversation, follow us on Twitter at OWC_Oxford

- Teachers and lecturers can order inspection copies quickly and simply via our website

www.worldsclassics.co.uk

American Literature

British and Irish Literature

Children's Literature

Classics and Ancient Literature

Colonial Literature

Eastern Literature

European Literature

Gothic Literature

History

Medieval Literature

Oxford English Drama

Poetry

Philosophy

Politics

Religion

The Oxford Shakespeare

A complete list of Oxford World's Classics, including Authors in Context, Oxford English Drama, and the Oxford Shakespeare, is available in the UK from the Marketing Services Department, Oxford University Press, Great Clarendon Street, Oxford OX2 6DP, or visit the website at www.oup.com/uk/worldsclassics.

In the USA, visit www.oup.com/us/owc for a complete title list.

Oxford World's Classics are available from all good bookshops. In case of difficulty, customers in the UK should contact Oxford University Press Bookshop, 116 High Street, Oxford OX1 4BR.

Bhagavad Gita

The Bible Authorized King James Version
    With Apocrypha

Dhammapada

Dharmasūtras

The Koran

The Pañcatantra

The Sauptikaparvan (from the
    Mahabharata)

The Tale of Sinuhe and Other Ancient
    Egyptian Poems

The Qur'an

Upaniṣads

ANSELM OF CANTERBURY	The Major Works
THOMAS AQUINAS	Selected Philosophical Writings
AUGUSTINE	The Confessions On Christian Teaching
BEDE	The Ecclesiastical History
HEMACANDRA	The Lives of the Jain Elders
KĀLIDĀSA	The Recognition of Śakuntalā
MANJHAN	Madhumalati
ŚĀNTIDEVA	The Bodhicaryàvatàra